French Conservatism in Crisis

FRENCH CONSERVATISM IN CRISIS

The Republican Federation of France in the 1930s

WILLIAM D. IRVINE

Louisiana State University Press
Baton Rouge and London

Designer: Albert Crochet
Type face: VIP Caledonia
Typesetter: G & S Typesetters, Inc.
Printer: Thomson-Shore, Inc.
Binder: John H. Dekker & Sons, Inc.

LIBRARY OF CONGRESS CATALOGING IN PUBLICATION DATA

Irvine, William D   1944–
  French conservatism in crisis.

  Bibliography: p.
  Includes index.
  1. Fédération républicaine.   2. Conservatism—France—History.   3. France—
Politics and government—1914–1940.   I. Title.
JN3007.F47I75   320.5'2'0944   78–27254
ISBN 0–8071–0555–4

To my parents
William and Mary Irvine

Contents

Maps

following page 42

Acknowledgments

A number of individuals and institutions have greatly assisted me in this project. I owe a considerable debt to Arno J. Mayer of Princeton University, who first sparked my interest in right-wing movements, supervised an early version of this book as a doctoral dissertation, and patiently and repeatedly reminded me of the need for conceptual rigor. Mme Louis Marin offered me her hospitality and her reminiscences many times in the summer of 1973 and kindly granted me permission to see selected cartons of the Louis Marin Papers. René Russier and Emmanuel Beau de Loménie shared their recollections of the 1930s with me. René Rémond made valuable suggestions about potential sources. John Cairns of the University of Toronto and Robert Soucy of Oberlin College read earlier versions of the manuscript and gave me encouragement and constructive criticism. Thomas Laqueur of the University of California at Berkeley and Steven Kramer of the University of New Mexico have for years offered me their insights on modern history as well as a much cherished comradeship.

Research for this project could not have been undertaken without the generous support of the Canada Council, which funded my stay in France in 1969–1971 and in the summer of 1973. The Minor Research Grants Committee of Glendon College of York University also provided research funds in 1972 and 1974. I would also like to thank *French Historical Studies* for permission to quote from my article, "French Conservatives and the 'New Right' During the 1930s," *French Historical Studies*, VIII (Fall, 1974), 534–62.

The greatest single source of intellectual stimulation and moral support has been my wife, Marion Lane. In particular, she read endless versions of this manuscript, accepted the utterly thankless task of criticizing the output of a fledgling author, and did so with rigor and energy. This book has benefited considerably, and I am deeply grateful.

Introduction

The Republican Federation of France was the largest and most important French conservative political party of the Third Republic. Tinged with neither the "radicalism" of the Alliance Démocratique nor the Christian socialism of the Parti Démocrate Populaire, the Republican Federation was the classic representative of the traditional French Right: Catholic, socially conservative, and intensely nationalistic. Led by some of the most prominent figures on the French Right, the party counted about one hundred deputies, or one-sixth of the Chamber of Deputies, among its adherents.

The Republican Federation was the preeminent party of the *modérés*. During the early years of the Third Republic the term *modéré* or *républicain modéré* identified those republicans whose loyalty to the regime was unequivocal but who simultaneously rejected the extreme anticlericalism and the more advanced social programs of the radical republicans. The *modérés*, as their leaders fondly observed, were republican moderates but not moderately republican. In the twentieth century the term generally designated those political groups that stood between the liberal Radicals and the monarchist Action Francaise. In practice it was more often a euphemism for right or conservative, although the *modérés* shunned both of these labels, which conjured up images of the early opponents of the Third Republic. The mystique of the word *left* had no counterpart on the Right. After 1900 no *Entente des droites* or *Union de la droite* challenged the *Bloc des gauches* or the *Cartel des gauches*. So pervasive was the cult of the Left and so aware were conservative politicians of Adolphe Thiers's adage that France was "center-left" that even moderate conservatives persisted in calling themselves "left republicans." No one, of course, denied that there was a Right, a nebulous realm inhabited by reactionaries, *chevaux-légers*, and other enemies of the Republic; but no one would admit to belonging to it. As one cynical commentator on the politics of the Third Republic remarked, one could no more find a man of the Right who labeled himself as such, than a can of peas labeled large. In the one case, the coarsest peas one could buy were medium or even semifine; whereas in the other, the most conservative politician would at best call himself a *modéré* or even a "left republican."[1]

Connoting reasonableness and the *juste milieu*, the label *modéré* continued to be a term of approbation among many conservatives during the 1920s and 1930s. Nonetheless, contemporary political commentators, when not damning them as ill-disguised reactionaries, often represented the *modérés* as solid French citizens having good qualities for everything except politics. Abel Bonnard, in his celebrated polemic, *Les Modérés*, portrayed the typical *modéré* as a gallic Squire Western with no political contribution to make except his vote in the Chamber of Deputies. He ironically observed: "The *modérés* are an indecisive troop. Their heads turn in the wind of debate like weathervanes trying to decide which breeze to obey. . . . When a minister utters the slightest sentence which does not show them too much disdain, they applaud frantically."[2] Henri Bazire, leader of the conservative Catholic Action Libérale Populaire, remarked in 1910 of the *modérés*: "When their death sentence is voted, they will propose an amendment requesting that the knife be dropped with moderation."[3] Others decried the point-

1. Albert Thibaudet, *Les Idées politiques de la France* (Paris, 1932), 16–17. It was considered to be an act of remarkable frankness when, in 1932, some moderately conservative deputies formed a group which actually entitled itself the *républicains du centre*. Jacques Debû-Bridel, "La crise des partis," *La Revue Hebdomadaire*, January 21, 1933, p. 333.

2. Abel Bonnard, *Les Modérés* (Paris, 1936), 17–18.

3. *La Libre Parole*, November 30, 1910.

less internecine quarreling of the *modérés*, their habit of dividing into a dozen indistinguishable groups, and their apparent unwillingness to accept change. As Jacques Fourcade observed: "'Divide so as not to rule:' thus could one formulate the motto of the *modérés*."[4]

Scorned by contemporary observers, the *modérés* have been virtually ignored by a subsequent generation of historians. Compared to the wealth of studies on movements and parties of the Left and of the fascist Right,[5] scholarly work on the traditional Right has been slight. René Rémond's brilliant sketch of the French Right places the *modérés* in their historical context and analyzes the several political traditions from which twentieth-century conservatives evolved. But Rémond's overview provides little information about the structure and dynamics of French conservatism, and he limits himself to quoting conventional contemporary wisdom about the conservative parties of the era. French conservatives, moreover, are frustratingly difficult to study. Their political formations were elusive phenomena, too often existing only on paper. Once in parliament, deputies of the same party would divide into a half-dozen or more separate groups, whose nuances only a parliamentary gossip columnist could distinguish. Just as contemporaries were often bewildered by the confusion that prevailed on the Right, the *modérés* still appear to constitute an anarchic morass into which an historian cannot profitably venture.

The *modérés*, furthermore, lack the obvious appeal of the political extremes. Many students of modern French history identify with the ideals of the parties of the Left and have a continuing interest in their fate. Similarly, the growing historical interest in fascism has recently focused attention on French

4. Jacques Fourcade, *La République de la province* (Paris, 1936), 81.
5. Among the more recent: William R. Tucker, *The Fascist Ego: A Political Biography of Robert Brasillach* (Berkeley, 1976); Robert Soucy, *Fascism in France: The Case of Maurice Barrès* (Berkeley, 1972); C. Stewart Doty, *From Cultural Rebellion to Counterrevolution: The Politics of Maurice Barrès* (Athens, Ohio, 1976); Zeev Sternhell, *Maurice Barrès et le nationalisme français* (Paris, 1972).

fascist intellectuals and has prompted an extended debate on the nature of fascism in France.[6] By contrast the *modérés*, unimaginative and utterly conventional, produced no Charles Maurras, Maurice Barrès, Pierre Drieu la Rochelle, or Robert Brasillach to catch the imagination of the intellectual historian.[7] Significantly, even so important a movement as the Croix de Feu awaits a serious scholarly study, probably because it seems to be, in substance if not in style, too close to the traditional conservatives.[8]

The history of the *modérés* is nonetheless important, for the response of conservative elites to the challenge of dramatic political, social, and economic change is critical to our understanding of modern European history. German historians in particular have directed attention to the strategies employed by conservatives in defense of the established order. The role and responsibility of the German conservative elite in the Nazi experience is a well-documented, if still-contested, subject. Much recent work has examined the pre-Nazi period, exploring in detail how conservatives sought to "modernize" their elitist political parties, create popular mass pressure groups, use racism as a tool

6. For the literature on this debate, see René Rémond, *La Droite en France* (2 vols.; Paris, 1968), esp. II, 424. For an opposing view, see Robert Soucy, "The Nature of Fascism in France," *Journal of Contemporary History*, I (1966), 27–55; Robert Soucy, "French Fascism as Class Conciliation and Moral Regeneration," *Societas*, I (1971), 287–97; Robert Soucy, "French Fascist Intellectuals in the 1930s: An Old New Left?" *French Historical Studies*, VIII (1974), 445–58; see also the special issue devoted to "Visages de Fascistes Français," *Revue d'histoire de la deuxième guerre modiale*, XCVII (1975).

7. Malcolm Anderson, *Conservative Politics in France* (London, 1975) is a recent general survey. Some of the leaders of the Center-Right have found their historian; for example, John M. Sherwood, *Georges Mandel and the Third Republic* (Stanford, 1970) and, to a lesser degree, Rudolph Binion, *Defeated Leaders: The Political Fates of Caillaux, Jouvenel and Tardieu* (New York, 1966). The Action Française is the subject of two major studies: Eugen Weber, *Action Française; Royalism and Reaction in Twentieth Century France* (Stanford, 1962) and Edward R. Tannenbaum, *The Action Française* (New York, 1962). Dieter Wolf has written an important history of Jacques Doriot, *Doriot, du communisme à la collaboration* (Paris, 1969).

8. Although Philippe Machefer and Robert Soucy are preparing major studies on the Croix de Feu, presently the sole work is the highly partisan Philippe Rudaux, *Les Croix de Feu et le PSF* (Paris, 1967). The Jeunesses Patriotes have been similarly neglected, the only study being Jean Philippet, *Les Jeunesses Patriotes et Pierre Taittinger, 1924–1940* (Paris, 1967).

for socially conservative integration, and manipulate foreign policy for socially conservative ends.[9] The behavior of Italian conservatives is more obscure, perhaps because their political formations were as invertebrate as those of their French equivalents. Yet recent writing on Italian fascism amply shows the symbiotic relationship between the Italian fascists and their conservative *fiancheggiatori*. Historians have probed the responses of Spanish conservatives to the chaos of the 1930s and their tacit alliances with protofascist movements. A particularly suggestive article has also examined the experiments of pre-1914 Russian conservatives with the mass politics of the "new" Right. Comparative studies have sought general patterns of conservative response, be they various alliances with counterrevolutionaries or efforts to recast the social, political, and economic order to ensure stability.[10]

By comparison with Germany, Italy, Spain, or Russia, France was a model of stability, threatened neither by dramatic socioeconomic change nor by genuine revolutionary disorder. After 1918 France had suffered no humiliating military defeat and harbored no irridentist appetites. Her middle classes were not yet severely dislocated by rapid industrialism, and their loyalties generally remained with the liberal republic. Her working

9. The literature is vast, but some of the most suggestive works include Hans-Ulrich Wehler, *Bismarck und der Imperialismus* (Cologne, 1969); Thomas Nipperdey, *Die Organization der deutschen Parteien vor 1918* (Dusseldorf, 1961); Thomas Nipperdey, "Die Organization der bürgerlichen Parteien in Deutschland vor 1918," *Historische Zeitschrift*, CLXXXV (1958), 550–602; Hans Jürgen Puhle, *Agrarische Interessenpolitik und preussischer Konservatismus im Wilhelminischen Reich* (Hannover, 1966); Dirk Stegmann, *Die Erben Bismarcks* (Cologne, 1970); Dirk Stegmann, "Zwischen Repression und Manipulation: Konservative Machteliten und Arbeiter-und Angestellten-bewegung, 1910–1918," *Archiv für Sozialgeschichte*, XII (1972), 351–423.

10. For Italy, see Francesco Leoni, *Storia dei partiti politici italiani* (Naples, 1971); Carlo Morandi, *I Partiti politici nella storia d'Italia* (Florence, 1968); Franco Gaeta, *Nazionalismo Italiano* (Naples, 1965); Adrian Lyttelton, *The Seizure of Power* (London, 1973); Renzo De Felice, *Mussolini il rivoluzionario* (2 vols.; Turin, 1965–68). Regarding Spain, see Martin Blinkhorn, *Carlism and Crisis in Spain, 1931–1939* (Cambridge, 1975); Richard A. H. Robinson, *The Origins of Franco's Spain* (London, 1970); Stanley G. Payne, *Falange: A History of Spanish Fascism* (Stanford, 1961). Also note Hans Rogger, "Was There a Russian Fascism?" *Journal of Modern History*, XXXVI (1964), 398–415; Arno J. Mayer, *The Dynamics of Counterrevolution in Europe* (New York, 1971); Charles S. Maier, *Recasting Bourgeois Europe* (Princeton, 1975).

classes were relatively small, largely unorganized, and until the mid–1930s politically weak. The democratic republic had a long history and deep roots; no imposing bloc of preindustrial or atavistic elites challenged the regime.

The chaotic decade of the 1930s, however, seemed to undermine this stability. The economic depression, although less severe than elsewhere, strained the limited competence of the French government and increased social unrest. Parliamentary impotence, tolerable during periods of social tranquility, raised questions about the viability of liberal democracy during sustained societal crisis. The mobilization of left-wing forces into the Popular Front, the substantial electoral victories of the Socialists and especially the Communists, and the dramatic growth of organized labor and its increased militancy seemed to presage major changes in French society. Although in retrospect the crisis of the 1930s seems less severe, to contemporary conservatives it augured a dramatic, and perhaps revolutionary, transformation of France. These real, if myopic, anxieties of French conservatives were magnified by the international crises. The *modérés* believed, not without some justice, that the French social order could not survive both the current domestic upheaval and the shock of war. Many came to believe that events both inside and outside France were conspiring to destroy the traditional social fabric and push France into a revolution.

The conservative perception of the crisis of the 1930s wrought fundamental changes in the outlook of most *modérés*. As the spiritual descendants of the liberal-conservative Orleanists, the *modérés* had accepted the democratic republic because it seemed a better guarantee of a stable society than the authoritarian alternatives of monarchist restoration or Bonapartist imperialism. They had been confident that in a liberal democratic system, with the aid of their entrenched social and economic position, they would be able to parry the latent threat from below. While preserving their republican posture, however, the *modérés* had grown increasingly ill at ease in the twentieth century. Both their much-vaunted social program and their rudimentary political organization remained better suited to an earlier era. When faced with the sudden changes and the threatened upheaval of the 1930s, many *modérés* fundamentally altered their political perspective. For the first time in the history of the Third Republic the essentially conservative consensus collapsed, and a new generation of *modérés* could no longer vouch for the social reliability of the republican regime.

To meet the challenge of the decade, conservatives adopted a twofold and fundamentally regressive strategy. First, they allied themselves with the growing forces of the so-called "new" Right, the antiparliamentary leagues. There is some debate, much of it definitional, about the applicability of labels like fascist or protofascist to movements like the Croix de Feu or the Jeunesses Patriotes (but not to Doriot's Parti Populaire Français). However, it is incontestable that the most moderate of the leagues represented a style of politics and an authoritarian ideal that the original *modérés* would have found repugnant. In the 1930s, however, insecure conservative elites found in the leagues a powerful base of mass support that could provide either invaluable electoral auxiliaries in a rapidly politicizing society or, if necessary, counterrevolutionary shock troops. Although most *modérés* never openly abandoned the parliamentary republic, their willingness to ally with a man of the background and temperament of the fascist leader, Jacques Doriot, bespoke at the very least a profound desperation and a cavalier disregard for democratic principles. Relations between the *modérés* and the leagues were often stormy, but it is striking that the one aspect of this "new" Right that never seriously worried traditional conservatives was its absolute contempt for parliamentary democracy.

The second, and related, dimension of the conservative defensive strategy was the appeasement of foreign fascism. Convinced by the mid-1930s that revolution was both the inevitable and the intended consequence of a war against Germany or Italy, most conservatives abandoned two generations of nationalistic and anti-German reflexes and clamored for peace at any price. War, they reasoned, had become the chosen vehicle for revolution in the twentieth century. Consequently, as long as the domestic Left was in the ascendancy and war promised to be an antifascist crusade, peace appeared as an essential condition for preserving order. Ultimately, the *modérés* feared Léon Blum more than Adolph Hitler and were unprepared to keep Hitler out of Prague as long as Blum and his allies ruled, or threatened to rule, in Paris. Most conservatives, although not all, found the prospect of a German conquest of eastern Europe to be disturbing but far less so than the risk of domestic social upheaval. To preserve France from revolution, or even radical reform, French conservatives passively accepted the imperialistic expansion of fascist Italy and Germany while they actively allied with protofascist elements in France.

Although circumstances in France differed from those found elsewhere, the basic reflexes of French conservatives resembled those of their German, Italian, Spanish, or Russian counterparts. The history of the French *modérés* during the last years of the Third Republic is thus part of the larger pattern of conservative response to the radical challenge of the twentieth century.

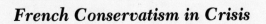

French Conservatism in Crisis

I. A *Party Profile*

In 1930 the perceptive political observer, André Siegfried, made the following analysis of the Republican Federation
of France:

> It could, in more than one respect, claim to be of the *progressiste*
> tradition, a true child of the moderate republic. But this is only a
> deceptive appearance for two decisive factors shift its center of grav-
> ity towards the right. On religious questions it represents the exist-
> ing social hierarchy. In a word, it is a party of social defense, in
> which big business (which is sometimes almost feudal) rubs shoul-
> ders with the Catholic (i.e. clerical) bourgeoisie and in which the
> strayed liberal republican would no longer recognize the republican
> tradition. Finally one finds in this conglomeration a hard core of
> nationalism, which appears to constitute the center of the most
> determined opposition to the policy of international understanding.
> In this heterogeneous mass a chemical analysis would reveal at least
> three colors: the color of the industrial feudality, that of intransigent
> nationalism and that of Catholic social defense. . . . By its general
> tone this segment of the Chamber evokes the distinct memory of
> the National Assembly although the nineteenth century style lib-
> eralism of that assembly was innocent of a certain influence of the
> Action Française which we believe to be rather at home here.[1]

Siegfried accurately caught the flavor of the Republican Federation and the diverse currents in the party during the 1930s. He
also correctly perceived that the conservatism of the Republican
Federation was no longer that of a previous generation of
modérés.

The Republican Federation of France had been founded

1. André Siegfried, *Tableau des partis en France* (Paris, 1930), 182–84.

1

twenty-seven years earlier by the right wing of the *progressistes*. The *progressistes* were conservative republicans, deeply committed to the Republic, profoundly hostile to the counter-revolutionary adventurism of the monarchists and Bonapartists, but also suspicious of the precipitous changes advocated by the Radical republicans. By 1898, with some 250 representatives in the Chamber of Deputies, the *progressistes* were the solid bulwark of the conservative republic, and the long premiership of one of their number, Jules Méline, symbolized their political ascendancy. The Dreyfus affair, however, disrupted the informal unity of the *progressistes*. In 1899, fearing for the security of the Republic, a minority of *progressistes*, led by Raymond Poincaré, deserted the relatively conservative government of Charles Dupuy for that of René Waldeck-Rousseau. Although Waldeck-Rousseau was a thoroughly moderate republican, his government included the Socialist, Alexandre Millerand, and relied on the Radicals for support. Jules Méline and the more conservative wing of the *progressistes* would not support such a government and joined the Catholic Right, only recently rallied to the Republic, in opposition. The rupture of the *progressistes* was consummated in 1901 when their left wing founded the Alliance Démocratique and openly allied with the Radicals. Two years later the right wing, reduced in numbers by the 1902 elections, formed its own party.

In response to the disruption and eclipse of their forces a number of prominent *progressistes* held a special congress on November 18, 1903. Eugène Motte, industrialist and deputy from the Nord, presided over the congress and proposed the creation of a Republican Federation. The Federation would unite former *progressistes* into a comprehensive political party that could meet more effectively the challenge presented by the Radicals and the growing Socialist movement. As the energetic young mayor of the textile town of Roubaix, Motte had twice defeated the prominent Socialist, Jules Guesde, in the legislative elections and had forged a large and powerful conservative electoral organization. Armed with these credentials, he stressed the need to replace the loose and informal organization of the *progressistes* with an elaborate and cohesive party that could mobilize the energies of the "industrialists, businessmen and merchants."[2]

The Republican Federation that emerged from the meeting was an amalgam of three political formations: the Alliance des Républicains Progressistes, Jules Méline's purely parliamentary union of deputies and senators, and two extraparliamentary associations, the Union Libérale Républicaine and the Association Nationale Républicaine. The Union, founded by the liberal lawyer Henri Barboux in response to the Boulangist agitation, had seen its task as the restoration of the political influence of the *grande bourgeoisie*. The Association had been founded in 1885 as a rallying point for moderate republicans by that cornerstone of the conservative republic, Jules Ferry. The republican credentials of the founders of the Republican Federation were excellent. Typically they had entered politics in the 1860s as republican or Orleanist opponents of the Empire and had rallied to the Republic from its foundation. Alexandre Ribot, Georges Picot, Edouard Aynard, Jules Méline, Paul Beauregard, Auguste Isaac, Joseph Thierry, and Henri Barboux had been mainstays of the moderate republic; and their prominence in the early Republican Federation clearly situated the party in the respectable republican center.[3]

The new party was undeniably socially conservative, rejecting most social legislation as "collectivist" and resisting bitterly the

2. On Motte see Myer Siemiatycki, "Guesdism and Anti-Collectivism in Roubaix-Wattrelos: A Study of the Legislative Elections between 1893–1906" (M.A. thesis, University of Sussex, 1971), esp. 57–61. *Journal des Débats*, November 20, 1903.

3. *Journal des Débats*, November 20, 1903; Pierre Cathala, *Eloge de Henri Barboux* (Mesnil sur l'Estrée, 1921); *Bulletin-Correspondance de l'Association Nationale Républicaine*, November 25, 1903; Charles Benoist, *Souvenirs* (2 vols.; Paris, 1934), II, 48; Josephe Buché, *Essai sur la vie et l'oeuvre d'Edouard Aynard* (Lyon, 1921); Alexandre Ribot, "Georges Picot," *La Revue Hebdomadaire*, February 11, 1911, pp. 141–70; Martin E. Schmidt, *Alexandre Ribot: Odyssey of a Liberal in the Third Republic* (The Hague, 1974); Antoine Olivesi, "La droite à Marseille en 1914: Aspects de la géographie électorale, de la structure sociale et de l'opinion politique des milieux modérés marseillais," *Provence Historique*, VIII (1957), 175–99; see also the assessment of the *Journal des Débats*, May 9, 1906.

proposed "inquisitorial" income tax. While reluctantly accepting the 1905 separation of church and state, the Federation opposed the pervasive anticlericalism of the period and urged a "generous and tolerant application" of the new law. Nonetheless, the party repeatedly insisted that its social conservatism and moderate Catholicism did not make it a party of the Right. It was, as its first president Eugène Motte maintained, a party of the Center with a greater affinity to its left-wing neighbor the Alliance Démocratique than to Jacques Piou's Action Libérale Populaire on its right. The latter consisted of Catholics who had abandoned their traditional hostility to the' republic and rallied to the regime in the 1890s.[4] Despite its nominal republicanism, Motte considered the Action Libérale Populaire to be at best a latecomer to the Republic without the historic republicanism of the Alliance or the Federation. For him it was of the utmost importance that the Federation be "an organization directed by republicans of the first hour." His successor, Joseph Thierry, maintained that the Federation was a party of republicans "from the time when the Republic was so beautiful."[5] At virtually every prewar congress delegates evoked the struggles of the Federation's founders against the forces of reaction. As late as the early 1920s, local leaders of the Federation, protesting real or imagined attempts to exclude them from the republican chapel, typically cited the republican credentials of their fathers or grandfathers.[6]

Behind these increasingly strident assertions of republican purity lay the fear that the Federation was gradually drifting toward the Right. During his presidency from 1906 to 1911, Joseph Thierry persistently declared the Federation to be a party of the Center. In 1910 he sought to clarify the party's position in a circular to members asserting that the Federation was

4. *Le Figaro*, November 26, 1906; Benjamin F. Martin, Jr., "The Creation of the Action Libérale Populaire: An Example of Party Formation in Third Republic France," *French Historical Studies*, IX (1976), 660–89.

5. *Journal des Débats*, November 20, 1903, November 25, 1909.

6. For example: *La Liberté du Morbihan*, December 30, 1923; *Journal de Rouen*, March 20, 1923.

open only to those who accepted all aspects of the Republic, including its religious laws. This circular, widely interpreted as a peace feeler toward Aristide Briand's moderate centrist government, stirred up a chorus of protests from the more conservative members of the Federation, who found republican loyalty quite consistent with intransigent opposition to the religious settlement.[7]

Early in 1911, Thierry and thirty other deputies seceded from the Federation's semiofficial parliamentary group, the *républicains progressistes*, to form a separate *union républicaine*. Ritualistically the new group claimed greater sensitivity to social questions than its predecessor but, as contemporaries recognized, the real issue was one of "political birth certificates." *Progressistes* like Thierry, who considered themselves to be native-born republicans, did not wish to be confounded with those who were at best "naturalized republicans." Fearing a gradual influx of former monarchists and nationalists into the ranks of the politically respectable but ideologically ambiguous *républicains progressistes*, the deputies of the *union républicaine* moved toward the Left. By 1914 most of them had left the ranks of the Federation for the Alliance Démocratique.[8]

The evolution of the Federation away from its liberal progressive origins reflected the leftward shift of the French political center of gravity, which inevitably altered the Federation's relative position on the political spectrum. The more moderate and genuinely republican elements, like Thierry, sought less equivocal formations, whose personnel were unambivalently republican. Their leftward migration resulted in part from a desire to avoid contamination by the former enemies of the republic and in part, as their conservative critics charged, from the more appealing electoral and ministerial opportunities offered by the Center-Left. At the same time, the departure of the more mod-

7. *La Lanterne*, November 14, 1910; *La Croix*, November 26, 1910; *La Libre Parole*, November 30, 1910; *La République Française*, December 1, 20, 1910.

8. *La République Française*, March 26, 1911. On the split within the *progressistes* see Malcolm Anderson, "The Parliamentary Right in France, 1905–1919" (D. Phil. dissertation, Oxford, 1961), 12.

erate conservatives made the Federation an attractive home for individuals whose political reflexes were very different from those of the founders of the party. The prewar rift marked the beginning of the evolution suggested by Siegfried, which by 1930 placed the Republican Federation on the extreme Right.

The First World War marks a break in the history of the Republican Federation. Not only had many of its earlier adherents changed political allegiances, but by 1918 many of the party's prewar leaders were dead or retired. Conservatives triumphed in the postwar elections; and the Federation, with approximately 125 deputies (twice its prewar representation), was well represented in the resulting *Chambre Bleu Horizon*. The party, however, made no effort to organize its deputies into a single group as it had in 1914 and instead joined other Catholic conservatives to form the 187-member Entente Républicaine Démocratique. A handful of provincial representatives continued to attend the party's modest annual congresses, and the executive still met at irregular intervals. But the Republican Federation had lost even the limited momentum it had enjoyed before the war.[9]

In 1924 the resounding victory of the electoral coalition of Socialists and Radicals, the Cartel des Gauches, shook the Federation out of its lethargy and demonstrated the need for firm leadership among conservatives. Since both Auguste Isaac, the president of the Federation, and François Arago, the ailing president of the party's parliamentary group, were defeated, the floundering Federation turned to the deputy from the Meurthe-et-Moselle, Louis Marin. Although Marin's undisciplined opposition to the Treaty of Versailles had made him something of a political pariah in 1919, he alone appeared to have the energy necessary to revive the party. He assumed leadership of the

9. Anderson, "Parliamentary Right in France," 95. The party had no official parliamentary group before 1914, and until 1910 deputies had been free to belong to more than one group. Consequently, it is difficult to establish exactly how many deputies belonged to the Federation. In 1906, forty-five of sixty-six *progressistes* adhered to the party (*Journal des Débats*, November 23, 1906); in 1914 the party counted forty-seven deputies.

Federation and its parliamentary group, founded *La Nation* (the party's house organ), and within a few years stamped the party with his energetic style. The Republican Federation became for many Frenchmen simply *le parti marin*, and Marin was considered the "second founder" of the party. His ragged and unkempt white moustache and his perennial blue and white polkadot bow tie provided contemporary cartoonists with an appealing symbol of the Republican Federation and the ultranationalist Right.[10]

Louis Marin was born in February, 1871, in the village of Faulx in Lorraine amidst military defeat, social revolution, and national humiliation. Marin's mother died shortly afterward of childbirth fever, a death that the Marin family ascribed to the forced absence of French doctors held as hostages by the Germans. The circumstances of his birth, a childhood marked by tragic accounts of the "terrible year," and the experience of the recently resettled refugees from German-occupied Lorraine left a lasting imprint on Marin and shaped his attitude toward Germany. The son of a notary, he first attended the communal school in Faulx and then, from 1881 to 1887, the Catholic College de la Malagrange near Nancy. It was at Malagrange, the alma mater of Maurice Barrès, that Marin began his friendship with the future industrial magnates, Henri de Peyerimhoff, Edouard de Warren, and François de Wendel, as well as with the historian Louis Madelin. The latter three were to collaborate with him in the Republican Federation. After three more years of study at the College of Saint-Sigisbert, Louis Marin moved to Paris where he received his law degree in 1892. His real interests lay elsewhere, however, and years spent in study and extensive travel aroused his desire to pursue ethnology and a teaching career. Marin remained active in the academic world throughout his life and was director of the Ecole d'Anthropologie in Paris from 1923 until his death.[11]

10. *La Nation*, October 1, 1938.
11. The best sources for the early career of Louis Marin are Mme. Louis Marin, *Louis Marin, 1871–1960: Homme d'Etat, Philosophe et Savant* (Paris, 1973); and Gaetan

In 1905, however, his main interest turned toward politics. That year, at the age of thirty-four, Marin began his political career as candidate for the second arrondissement of Nancy. Although a member of the Republican Federation since its inception, Marin ran as an independent liberal. He was not, as his friend Louis Madelin later observed, "one of those classic candidates, carefully catalogued and designated by congresses, rubber stamped by the parties and supervised by committees."[12] Supported by a committee of three friends, he campaigned vigorously, pedaled his way around the constituency on his bicycle, and successfully outdistanced his seven rivals. Once in the Chamber, Marin associated himself with the other deputies of the Republican Federation, and in 1906 he was elected one of the secretaries of the *républicains progressistes*. It was the beginning of a forty-six-year parliamentary career.

Marin soon earned the reputation of a first-class parliamentarian. Although his political views were often extremely unpopular with his colleagues, he enjoyed the personal respect and professional esteem of even his most extreme political opponents. A meticulous and hardworking representative, almost always seen with a sheaf of documents under his arm, Marin was one of the best-informed deputies in the hemicycle. His discourses and interventions in parliament revealed a profound and extensive grasp of contemporary problems, in particular those of foreign policy. During his parliamentary career Marin presented

Sanvoisin, "L'Oeuvre de M. Louis Marin," *La Revue Hebdomadaire*, February 27, 1932, pp. 473–93. Other sources, most of which rely heavily on Sanvoisin for the period before 1932, include: L. Dumont-Wilden, *Louis Marin* (Paris, 1936), a brief and uncritical "campaign biography"; André François-Poncet, "Notice sur la vie et les travaux de Louis Marin," *Institut de France, Académie des Sciences Morales et Politiques*, 1964, no. 3, pp. 1–32; Pierre Renouvin, "Discours prononcé le 25 avril 1967 à l'occasion de l'inauguration de la Place Louis Marin," *Institut de France, Académie des Sciences Morales et Politiques*, 1967, no. 6, pp. 1–12; Paul Faber, *Discours, Paris, Conseil Municipal, Inauguration officielle de la Place Louis Marin* (Paris, 1967); Henri Lalevée, "Un grand Français d'origine vosgienne: Louis Marin, 1871–1960," *Bulletin de la Société Philomathique Vosgienne*, LXIX (1966), 97–106; Monique Vivenot, "Un homme politique lorrain: Louis Marin et l'Allemagne, 1905–1933," *Bulletin de l'Association Interuniversitaire de l'Est*, VIII (1966), 295–303.
   12. Cited in Mme. Marin, *Louis Marin*, 152.

over five hundred reports or bills before the Chamber, a record in the history of that body. He presided over a number of commissions, including Poincaré's commission on economic reforms in 1923 and the commission of enquiry into the Oustric scandal in 1931. He was six times a cabinet minister, frequently the sole representative of the Republican Federation in the government.

Despite his prominence, the major cabinet posts (the so-called "levers of command") always escaped him. He was invariably assigned the lesser portfolios, such as the Ministry of Liberated Areas or the Ministry of Pensions or the primarily symbolic ones like the Ministry of State. Marin's extreme nationalism made him a liability in most governments and tended to frighten away the Center elements in parliament. Marin usually received posts in the broad coalition governments that extended from the Radicals to the Republican Federation, known as governments of "national union." Here, Marin's presence was necessary to assure the support of the Republican Federation. But, given the political balance of the interwar years, even the most conservative premier could not hope to form a viable government with Louis Marin in a major post.

Louis Marin's most characteristic trait was his traditional and unbending nationalism. His experiences in his native Lorraine instilled in him a profound distrust of Germany and an abiding concern for French security. His writings abounded with references to "the desire for domination and conquest" that "has always haunted the German mentality," and to the "warlike tendencies of the German people already noticed by Julius Caesar." In 1919 he and his friend Henri Franklin-Bouillon bitterly opposed the Treaty of Versailles as too lenient and were the only non-Socialists to vote against its ratification. During the interwar years Marin's Germanophobia was legendary. Emmanuel Berl once observed that, for Louis Marin, "French diplomacy is bad by virtue of existing at all. To discuss is already a concession, a first step down the road to disaster. To listen is a second concession, more serious than the first. To reply is a third concession and tantamount to the complete surrender of national dignity."[13]

For Marin the distinction between good and bad Germans was absurd. The "good" Gustav Stresemann was simply a German statesman pursuing that nation's traditionally aggressive foreign policy by more subtle means. Marin particularly condemned the perennial French foreign minister of the 1920s and early 1930s, Aristide Briand, whose desire to treat Germany as a worthy member of the international community struck Marin as naïve and dangerous. Marin regarded German aggressiveness as a given of international politics, and he refused to believe that either a change of regime in Germany or pious proclamations by its leaders could alter this harsh reality. The only appropriate policy for France was eternal vigilance and an insistence on the rigorous application of the peace treaties, which, even if imperfect, were the only means of preserving the victory for which France had sacrificed so much.

Marin's trademark was his stubborn and uncompromising stance on a broad range of "matters of principle." As one journalist noted, he could compile "the most impressive honor role of 'voted againsts'" of anyone in politics.[14] Although Marin's intransigence appealed to those conservatives who decried the vacillation of most modérés, it made him a difficult colleague. He regarded the Republican Federation as *his* party and was intolerant of dissenting views. He could display a Robespierre-like self-righteousness when defending his position and would condemn as opportunists—if not as outright traitors—those who deviated from his often intemperate and inflexible principles. Marin's speeches and writings were marred by a penchant for moralizing that not only irritated his colleagues, but often obfuscated the issue. A voluble rather than eloquent speaker,

13. *La Nation*, May 14, 1938; *Le Jour*, November 24, 1938. Marin catalogued his objections to the treaty in Louis Marin, *Le Traité de paix* (Paris, 1920). Emmanuel Berl, *La Politique et les partis* (Paris, 1932), 31–32.

14. André Stibio, "Louis Marin: Un Parlementaire 100%," *Vendémiaire*, May 5, 1937.

Marin tended to obscure his points with long and irrelevant digressions. The ardor of his convictions was seldom in doubt, but he frequently devoted more energy to the elucidation of some moral law or to the justification of his past actions than to discussing the point at issue.

Marin's self-righteousness intensely exasperated those who suspected that he could be far more flexible when there was a chance of his being offered a cabinet post. His principled opposition, they observed, tended to be most intense when he was excluded from the cabinet of the day. In 1931 Aristide Briand effectively cut short one of Marin's harangues about his criminal foreign policy by observing that the foundations of that same policy had been laid while Marin was a colleague of his in Poincaré's 1926–1928 government. He noted that Marin had not at that time been distressed to the point of resigning his portfolio in protest.[15] Similarly, the alacrity with which Marin entered Pierre-Etienne Flandin's 1934 cabinet disturbed some members of the Federation, who considered it to be a government of unprincipled ambition.[16]

Although Marin's lack of tact and diplomacy provoked serious ruptures within the Federation during the early 1930s, his reputation for intransigence earned him the respect of many *militants*, some of whom accorded him an immoderate degree of devotion.[17] Despite his disruptive actions, he was the closest thing to a unifying symbol the Republican Federation ever had.

The leaders of the Republican Federation fell into three general categories: Marin's loyal supporters, those who resisted his inflexible nationalism, and those who represented a style of poli-

15. *Journal Officiel: Débats parlementaires, Chambre des Députés*, August 8, 1931, p. 2668. Unless otherwise indicated, all future references to the *Journal Officiel* are to the debates of the Chamber of Deputies.

16. Many commentators, particularly on the Right, suspected that Flandin had connived with the Radicals in the fall of 1934 to defeat the government of Gaston Doumergue. Doumergue had come to power after the right-wing riots of February 6, 1934, and was seen as something of a savior by many conservatives.

17. For a particularly effusive example see *L'Union Républicaine du Rhône*, February 5, 1933.

tics quite alien to that of the founders of the party.[18] Marin's principal lieutenant was Camille Blaisot, deputy from the Calvados and vice-president of the Federation. More tactful than his leader, Blaisot identified closely with Marin and often served as the party's token representative in conservative governments. The leaders of the Federation's larger departmental organizations, particularly Victor Perret from the Rhône, Jean Baudouin from the Seine-Inférieure, and Charles-Maurice Bellet from the Seine, consistently supported Marin. Some of his most loyal followers had entered politics on the extreme Right. The Parisian deputy, Joseph Denais, began his political career in the Action Libérale Populaire and had served as editor of the anti-Semitic *La Libre Parole* before 1914. The journalist, Jacques Debû-Bridel, made his political debut with the Action Française before coming to the Federation in the 1930s. In spite of their

18. The prosopographical data in this chapter are drawn primarily from the following sources. Jean Jolly (ed.), *Dictionnaire des parlementaires françaises* (7 vols.; Paris, 1960–72) gives biographical information on all French parliamentarians between 1889 and 1940. However, many of the sketches are uneven in quality, providing little information about family or social background. More informative in this respect is the monumental exercise in muckraking by Augustin Hamon, *Les Maîtres de la France* (3 vols.; Paris, 1937). Hamon, a left-wing critic of finance capitalism, provides a remarkable look into the interconnections between the various segments of the French elite and is particularly informative about the marriage alliances between deputies of the Federation and landed and industrial wealth. It is a highly polemical work and not free from errors of fact. A more reliable source, and one that Hamon relied heavily upon, is the periodical *Les Documents politiques, diplomatiques et financiers*, directed by R. Mennevée. This journal, which appeared monthly from 1920 until 1939, provides a detailed and careful examination of French and international capitalism. Of particular interest are its special issues entitled "Parlementaires et Financiers" (April, 1928, April, 1930, March, 1932, August, 1933, February, 1936), which listed all deputies and senators sitting on the board of directors of one or more business firms. Additional information can be drawn from the thumbnail portraits of all deputies that appeared in the right-wing weekly *Le Charivari* prior to the elections of 1932 and 1936 (every week from August 1, 1931, to April 23, 1932, and from January 18, 1936, to April 25, 1936). The brief sketches were written by a well-informed but anonymous and highly biased correspondent. Further information can be drawn from Gilles Norman, *Politiques et hommes politiques* (2 vols.; Paris, 1925), II. Two final sources, although the least reliable, are Henry Coston (ed.), *Partis: Journaux et hommes politiques d'hier et d'aujourd'hui* (Paris, 1960) and Henry Coston (ed.), *Dictionnaire de la politique française* (Paris, 1967). Coston was a notorious Vichyite and a right-wing critic of finance capitalism. He was very familiar with ultraconservative and Fascist circles. Although his works contain a number of errors, they provide some useful information about members of the Federation.

origins, however, by the late 1930s these men were among the more loyal republicans in the party.

The most notorious of Marin's intimate colleagues was his boyhood friend and fellow deputy from the Meurthe-et-Moselle, François de Wendel. One of the leading figures in French mining and metallurgy, de Wendel was, from 1918 to 1940, secretary-general of the powerful iron and steel cartel, the Comité des Forges. A symbol of the famous two hundred families (after the two hundred directors of the Bank of France) who allegedly controlled France, de Wendel's purported influence in government was a persistent source of controversy in the 1920s and 1930s. Critics of the Federation did not hesitate to charge that de Wendel was the real master of the party and that Marin's insistence on the rigorous enforcement of the Treaty of Versailles merely reflected the economic interests of the de Wendel steelworks. De Wendel did contribute financially to the Federation, but recent scholarship has shown that his influence both in the government and in the Federation was less than either critics claimed or de Wendel desired.[19]

Opponents of Marin's dictatorial style and unyielding nationalism gathered around the deputy from the Doubs, Georges Pernot, and the journalist Henri de Kerillis. Pernot, a vice-president of the party, was a devoted Catholic and maintained close relations with the Christian democrats of the neighboring Parti Démocrate Populaire and the liberal Catholic review, *Politique*. Pernot shared some of the internationalism of these liberal Catholics and enjoyed cordial relations with the architect of French foreign policy, Aristide Briand. He increasingly found

19. The special edition on the "200 Familles" in *Crapouillot*, February 6, 1936, begins with full-page pictures of François de Wendel and his nephew Guy de Wendel. By far the most authoritative study of de Wendel, based on hitherto unavailable private papers, is Jean-Noël Jeanneney, *François de Wendel en République: L'argent et le pouvoir, 1914–1940* (Paris, 1976). Jeanneney's study effectively refutes most of the sinister and conspiratorial theories about de Wendel put forth by contemporaries and by historians, such as Emmanuel Beau de Loménie, *Les Responsabilités des dynasties bourgeoises* (5 vols.; Paris, 1943–73), esp. III, *La Guerre et l'immediat après guerre* (1954), 87–88, and V, *De Hitler à Pétain* (1973), 246–47.

Marin's nationalism to be excessively rigid and counterproductive and led a revolt against him in the early 1930s. Kerillis, a World War I aviator and self-proclaimed member of the *génération du feu*, was for most of his career the enfant terrible of the French Right. As political director of the conservative *Echo de Paris*, Kerillis bemoaned the ineffectiveness of the *modérés* and created the Centre de propagande des républicains nationaux with a view to modernizing the electoral efforts of conservatives. In the early 1930s he was an outspoken member of the Federation's executive committee, protesting both the party's incoherent organization and Marin's autocratic leadership.

By the 1930s some of the survivors and many of the spiritual heirs of the virtually defunct antirepublican Right had entered the Republican Federation. Some had an importance, or a notoriety, that was independent of their role in the party. Three vice-presidents of the Federation, Pierre Taittinger, Edouard Soulier, and Jean Ybarnegaray, were better known for their activity in the Jeunesses Patriotes. Taittinger, who entered politics as a deputy from the Bonapartist stronghold of the Charente-Inférieure and later represented the first arrondissement of Paris, founded the Jeunesses Patriotes in 1925 and presided over the right-wing league throughout its history. Soulier, a Protestant minister and deputy from Paris, was honorary president of the league. In the early 1930s both men publicly differed with Louis Marin over foreign policy but remained within the party. The big and robust deputy from the Basses-Pyrénées, Jean Ybarnegaray, was among the most popular deputies in the Chamber. "Ybar" was an easygoing, generous figure whose personal warmth compensated for his legendary laziness. After 1934 Ybarnegaray drifted away from both the Federation and the Jeunesses Patriotes and gravitated into the Croix de Feu and the Parti Social Français.

During the 1930s a new generation of leaders emerged. Jacques Poitou-Duplessy, Xavier Vallat, and Philippe Henriot, all three vice-presidents of the Federation, brought a new energy to the party and also helped to change its tone. In both temperament and political origins, these men had little in common with the moderate *progressistes* who founded the Republican Federation. Their increasing prominence in the party symbolized its gradual evolution toward the extreme Right. Jacques Poitou-Duplessy came from a family of wealthy landowners in the Charente. The Charente had a powerful Bonapartist tradition, and Poitou-Duplessy's brother, Roger, had been a Bonapartist deputy from the department. After war service in the air force, he ran for parliament and represented his brother's former constituency from 1919 to 1924 and from 1936 until 1940. During the interval he served as the Federation's delegate-at-large for propaganda and became vice-president in 1935. Upon his reelection in 1936 he quickly became one of the most strident opponents of the Popular Front. He also typified those deputies whose opposition to communism, both domestic and foreign, gradually led them to abandon their traditional hostility toward Germany and concentrate their energies on the "Russian peril."

Xavier Vallat was among the most notorious public figures in interwar France. He was the son of a public school teacher, whose monarchist convictions caused him to be constantly harassed by local school authorities. During World War I, Vallat was five times wounded and lost a leg and an eye. Elected as a monarchist deputy from the Ardèche in 1919, he was beaten in 1924 and reelected in 1928. Vallat was a monarchist, a devoted Catholic, an extreme nationalist, and an anti-Semite. In the 1920s he dabbled in most of the groups of the extreme Right including the fascist Faisceau, the Action Française, and the Croix de Feu. In the Chamber he sat as an independent with a small group of monarchists until 1933 when he quietly joined the Republican Federation. Motivated by opportunism rather than Republican conviction, he admitted after the war that he had been willing to feign a lukewarm republicanism in the 1930s because he saw no immediate possibility for the restoration of the monarchy.[20] The intense and unbending nationalism of Louis Marin also attracted him.

His unlikely background notwithstanding, Vallat became an active member of the Republican Federation and was elected vice-president in 1936. A popular speaker with a wry sense of humor and a blunt, precise style, Vallat became a favorite at party rallies where he energetically defended the Federation against attacks from both the Left and the "new" Right. He enjoyed friends on all sides of the hemicycle, but parliamentary amenities did not deter him from commenting on the racial origins of Léon Blum. Writing in the local paper in his constituency of Annonay, he pointedly spat out his hatred for Freemasons, financiers, and Jews. He also shared Louis Marin's hatred for the Germans, although he allowed this hatred to be surpassed by his greater fear of Communist Russia.

The most energetic figure in the Republican Federation was Philippe Henriot. The son of a modest infantry officer and the product of the Catholic *école libre*, Henriot began his career as a professor of English in the college of Sainte Foy la Grande in Bordeaux. In 1914 a fortunate marriage made him the owner of a comfortable landed estate in the Bordeaux region. He did not enlist in World War I and devoted the next ten years to viticulture and writing novels and poetry.[21] In 1925 Henriot entered political life in association with the conservative deputy from the Gironde, the Abbé Bergey. He helped Bergey establish the Republican Union of the Gironde, which affiliated with the Republican Federation in 1927. He subsequently rose in the Federation's organization, becoming successively a member of the National Council, a member of the executive, and in 1932 a vice-president. In the same year he replaced Bergey as deputy from Bordeaux.

20. Xavier Vallat, *Le Procès de Xavier Vallat (presenté par ses amis)* (Paris, 1948), 20; see also his autobiographical Xavier Vallat, *Le Nez de Cléopâtre* (Paris, 1957).

21. The satirical monthly, *Crapouillot*, January, 1935, p. 44, dubbed him the "unknown soldier." For a general outline of Henriot's early career see Jean and Bernard Guerin, *Des hommes et des activités autour d'un demi-siècle* (Bordeaux, 1957), 365–66.

Henriot's principal asset as a politician was his remarkable gift of oratory. Although an ugly and ungainly figure, he could captivate an audience with his compelling rhetoric; and within two years of entering the Chamber, he earned the reputation of being the most effective speaker on the Right. His speaking skill, however, was not matched by a corresponding degree of political acumen. Jean-Pierre Maxence described him as "lashing, effective, magnificent when leading a precise assault" but "vague, verbose, and even uncertain on questions of general politics." As even he seems to have realized, Henriot lacked substance and never really understood politics. The harshness of his rhetoric, the vagueness of his ideas, and his ill-disguised impatience with parliamentary tradition sounded faintly fascist and led contemporaries to wonder what Philippe Henriot was doing in the party of Louis Marin. Although his relations with Marin were cool, Henriot nonetheless professed a stubborn fidelity to the Federation and until 1940 defended it against its younger rivals on the Right.[22]

In the conservative, nationalistic, and Catholic Republican Federation of Louis Marin, François de Wendel, and Georges Pernot, others of more questionable republicanism could find a comfortable home. Observers of the Left and the Right often treated the Federation of the 1930s as an unholy alliance. The influx of former Bonapartists and members of the Action Française into the Federation scandalized liberal Catholics. On the extreme Right, François Le Grix of *La Revue Hebdomadaire* was distressed to find such dynamic figures as Xavier Vallat and Philippe Henriot "bogged down" in a party like the Republican Federation.[23] Significantly, these apparent ideological incongrui-

22. Jean-Pierre Maxence, *Histoire de dix ans* (Paris, 1939), 245; Jacques Debû-Bridel, *L'Agonie de la Troisième République* (Paris, 1948), 185–93; *L'Ordre*, April 23, 1937; Emmanuel Beau de Loménie, *La Revue Hebdomadaire*, October 19, 1935, pp. 325–26. For a long speech about the eternally young Federation, see *La Réveil Charentais*, June 13, 1937.

23. *Le Petit Démocrate*, January 24, 1937; *La Revue Hebdomadaire*, June 12, 1937, p. 251.

ties never perturbed the ranks of the Republican Federation—a comment on the state of conservative republicanism by the 1930s.

In the 1930s between 80 and 100 of the 600 deputies in parliament were affiliated with the Republican Federation.[24] These figures need qualification, however, since the number of deputies actually sitting with the parliamentary group was often significantly smaller. In 1928, 102 deputies sat with the parliamentary group of the Federation; in 1932, 43 deputies; in 1936, 60 deputies. The apparent decline in electoral representation in the 1930s was due primarily to internal dissensions and the resultant defection of deputies, rather than to any drastic change in electoral fortunes. In 1932 the Federation actually elected some 80 deputies; but nearly half of them, largely for personal reasons, chose not to sit with the official group of the party. After the 1936 election, the headquarters of the Federation drafted a list of 95 deputies, who it felt might reasonably be expected to sit with the party.[25] That only 60 did so can be attributed mostly to personal rancor dating from the early 1930s. In any case, many former members of the Federation had political reflexes and voting records that were virtually identical with those of the "official" members of the party.

The deputies of the Republican Federation were drawn by and large from the social and economic elite of France. Titled and landed wealth was well represented in the party. During the 1930s at least eleven counts, five marquises, four barons,

---

24. The Republican Federation also had 56 senators in 1924 and 30 by 1938. Its senators sat in two separate groups, the Union Républicaine and the Gauche Républicaine; the Federation did not play a distinct role in the Senate. Senators such as General Auguste Hirschauer (Moselle), Gustave Gautherot (Loire-Inférieure), Maurice Hervey (Eure), Manuel Fourcade (Hautes-Pyrénées), François de Wendel (Meurthe-et-Moselle), and Charles Desjardins (Aisne) were nonetheless active in the internal life of the party.

25. This list would appear to represent a realistic estimate, including former (and future) members of the party, as well as those who had received financial aid from the Federation. It carefully omitted those whose rupture with the party had been bitter and definitive. The list is in the private collection of Louis Marin's papers (Archives Nationales, carton 85).

two dukes, and a prince were deputies of the party.[26] Most of them, as well as many other untitled deputies, had substantial holdings of landed property and one or more country chateaux. The Federation had no monopoly on deputies of this kind: Count André de Fels was a leading director of the Alliance Démocratique; and François-Xavier de Reille-Soult, Duke of Dalmatia, was a deputy of the Parti Démocrate Populaire. Nonetheless, this element of French society was best represented by the Federation. Of the twenty-four deputies listed by Augustin Hamon to show the connection between deputies and landed property, nineteen were members or former members of the Republican Federation.[27]

By the twentieth century, French landed, commercial, and industrial wealth had become intermixed. For example, the daughter of de Wendel, the steel magnate, married a de Montaigu of the wealthy aristocratic family from the Vendée. A daughter of this union married into the aristocratic du Luart family, which had intimate connections with the world of finance and industry. All three families provided deputies for the Republican Federation: François de Wendel, Hubert de Montaigu, and Jacques du Luart. Some aristocratic deputies of the Federation had indirect relations through marriage with the French financial and industrial oligarchy. Count Bertrand d'Aramon, for example, was the son-in-law of Jacques Stern, director of the Banque de Paris et des Pays-Bas. Marquis Lionel

---

26. Counts: Bernard d'Aillières (Sarthe), Bertrand d'Aramon (Paris), Bernard de Coral (Basses-Pyrénées), Jacques du Luart (Seine-Inférieure), Hubert de Montaigu (Loire-Inférieure), Jean' de Tinguy du Pouët (Vendée), Pierre de Chabot (Vendée), Ernest de Framond de la Frammondie (Lozère), Edouard de Warren (Meurthe-et-Moselle), François de Wendel (Meurthe-et-Moselle), Victor Rillart de Verneuil (Aisne), Charles de Lasteyrie (Paris). Marquises: Lionel de Moustier (Doubs), Henri de Saint-Pern (Maine-et-Loire), Pierre de Haut (Jura), Henri de la Ferronnays (Loire-Inférieure), Jacques de Juingé (Loire-Inférieure). Dukes: Etienne d'Audiffret-Pasquier (Orne), François de Harcourt (Calvados). Barons: Georges de Grandmaison (Maine-et-Loire), Guillaume des Rotours (Calvados), Henry des Lyons de Feuchin (Somme). Princes: François de Polignac (Maine-et-Loire).

27. Hamon, *Maîtres de la France*, II, 318–24.

de Moustier married Suzanne de Ligne, daughter of a Belgian millionaire; and the Marquis de Juingé married a daughter of a leading steel producer, Eugène Schneider.

For other aristocratic deputies there was a direct family connection with business and industry. Pierre de Monicault, deputy and large-scale agriculturalist from the Ain, was the brother of Gaston de Monicault—a leading director of the largest insurance company in France, the Assurance Générale. The Marquis Pierre de Haut was associated with a number of important mining and metallurgical interests in the Franche-Comté and was the vice-president of the insurance firm Abeille. Count Charles de Lasteyrie inherited a seat on the board of directors of the Chemin de Fer de l'Ouest. A former inspector of finance, Lasteyrie was also a principal director of the insurance company Providence, controlled by "nobles representing agrarian and landed capitalism."[28] Henri Fournier-Sarlovèze, deputy for the Oise, was vice-president of another major insurance firm, the group Urbaine.

A number of deputies were well-known industrialists. Auguste Isaac, Marin's predecessor as president of the party, was an important entrepreneur and financier in Lyon. François de Wendel was the most notorious representative of big business in the party, but several other deputies also played a leading role in French heavy industry. Jean Plichon, deputy from the Nord, was vice-president of the powerful Comité Central des Houillères de France, chairman of the board of directors of the Mines de Bethune, and a member of the boards of the Union des Industries Métallurgiques et Minières, Crédit Industriel et Commercial, and at least eleven other firms in the fields of mining, metallurgy, and banking. His fellow deputy from the Nord, Louis Nicolle, sat on the board of directors of no less than sixteen companies in textiles, distilling, metallurgy, and transport. Pierre Amidieu du Clos, deputy from Meurthe-et-Moselle, came from a long line of metallurgical entrepreneurs and was

28. *Ibid.*, 57–58.

the director of a sizable mining complex. Of the 102 deputies of the Federation in the 1928–1932 legislature, 43 sat on the boards of directors of one or more private companies.[29]

By no means, however, did all these deputies represent large-scale capitalism. Many were heads of small family firms and represented the interests of small and medium-sized business. Edmond Bloud, deputy for the Seine, collaborated with Francisque Gay in a small publishing house which specialized in Catholic literature. His fellow Parisian deputy Louis Dubois also owned a small printing house. Auguste Sabatier, deputy from Paris, headed a wholesale butcher shop catering to the Parisian restaurant trade; Victor Rochereau, deputy from the Vendée, sat on the board of directors of the Fabrique Vendéenne de Bonneterie; and Robert Serot, deputy for the Moselle, sat as an agronomist on the board of the Caisse Regionale de Crédit Agricole Mutuelle. Louis Dumat, deputy for Paris, was director of the Société d'Habitation à Bon Marché; Pierre Vallette-Viallard from the Ardèche was a building contractor; and André Daher from Marseilles was a ships' outfitter, who expanded into maritime insurance and transport.

Such connections with the business community were not unique to the deputies of the Republican Federation. In the 1928–1932 legislature, approximately 150 deputies were sitting on the boards of one or more companies, and the parties of the Center and the Center-Right were as well represented in the nation's boardrooms as was the Republican Federation. Furthermore, many leading figures in the party had little overt connection with big business. Louis Marin, Edouard Soulier, Camille Blaisot, Gustave Guerin, Georges Pernot, Xavier Vallat, and Philippe Henriot were all men of relatively modest origin, who were important almost exclusively for their political activities. Conversely, some who had the most intimate links with the business world played little or no role either in the Chamber or in the party. The son-in-law of Jacques Stern, Bertrand d'Ara-

29. *Les Documents politiques*, April, 1928, April, 1930, March, 1932.

mon, for example, sat for years in parliament without once opening his mouth.

Nonetheless, very few of the Federation's deputies could be
classed as plebeian. The only member of working-class origins
was Gaston About, a former railroad engineer, who represented
the Haute-Savoie from 1919 to 1932. Charles Coutel from the
Nord had worked as a cookie cutter before entering parliament.
Clovis Macouin from the Deux-Sèvres was a former postman,
and Alphonse Thibon from the Ardèche was described in 1936
as the only real peasant in the Chamber.[30] The typical deputy
of the Republican Federation, however, was more likely to be a
professional man. Many of those who had studied law or medi-
cine had alternate sources of income, of course, but a number of
deputies had been no more than local practitioners before entering parliament. Several were graduates of advanced technical
schools. André Baud, for example, left the Ecole Polytechnique
to work as an administrator for the Creusot steelworks before
winning a seat for the Jura in 1936. With the exception of
Charles de Lasteyrie, a former inspector of finances, and Félix
Grat, the deputy from the Mayenne who opted to teach cartog-
raphy at the Ecole des Hautes Etudes after graduating from St.
Cyr, very few deputies of the Federation made careers in the
civil service or in national education. A number, including
Joseph Denais, Jacques Poitou-Duplessy, Désiré Ferry from the
Moselle, and Désiré Bouteille from the Oise, had careers as
professional journalists.

A number of the party's deputies retained connections with
the professional military. Several of the western nobility, including Grandmaison, de Polignac, and de Coral, had been career
officers in the cavalry. General de Saint-Just, deputy from the
Pas-de-Calais, and Lieutenant Colonel Alexis Calliès, deputy
from the Haute-Savoie, were treated by the Left as the symbols
of the militarist tradition in parliament during the 1930s.
Charles des Isnards, former colonel in the cavalry and the air

30. *Le Charivari*, June 6, 1936.

force, acted as the Federation's spokesman on military questions during the late 1930s. Philippe Henriot, François Martin from the Aveyron, and Pierre de Monicault from the Ain were all from professional military families.[31]

Two further characteristics distinguished the deputies of the Republican Federation. An extraordinary number of them came from what might be called parliamentary families. At least twenty were the sons or grandsons of deputies and, in the case of families like the de Moustiers, the d'Andignés, the Saint-Justs, the Roulleaux-Dugages, and the Grandmaisons, the parliamentary seat had become a virtual fief that was passed down from one generation to the next. Secondly, although the Federation habitually insisted that it was still a young party, its deputies were old. The average age of the party's deputies in 1933 was fifty-seven years and nine months, making the party the oldest in the Chamber. The next oldest was Georges Pernot's group of dissident members of the Federation, which on the average was two months younger. This gerontocratic leaning was somewhat redressed, however, in 1936 when the party elected twelve deputies between the ages of twenty-six and forty.[32]

The deputies of the Republican Federation were, in general, both wealthy and socially respectable. Their social prestige gave them access to funds and influence that were an inestimable advantage in assuring their election or reelection. In addition, many deputies belonged to families which had traditionally dominated their region of France, both economically and politi-

31. The links between the Federation and the professional military are hard to uncover. General Auguste Hirschauer, senator and former military governor of Strasbourg, was a vice-president of the party. Maxime Weygand was a friend and frequent visitor of Louis Marin. Jean Fernand-Laurent claimed that he belonged to the Federation and participated in the party's deliberations on national defense. Jacques Weygand, *Weygand mon père* (Paris, 1970), 256–57; Camille [Jean] Fernand-Laurent, *Un Peuple ressuscite* (New York, 1943), 116.

32. *Marianne*, July 19, 1933. Deputies: François Valentin (Meurthe-et-Moselle) 26, François Boux de Casson (Vendée) 27, Jean Crouan (Finistère) 30, Edouard Frédéric-Dupont (Paris) 33, Bernard de Coral (Basses-Pyrénées) 32, François Martin (Aveyron) 35, Emmanuel Temple (Aveyron) 39, Henri Becquart (Nord) 39, François de Saint-Just (Pas de Calais) 40, Félix Grat (Mayenne) 40, André Parmentier (Nord) 40, André Daher (Bouches-du-Rhône) 40.

cally. The comparative electoral security of the party's deputies was amplified by their geographical distribution. As Maps 2, 3, 4, and 5 indicate, the deputies of the Republican Federation came principally from three major areas: the northeast, including the Franche-Comté; the west, particularly Normandy and Anjou; and the southern edge of the Massif-Central. With the exception of Paris itself, the party was almost unrepresented in the Parisian basin, the Midi, or the extreme southeast.

There is no simple explanation for the geographical distribution of the deputies of the Republican Federation. As students of French electoral geography have noted, voting patterns are usually not congruent with the social and physical geography of France.[33] This was generally true of the Federation's electoral strength. In some areas, of course, social factors were obviously the determining variable. Within Paris, for example, the Federation was the major party in the middle- and upper-middle-class central and western districts (the first, sixth, seventh, eighth, ninth, fifteenth, sixteenth, and seventeenth arrondissements); whereas, particularly by 1936, it was almost unrepresented in the predominantly working-class eastern arrondissements or in the suburbs. Similarly, in Lyon the party's strength lay in the middle-class quarters. In the Meurthe-et-Moselle, on the other hand, five deputies out of seven adhered to the Federation during the early 1930s, and four of them represented industrial, working-class constituencies. Where constituencies combined rural and urban regions, there was no significant difference between the performance of the Federation in the rural and urban cantons. In fact, at the national level there was little correlation between the social and political geography of the party. Political lines cut across social demarcations, and regions with similar social compositions had diametrically opposed voting patterns. The Federation, for example, had many deputies

33. Goguel discusses the problem of the general absence of any correlation between the social and physical geography of France and its political geography in François Goguel, *Géographie des élections françaises, de 1870 à 1951* (Paris, 1951), 131–34. See also the extended discussion in Georges Dupeux, *Le Front populaire et les élections de 1936* (Paris, 1959), 157–91.

from primarily agricultural departments like the Vendée, the Morbihan, the Mayenne, and La Manche; but they had none at all in the equally agricultural departments of the Creuse, the Corrèze, and the Drôme. Similarly, the Federation was comparatively weak and growing weaker in the north of France, but it remained strong in the east even though both regions were heavily industrialized.

Religious factors, on the other hand, appear to have been a more significant determinant of party appeal. There was a very clear correlation between the distribution of practicing Catholics and the geographical distribution of the Federation's deputies.[34] The party, along with the small Parti Démocrate Populaire, was alone in actively defending the Church, which made it appealing in the remaining Catholic regions of France. Finally, the intense nationalism of the party made it politically attractive in the eastern departments where the traditional anti-German sentiments had been accentuated by the devastation of World War I.

During the 1930s the areas of party strength, measured both by popular vote and by the number of deputies elected, shifted toward the west. In 1932 the party experienced a net loss of over twenty seats, most of them in the north, the Parisian region, and the southeast. Socialists and Radicals usually took the seats from the Federation, but several were lost to the Parti Démocrate Populaire. In areas of traditional party strength— the Meurthe-et-Moselle, the Bas-Rhin, and the Mayenne— the Catholic Parti Démocrate Populaire could make inroads among the electoral clientele of the Federation. In 1936 the party lost seven seats, all but one of them in the industrial north or in the Parisian basin. At the same time it gained seventeen seats, mostly in the west (Mayenne, Vendée, Loire-Inférieure, Manche, Charente, Maine-et-Loire, Sarthe) and to a lesser extent in the east (Meurthe-et-Moselle, Belfort, Haute-Savoie, Jura, and the Vosges) and in the Massif-Central (two additional seats in the Aveyron). The adhesion of eight former independent

34. For the religious geography of France, see F. Boulard, *Essor ou déclin du clergé français* (Paris, 1950), 169; Goguel, *Géographie des élections françaises*, 135.

monarchists to the Federation also increased the party's strength in the west. The gradual loss of influence in the north and the southwest corresponded to a long-run secular shift in French voting patterns.[35] The economic crisis of the mid-1930s accentuated the growing weakness of the Federation in industrial areas. At the same time, the polarization of French society, resulting from the formation of the Popular Front, assisted the party's candidates in the west and the Massif-Central.

The geographic distribution of the Federation's deputies, as well as the pattern of its popular vote, clearly shows that the party drew its support from the traditionally conservative, Catholic, and nationalistic regions of France. Although the decade of the 1930s was in most respects a frightening one for the Federation, the party retained much of its parliamentary strength. Reduced somewhat but hardly decimated by the changing electoral patterns of the 1930s, the deputies of the Republican Federation constituted the core of the traditional French Right. Because its deputies usually represented the comparatively impenetrable bastions of conservatism, the Republican Federation enjoyed a parliamentary representation that was out of proportion to its achievements as an organized political party. For although the Federation's parliamentary strength was substantial, as the next chapter demonstrates, the party itself was weak.

---

35. Goguel, *Géographie des élections françaises*, 128–29.

II. *Organization and Structure*

In France, elaborately articulated mass parties are rare. Although differing in their morphology, their distribution of power, and their goals, most French political parties had in common a relatively modest membership. This was particularly true on the Right, where conservatives considered the mass party to be unnecessary and politically uncongenial. Instead of mobilizing mass support by creating large integration parties, they chose to rely on the social and political influence of local *notables*. In the twentieth century, however, the influence of these *notables* waned, and the older elites appeared increasingly to be challenged by the growing cadres of the Left. Members of the Republican Federation complained of the unionized, lay-educated, and left-leaning officials in the prefecture, the administration, the police, the judiciary, and the educational system. The party believed that these new *notables* directly or indirectly reinforced the political Left and demoralized the *modérés*.[1]

The Federation of course exaggerated the leftist role of civil servants, but it was undeniable that, where traditional elites had

1. René Rémond, *La Droite en France* (2 vols.; Paris, 1968), 176–77; Maurice Duverger, *Political Parties* (New York, 1963), 20–23; Georges E. Lavau, *Partis politiques et réalités sociales* (Paris, 1953), 138–62; R. von Albertini, "Partei-organization und Parteibegriff in Frankreich, 1789–1940," *Historische Zeitschrift*, CXCIII (1961), 529–600; Jean Charlot, *L'U.N.R.: Etude du pouvoir au sein d'un parti politique* (Paris, 1967). For a particularly insightful analysis of the German equivalent of the cadre party, the *Honoratiorenpartei*, see Thomas Nipperdey, "Die Organization der bürgerlichen Parteien in Deutschland vor 1918," *Historische Zeitschrift*, CLXXXV (1958), 550–602; Thomas Nipperdey, *Die Organization der deutschen Parteien vor 1918* (Dusseldorf, 1961). Jacques Debû-Bridel, "La crise des partis," *La Revue Hebdomadaire*, January 21, 1933, pp. 337–38; Victor Perret, *Rapport sur la politique générale fait au congrès de la fédération républicaine*, 1934, in Marin Papers, Archives Nationale, carton 82. A classic statement of this view is Albert Thibaudet, *La République des professeurs* (Paris, 1927).

lost or were losing their influence, conservatives had to rely on more effective and more popular instruments to combat the growing strength of the Left. As a member of the Federation's executive committee noted in 1926, the time for an elite bourgeois party was now past, and the "organization of the F. R. therefore must be democratic and largely open to workers and peasants."[2]

Since its foundation, leaders of the Republican Federation had insisted that the *modérés* could no longer rely on a few outstanding *notables* but needed an elaborate electoral and propaganda organization "in each city, town and village."[3] The party, however, never translated such pronouncements into action; and the Federation remained an elite party dominated by deputies, senators, the mayors of important cities,[4] a few general councilors, newspaper editors, industrialists, and presidents of regional chambers of commerce. Only in 1924 did the new secretary-general, Jean Guiter, make a sustained effort to create "a real party." Arguing that conservative parties could no longer remain loose and ephemeral associations of deputies, he proposed to infuse new life into the moribund party structure, create "active and well organized departmental committees," and convert the Federation into a party "worthy of the name." By the late 1920s *La Nation* regularly boasted of the Federation's organizational initiatives and burgeoning committee structure. Some enthusiastic *militants* even sought to emulate the zeal and discipline of their counterparts on the Left.[5]

Yet the Federation did not intend to become a democratic party, in which the rank and file would play a significant role in decision making within the party. While recognizing the dangers of remaining an *état major sans troupes*, the leaders of the Federation expected the troops to limit themselves to winning

2. *Le Journal de Rouen*, June 5, 1926.
3. *Journal des Débats*, November 22, 1905.
4. Including Lille, Rouen, Marseilles, Le Havre, Nancy, Aix en Provence, Beauvais, Brest and Roubaix.
5. *La Nation*, October 15, 1925. For example, Robert Pimienta (leader of the Federation in the Oise), *L'Oise Nationale*, February, 1936; also *La Nation*, May 16, 1931.

elections and spreading conservative ideas. They were effectively excluded from major decisions of party policy and prevented from encroaching on the prerogatives of the party's elite or its deputies. The Federation had pretensions to creating a large and powerful political party but rarely succeeded in becoming more than a loose association of deputies bolstered by a limited number of prominent provincial conservatives.

The central organs of the Republican Federation consisted of a National Council, an executive committee (Conseil Directeur), and an executive (Bureau). In theory the National Council, with 100 members in 1924 and 275 in 1938, administered and directed the party. In practice, except during political crises, the Council delegated its governing powers to the executive committee and the executive. The latter included a president, treasurer, secretary-general, and from six to fourteen vice-presidents. At the party's headquarters at 34 Rue de Varenne, the executive had at its disposal a permanent paid staff, which acted as a secretariat and directed the party's propaganda activity.[6]

The governing bodies of the Republican Federation were co-optive oligarchies. Deputies, senators, and presidents of departmental branches of the party belonged to the National Council *ex officio* and predominated; the rest were selected from among "*notables* distinguished by their political competence" or their "professional interest."[7] In the executive committee and the executive, the great majority were parliamentarians. These, plus a handful of important departmental presidents, dominated the deliberations.

In principle, the executive organs of the Federation were re-

6. The one reference to the secretariat in the Marin Papers indicates that in 1927 it employed ten full- or part-time staff; for 1928 the figure was eight; in Marin Papers, carton 74.

7. In 1924, 58 of 99 members of the Council were deputies and senators; 7 were presidents of local branches. For 1929 the figures were 82 and 62 respectively out of a total of 194; for 1935 there were 87 parliamentarians and 109 local officials out of 231. Composition of directing organs was usually given in the published reports of annual congresses, in Marin Papers, carton 82; see also *L'Union Républicaine du Rhône*, May 17, 1931. *La Nation*, February 18, 1939.

quired to submit their decisions for the approval of the party's
annual congress. But in spite of the fanfare with which the Federation announced its congresses, their importance was almost
entirely symbolic. The average party member exercised little influence at congresses, and the resolutions of those congresses
meant little. The congresses represented no one in particular
and made no attempt to ensure that representation of delegates
was proportionate to the population or to the party's electoral
strength in various departments. Delegates came from most
parts of France but usually represented only themselves.[8] Potentially controversial issues rarely received preliminary discussion in the local branches, the branches never mandated
delegates, and most who attended congresses did so as spec-
tators. This suited the leaders of the Federation, who regarded
any unnecessarily spirited discussion as a sign of discord and dis-
union. Congresses were the occasion for bonhomie and morale-
boosting discourses, not debates over tactical or ideological differences. They manifestly were not the place where deputies or
the party executive ought to be held to account for their actions.

The Federation's 1929 congress at Rouen reveals the nature of
the Federation's annual deliberations. Prior to the Rouen congress the Federation was critically divided between opponents
and supporters of the Poincaré government on the issue of the
controversial interallied war debts. The fate of the government
and the post-1928 conservative coalition hinged on the votes of
the Federation's deputies. For once, political observers, expecting a significant debate, paid careful attention to the party's congress. Leaders of the Federation, however, sat all night prior to
the opening of the congress to arrive at a compromise formula
that would obviate an acrimonious debate on the floor. In the
relatively restrained debate the next day, virtually all deputies
indicated that they intended to retain their liberty once in the
Chamber, thus reducing drastically even the significance of the

8. The 1938 congress at Paris attracted 1,127 delegates from seventy-six departments, although half came from the department of the Seine. The register has survived
in Marin Papers, carton 88.

compromise formula. As the Federation's arch partisan, the *Journal de Rouen*, noted: "The congresses of the Republican Federation do not resemble those of certain parties . . . at which the most obscure *militants* . . . can be seen giving orders to and imposing their will on their chiefs."[9]

In the early 1930s some *militants* complained about the sterile character of the Federation's congresses and argued for a greater participation in its deliberations. They contended that if delegates were mandated, represented proportionately, and in possession of "the kind of information [about the party] possessed by the most obscure cardholder of the SFIO [the Socialist party]," the congresses might be more productive and have more authority vis à vis the deputies.[10] The leadership predictably ignored these suggestions, and the congresses remained somnolent. A sharp exchange at the 1937 congress over the question of the Parti Social Français startled a Parisian press that had learned to sleep through the party's proceedings. The congresses of the Republican Federation mirrored the general sclerosis in party life.

The Republican Federation attempted to broaden its base and attract certain critical constituencies by establishing a number of auxiliary organizations. Some, like the Republican Federation of Mayors and Municipal Councilors, had only the loosest connection with the party. More significant was the women's section. Believing that it would capture a disproportionate share of women's votes, the Federation advocated the introduction of women's suffrage. In 1935, in collaboration with the conservative National Federation of Women the party created the Women's Section of the Republican Federation. By 1938 the section claimed representatives in sixty-five departments, although in 1936 it reported only 1,625 subscribers to its monthly bulletin, *Les Devoirs des Femmes*. *Les Devoirs* made unexceptional read-

9. *Le Journal de Rouen*, June 9, 13, 1929.
10. *La Nation*, June 22, 1929; *L'Echo de Paris*, May 1, 1930; Jean Guiter to Louis Marin, August 30, 1929, in Marin Papers, carton 82; minutes of the Republican Federation of the Seine, February 21, 1933, June 14, 1934, in Marin Papers, carton 82; *L'Union Républicaine du Rhône*, July 23, 1933.

ing, consisting mostly of reprints from *La Nation*, articles on the importance of the home and family, and diatribes against the author of *Du Mariage*.[11]

Far more important and interesting was the Jeunesse de la Fédération Républicaine. During the 1920s the Federation had seen no need for a youth formation because it considered the Jeunesses Patriotes to be an adequate representative of conservative youth.[12] By 1935, under attack as an old party and outbid by the youthful right-wing leagues, the Federation decided to create a youth group. A number of previously existing departmental youth groups federated under the leadership of the party's young Turk, Philippe Henriot, who worked to create a movement attracting young men between the ages of seventeen and thirty. *Jeunesse*, the biweekly journal of the party's youth group in the Gironde, became the official organ of the Jeunesse de la Fédération Républicaine.

Significantly, the Federation did not expect the youth group to rival the growing right-wing leagues in size. René Russier, the secretary-general of the group, admitted that the masses would be attracted to the leagues. The youth group, far from providing the party with a mass base, was designed to draw a stratum of French conservative youth into the directing circles of the Federation to regenerate the cadres of the party. Still, the formation of a youth movement was not without its perils in the 1930s when young people were searching for dynamic alternatives. Old parties and the liberal democratic approach to politics were no longer fashionable, and even a thoroughly republican party like the Radical-Socialists found its youth group attracted to an authoritarian and nationalistic mystique.[13] A similar, if not more pronounced, evolution might have been expected from the young conservatives of the Jeunesse de la Fédéra-

---

11. *La Nation*, February 18, 1939 (supplement); minutes of the executive committee of the Women's Section of the Republican Federation, April 4, 1936, in Marin Papers, carton 82. The author of *Du Mariage*, an early advocate of women's sexual emancipation, was the Socialist leader, Léon Blum.

12. *La Nation*, June 22, 1929.

13. *Le Temps*, March 24, 1935. Peter J. Larmour, *The French Radical Party in the 1930's* (Stanford, 1964), 222–24.

tion Républicaine, particularly in the light of the subsequent record of Philippe Henriot.

There were differences between the Federation and its youth group, but they were of tone, not substance. *Jeunesse* alluded occasionally to gerontocracy on the Right and published a number of articles devoted to Franco, Salazar, Degrelle, Ionescu, Mussolini, Mosley, and other European fascists or protofascists. The journal evinced a greater degree of enthusiasm for these authoritarian leaders than was usual in the Federation, and a young Maurice Duverger ended a series of articles on Mussolini's corporate state with the cautious suggestion that France could learn something from this model. But in general even the most open admirers of foreign authoritarian regimes in the Jeunesse tempered their enthusiasm with the judgment that these models were not for export and accorded ill with the French tradition.[14] During the Federation's sustained feud with the Parti Social Français in the late 1930s, no one in the youth group moved to support the younger and more exciting party.

The general identity of views between the Federation and its youth group was not accidental. Aware of the experience of the Jeunesses Radicales, leaders of the Federation loaded the executive of the Jeunesse de la Fédération Républicaine with *ex-officio* members from the central party. These soon dominated the pages of *Jeunesse* and were given to moralizing admonitions about the perils of impatient youth. By 1937 some of the original founders of the youth group, restless under the increasingly strict tutelage of the Federation, resigned in protest against the deliberate stifling of youthful ideas. They protested in vain, and the Jeunesse de la Fédération Républicaine, far from being a new and exciting vehicle for impatient young conservatives, remained a prosaic copy of the Republican Federation.[15]

La Nation reflected the elitist quality of the Federation. Of-

14. *Jeunesse 34*, April, July–August, 1934.
15. *La Nation*, February 18, 1939. Robert Cassagnac (a vice-president of the youth group and a leader of the protest) to Marin, November 21, 1937, in Marin Papers, carton 75. The youth group adhered closely to the social norms of its elders. When in 1938 it organized a youth cruise, individual members were offered a choice of first, second, or third class accommodations.

ficially subtitled *organe officiel de la Fédération Républicaine*, *La Nation* was really the official organ of Louis Marin. Dissenting views within the party never appeared in *La Nation*, and even their existence was only furtively recognized. The house organ featured a relatively high quality of political, social, and economic journalism but was usually silent about the internal affairs of the party. It announced party congresses and reprinted speeches, gave brief summaries of meetings of the executive, and periodically published reports from some of the party's departmental sections. Yet the reader never learned how many members the party had, which departments were organized, how the party treasury stood, or even which deputies belonged to the Federation. Neither in 1932 nor in 1936 did *La Nation* bother to list the official candidates, still less did it feel the need to publish the results. In a few departments the party had local press organs that were more informative, but in general the press of the Federation rarely gave *militants* the impression of being active participants in the life of a party.

Financially the Republican Federation was independent of all but a handful of its members. Predictably, the Federation never published information about its finances beyond insisting that the party was poor, dependent on the modest resources of its *militants*, and ignored by the *puissances d'argent*. Contemporary commentators dismissed these ritualistic utterances and generally insisted that the Federation was in the hands of the French business community and, in particular, of François de Wendel, secretary-general of the Comité des Forges. A subsequent generation of scholars was unable to document these charges, but with the recent appearance of Jean-Noël Jeanneney's monumental study of de Wendel it is now possible to speak with some precision about the size and source of the Republican Federation's funding.[16]

16. *La Nation*, September 12, 1936; *Voir Clair en Politique*, March 1, 1936; *L'Union Républicaine du Rhône*, May 18, 1935; Jean Meynaud, *Les Groupes de pression en France* (Paris, 1958); Jean Meynaud, *Nouvelles études sur les groupes de pression en France* (Paris, 1961); Raymond Fusilier, "Les finances des partis politiques," *Revue politique et parlementaire*, CCXI (1953), 258–76; Jean-Noël Jeanneney, *François de*

The Federation had three major expenses: the operating budget of the party's headquarters, *La Nation*, and electoral campaigns. The annual cost of the secretariat, propaganda rallies, and the party's congress rose from 143,000 francs in the mid-1920s to 350,000 francs in 1936. *La Nation* cost rather more, although the Federation's erratic bookkeeping makes it impossible to give an exact figure. Elections represented the largest single expense. In 1928 the Federation gave its official candidates 1,891,000 francs; in 1932 and 1936 the figures were 805,000 and 1,441,000 francs respectively. Since the Federation actually contested less than one-third of the six hundred constituencies, the direct financial support per candidate averaged about 5,000 francs—more than a nominal sum but far less than was needed to finance a campaign by the late 1930s.[17]

The nominal membership dues of the party could not cover any of these expenses because the money was retained by the local branches of the Federation. Individual members could and did make substantial special contributions to the party's treasury, and the Federation actively canvassed sympathetic figures in the business community. Yet the donations received from these sources were usually modest and irregular. The most consistent source of revenue for the Federation was the Union des intérêts économiques directed by Ernest Billiet. Founded in 1919, the Union channeled money from commerce and industry into conservative and centrist political organizations, principally

Wendel en République (Paris, 1976). Unless otherwise indicated the source for the next three paragraphs is from pp. 440–54 of this work.

17. The total expenses of *La Nation* in 1937 amounted to 752,237 francs. Jeanneney, *François de Wendel*, p. 443, n. 70. Because of the extreme vagueness of electoral labels in many departments, it is impossible to establish how many candidates the Federation actually presented in elections. In 1914 it presented 116 official candidates (*Le Temps*, April 27, 1914). For 1932 the party gave the figure of 150 official candidates (*Rapport sur la politique générale fait au congrès de la fédération républicaine, 1933*, in Marin Papers, carton 82). The Ministry of the Interior lumped candidates of the Federation with other unclassifiable conservatives under the label of the Union Républicaine Démocratique (after the party's parliamentary formation in the 1920s). In 1932 there were 194 candidates of the URD in 605 constituencies; in 1936 there were 229 in 608. On the financial demands of candidates see, for example, Guiter to Marin, August 22, 1932, Pierre Poussard to Marin, May 8, 1932, Poussard to Guiter, April 8, 1932, all in Marin Papers, carton 79.

but not exclusively for electoral purposes. In 1932 and 1936 three-quarters of the Federation's campaign funds came from the Union. Billiet's organization also provided 10,000 francs a month for the party's secretariat and as late as 1936 subsidized *La Nation* to the extent of 20,000 francs a month. Although the Union des intérèts économiques was the financial backbone of the Federation, the organization actually funded all political groups to the right of the Socialists—most of them more generously than the Federation. Billiet, essentially a moderate centrist, was quite prepared to suspend his subventions in response to Marin's refractory nationalism. He also used his considerable economic clout to force the Federation to support candidates of the Center-Right rather than put forth its own candidates.[18]

Contemporaries who charged that the Federation was dominated by de Wendel gold were partly right. As an important contributor to the Union des intérèts économiques, de Wendel could often ensure that an otherwise reluctant Billiet would direct funds to the Federation. He was also prepared, albeit unenthusiastically, to make direct contributions to the party whenever its financial situation appeared to be desperate. He preferred, however, to act indirectly. During the 1932 elections, de Wendel persuaded the premier, André Tardieu, to channel some 150,000 francs (originally donated by the Comité des Forges to the government's secret funds) into the totally depleted campaign chest of the Federation. Nonetheless, the evidence from the Marin and de Wendel Papers indicates that de Wendel neither was nor wished to be the principal financier of the Republican Federation and that his contributions were less than his critics charged and less than Marin desired.

The Republican Federation incontestably received financial support from the industrial and commercial establishment, and Marin clearly enjoyed a privileged relationship with de Wendel. Despite such aid, however, the Federation never enjoyed a very healthy treasury, and Jean Guiter repeatedly lamented the pre-

18. Guiter to Marin, January 28, 1928, in Marin Papers, carton 75.

cariousness of the party's finances.[19] The Federation's periodic complaints about being abandoned by the financial oligarchy and the major *bailleurs des fonds* did contain a grain of truth. From the point of view of France's business community, the Federation must have appeared as a quixotic and unreliable ally, prone in the early 1930s to disrupting conservative coalitions by fighting lost causes and undermined in the later 1930s by the more dynamic "new" Right. It made more sense to concentrate support on parties of the Center, such as the Alliance Démocratique, which wholeheartedly supported business interests and were far more likely to occupy a position of real power.

The weak articulation of the Republican Federation reflected not only the desire of its conservative leadership to retain power in the hands of a select oligarchy but also the relative weakness of the *militants*. There were local organizations of *militants* in most parts of France, but they were neither numerous nor strong and their role was primarily passive. Even had the *militants* been temperamentally so disposed—and they rarely were —they were generally too feeble to insist on greater influence in the party. A few local organizations were sometimes sufficiently large and cohesive enough to challenge the actions of their leaders, but nowhere were the rank and file powerful enough to control their deputies effectively.

Although the Federation often spoke of its *militants*, it never gave any definitive figure about the size of its membership, apart from the odd, wildly improbable guess. The most plausible estimate would put the party's membership no higher than (and probably equal to) the circulation of *La Nation*, which in the 1930s did not greatly exceed 10,000.[20]

19. In 1936, for example, the Federation was unable to continue its very modest subventions to its women's section. Minutes of the women's section, January 7, 1936, in Marin Papers, carton 82.

20. The party occasionally suggested that its membership was comparable to the 100,000 of the Socialists. *La Nation*, June 19, 1926; Raymond Millet, "Notes sur les partis modérés," *L'Esprit*, June, 1939, p. 210. Fragmented evidence suggests that the Federation considered all subscribers to *La Nation* to be members even if they did not formally fill out the party's membership form. Although figures of 40,000 (*La Nation*,

Jean Guiter often spoke of marshaling these militants into a coherently organized network of departmental federations, with branches at the cantonal and even communal level, meeting regularly, "spreading the ideas of the Republican Federation among all classes and into the most remote villages."[21] Here and there the Federation established departmental organizations that approximated Guiter's ideal. The real picture of the Republican Federation outside of Paris, however, was very different. Committees certainly existed but not in all departments and rarely outside of the principal towns. Some identified closely with the Federation, even calling it affectionately the Fédé; just as often they were at best loosely affiliated with the party. A few had long histories, going back to the early days of the Federation or beyond, but more were ephemeral affairs, the product of the momentary zeal of a prominent *notable* or parliamentary aspirant. Some local committees met regularly and had a permanent party headquarters; more typically, committees sprang to life only for the annual banquet and the legislative elections. Judging by the activities column of the party's provincial press, some *militants* participated in something like an active party life; more often a *militant* of the Republican Federation was a local conservative who subscribed to *La Nation*.

In the departments, Parisian political nuances lost much of their significance. One was simply a *modéré*, opposed to the Cartel des Gauches; the particular shade of conservatism was less important. To preempt distasteful doctrinal dissension, local conservatives of all colors often formed a single departmental *comité d'entente*. Even when they belonged to the Federation, local politicians often preferred such vague political labels for fear that an exclusive identification with the Federation might alienate more moderate conservative support. Although the headquarters of the Federation chose to consider the Union of

July 24, 1926) and 80,000 (*Le Temps*, June 2, 1937) were given for the circulation of the journal, its circulation in 1933 was 11,756. Jeanneney, *François de Wendel*, p. 442, n. 66.

21. *La Nation*, August 25, 1925.

Independent and National Republicans in the Tarn, the Republican Alliance of the Marne, the Social Union of Berry in the Cher, the Republican Federation of Poitiers and Vienne, and the Republican and Social Federation of the Central Plateau for the five departments of the Massif-Central as their departmental branches, in fact they represented all conservative elements to the right of the Radicals. The National Republican Union of the Ardèche, whose president Pierre Vallette-Viallard was a deputy of the Federation, gave as its mission: "to unite, without delving into their souls, all honest men and all those that constitute the party of order."[22] In the Ardèche, where many men of order were thinly disguised monarchists, the local branch of the Republican Federation had good reason for not delving too deeply into souls. In many departments the Federation's committees represented primarily "honest men" and only secondarily the Republican Federation.

The Federation did, nonetheless, have some coherent departmental organizations that closely identified with the main party. The most vigorous and best organized was the Republican Federation of the Rhône. In the Rhône, the *modérés* needed an effective organization. Dominated by the large industrial city of Lyon, the fief of the Radical leader Edouard Herriot, the department was distinctly a stronghold of the Left. Its predominantly leftist electorate had traditionally voted Radical, shifting gradually in the 1930s to the Socialists and the Communists. Ten of its fourteen seats were firmly in the hands of the Left.[23]

The Republican Federation of the Rhône was founded in 1903 and formally adhered to the national Republican Federation in 1905. During the 1920s, under the leadership of Victor Perret, it became the organizational showpiece of the party. Perret, a textile manufacturer, sought to form committees in each of the departments' cantons and in many of its communes. He founded a number of auxiliary organizations, established a weekly

22. *Ibid.*, March 2, 1929.
23. It ranked sixty-seventh out of eighty-eight departments in percentage of *modéré* vote. B. Léger, *Les Opinions politiques des provinces françaises* (Paris, 1936), 259–60.

newspaper, and created a permanent and active party headquarters. During the 1930s Perret and other organizers traveled the communes of the department each Sunday, forming new committees and addressing old ones. He also extended his organizational abilities to the neighboring departments of the Isère and the Loire.

By the 1930s the Federation of the Rhône theoretically maintained committees in each of the department's 33 cantons and in most of its 268 communes. The cantonal committees held annual congresses and delegated representatives to the executive committee. The executive committee elected a smaller executive, which met weekly. The annual congresses of the Federation of the Rhône often attracted five or six hundred delegates and as many as thirty deputies. Admittedly, eight or ten of the cantonal committees existed only on paper, and well over one-third of the communes had no permanent committees.[24] But the columns of the party's weekly, *Union Républicaine*, revealed many active and flourishing committees and a party life marked by genuine vitality.

In an attempt to broaden and democratize its appeal, the Federation of the Rhône founded workers' associations, social centers, and a youth group. The Comité des ouvriers et employés met monthly to discuss political issues, as well as more general problems of social insurance, hospitalization, and apprenticeship. Members of the group enjoyed access to free legal advice from lawyers in the Federation. In the 1930s the party opened several social centers in Lyon containing restaurants, bars, recreation rooms, lecture halls, and libraries. Open to members of the Federation "without distinction as to social class," the centers were intended to encourage "a greater collaboration and better understanding between employers and workers." Characteristically, leaders of the Federation credited the centers with helping them learn "to appreciate the humble people and the workers."[25] They were more at ease with the middle-class stu-

24. *La Nation*, January 19, 1929.
25. *L'Union Républicaine du Rhône*, August 14, November 6, 1932.

dents of Lyon, among whom they established a large and flourishing youth movement.

Much of the undeniable energy of the Federation of the
Rhône was directed less toward conquering the bastions of the
Left than toward consolidating the Republican Federation's predominance among the *modérés*. For example, Alexandre Bosse-
Platière, a wine grower in the Beaujolais and a leading *militant*,
conducted a protracted struggle against the multipartisan conservative committees, which went under names like *union nationale* or *concentration républicaine*. The center of gravity of
such committees was to the left of the Republican Federation,
and they often considered it expedient to exclude candidates of
the right-wing Federation in local and national elections. After
years of infighting, Bosse-Platière gradually established the
Federation's dominance in his constituency of the Villefranche
and demonstrated that those who campaigned under the party
label did no worse, although not significantly better in that left-
leaning area, than those who ran under more ambiguous labels.
By the 1930s the Federation was the major conservative party in
the department. In 1934, for example, twelve of seventeen conservatives on the departmental council, the Conseil Général,
belonged to the Federation. In the legislative elections of the
1930s the Federation virtually monopolized the conservative
candidacies.

The actual electoral performance of the Federation of the
Rhône was less impressive. In contrast to the national party, it
did contest all constituencies. Until 1936, however, it elected
only two deputies: François Peissel in the tenth constituency of
Lyon, the suburb of Villeurbanne, and Antoine Sallès in the second arrondissement. These were both deeply conservative,
Catholic constituencies that had long been in the hands of the
modérés. Since Peissel and Sallès had been deputies for a long
time, they did not owe their elections to the Federation. In 1936
the party captured the sixth arrondissement of Lyon, a mixed
quarter including both working classes and a substantial minority of conservative bourgeoisie, who had traditionally given the

Radicals a slim majority.[26] Pierre Burgeot, a prominent *militant* in the Federation, wrested the conservative candidacy that year from its traditional bearers in the Alliance Démocratique and subsequently defeated the Radical incumbent—an impressive achievement in Edouard Herriot's hometown in the year of the Popular Front. Elsewhere the Federation's candidates labored mightily—one even scored a first ballot victory over Herriot in 1936—but never threatened the electoral predominance of the Left.

Notwithstanding its limitations, had the Republican Federation of the Rhône been typical of the Federation's departmental branches, the party would have enjoyed a considerable local power base. But it was not. None of the party's other departmental federations, even in the largest departments, could compare with the Rhône. In the Loire-Inférieure, the Gironde, the Loir-et-Cher, the Charente, the Alpes-Maritimes, the Maine-et-Loire, the Bouches-du-Rhône, and the Seine there were branches that met regularly, pursued their propaganda activity more or less continuously, and took seriously their claims to be the local federations of a national party. There were also isolated strongholds in towns like Calais and Hazebrouck. But none of them approached the Federation of the Rhône. The Republican Federation of the Seine, for example, repeatedly complained of a "general malaise" among its committees, lamented its lack of financial support, and regretted its inability to emulate its counterpart in Lyon.[27]

More typical still was the Republican Federation of the Aude, which shortly after its foundation in 1926 established some 150 communal committees yet faded away within eighteen months. The Federation of the Haute-Garonne, created by an ambitious

---

26. Léger, *Les Opinions politiques*, 140–43; Pierre de Pressac, *Les Forces historiques de la France* (Paris, 1928), 101–108; André Kleinclausz, *Histoire de Lyon* (3 vols.; Lyon, 1952), III, 272–76.

27. *L'Action Sociale et Nationale*, May 5, 1930, March 1933; minutes of the Republican Federation of the Seine, October 26, 1932, May 11, 1933, in Marin Papers, carton 82; see also the complaints of a former secretary-general of the branch, 1938?, in Marin Papers, carton 79.

Map 1

Departments of France

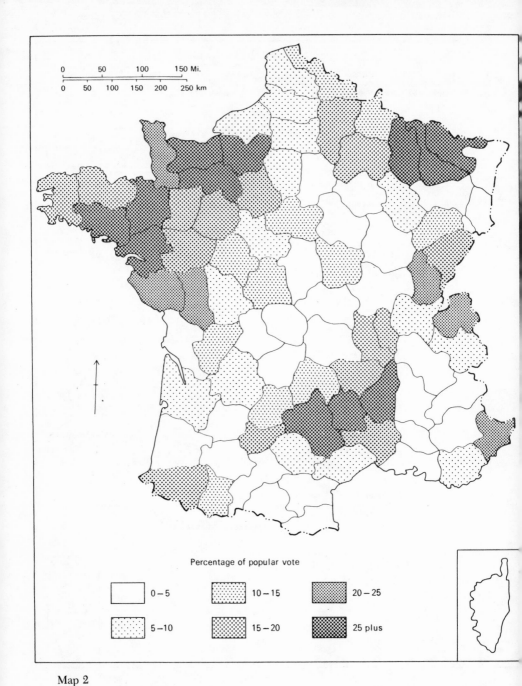

Map 2

Distribution of the Republican Federation's Popular Vote by Department in 1932

Percentages are based on the official figures, which in 1932 included all *modérés* under the label of URD (Union Républicaine Démocratique). Votes cast for candidates of the Parti Démocrate Populaire have been subtracted from the totals. Source: Georges Lachapelle, *Elections législatives des 1ᵉʳ et 8 mai 1932, Resultats Officiels* (Paris, 1932).

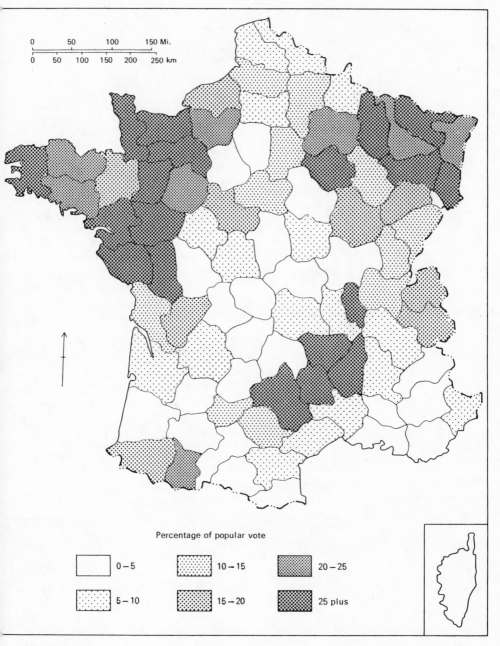

Percentage of popular vote

0 – 5	10 – 15	20 – 25	
5 – 10	15 – 20	25 plus	

Map 3

Distribution of the Republican Federation's Popular Vote by Department in 1936

The above figures include the popular vote for the Republican Federation, the Républicains d'action sociale, the groupe agraire, and the Indépendants d'action populaire. The last three groups had programs that were close to that of the Federation and attracted a number of its former members. Source: Georges Lachapelle, *Elections législatives des 26 avril, 3 mai 1936, Resultats Officiels* (Paris, 1936).

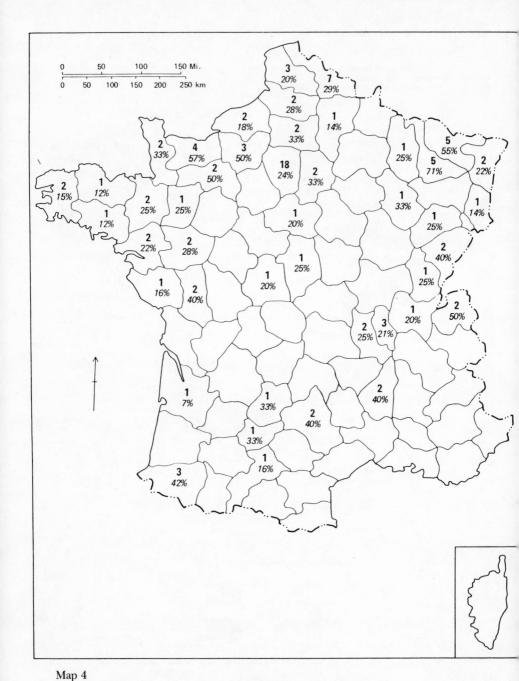

Map 4

Distribution of the Deputies of the Republican Federation in 1931

The second figure for each department gives the party's representation as a percentage of the total number of deputies in the department. Source: Membership list of the party published in *L'Union Républicaine du Rhône*, May 17, 1931.

Map 5

Distribution of the Deputies of the Republican Federation and "Sympathizers" in 1936

The second figure for each department gives the party's representation as a percentage of the total number of deputies in the department. The above figures include the ninety-five deputies that the Federation's headquarters anticipated would join the official group of the Federation in June, 1936. Only sixty did, but the rest were ideologically, programmatically, and often personally very close to the Federation. Source: Pierre Renouard to Louis Marin, in Marin Papers, carton 88.

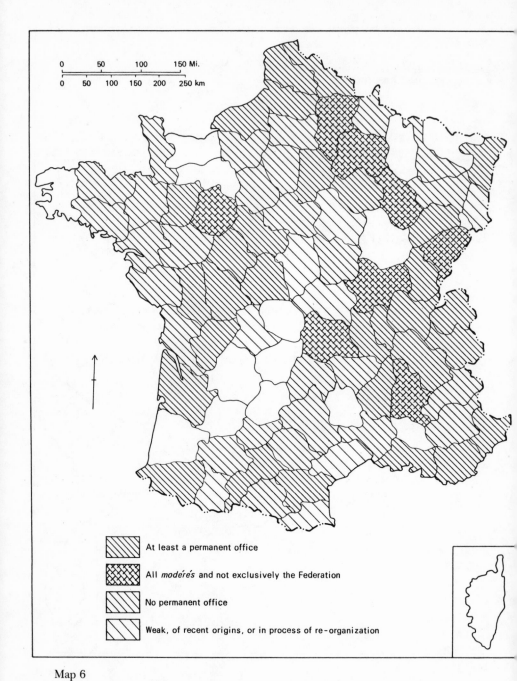

Map 6

State of the Departmental Organization of the Republican Federation in 1939

Source: René Russier's private file for June, 1939, preserved in Marin Papers, carton 75.

local politician in 1933, boasted of 1,700 members and committees springing up "like magic" but also folded after the aspiring deputy's electoral defeat in 1936. The true face of the Republican Federation appeared in the Federation of the Ardennes, which reported that it worked *sans grand bruit*; that of the Nièvre, which complained that "the calm and reserved temperament of our rural populations" was "unfavorable to continuing activity"; or that of the Haute-Saône, which restricted itself to meetings that were "essentially private but open to friends of our friends." Local branches rarely escaped the general torpor that haunted *modérés* in the 1930s, constantly bemoaning the lack of money, *militants*, and enthusiasm. Many like the Republican Federation of Morbihan could report having little except "devoted members who silently defend [the party's] ideas and work to make them triumph." Even committees like the Republican Federation of Rambouillet, which showed a rare degree of zeal and an outspoken antagonism to the incumbent deputy, could not decide whether or not to contest the 1932 election until eighteen days before.[28]

Jean Guiter's files for 1939 list branches of the Federation in seventy-five departments.[29] In at least nine of them, however, the organizations cited represented all *modérés* and not just the Federation; another ten were of recent vintage or limited importance (see Map 6). Only twenty-nine departmental affiliates listed a permanent address, as opposed to the personal address of the president or secretary-general. Even the active committees were lackluster and stodgy. The Republican Federation of Calais, for example, once filled one-quarter of the front page of its monthly bulletin with a notice announcing that an umbrella had been left behind at the last meeting of the central committee,

28. *La Liberté de l'Aude*, October 24, 1926, January 9, 1927; *Le Sud-Est Républicain de Toulouse*, January 17, 1933, April 24, 1934; *Bulletin Mensuel de la Fédération Républicaine du Calaisis*, April, 1930; *Bulletin Mensuel de la Fédération Républicaine de Rambouillet*, July, 1932; *L'Indépendant de l'Arrondissement de Rambouillet*, April 22, 1932; *La Nation*, December 14, 1934, October 5, 19, 1935, December 28, 1935.

29. Guiter's files on the state of departmental organizations in 1939 have survived in Marin Papers, carton 75.

requested that it be reclaimed, and added: "As is customary, there will be no charge for storage."[30] Dominated by lethargic provincial conservatives and silent defenders, the local organizations of the Republican Federation rarely rose above the level of glorified corresponding societies. As such they might have sufficed in another century but were clearly insufficient for the 1930s.

The lack of a coherent infrastructure of *militants* helps account for the prevailing insecurity during the crises of the 1930s and the party's tendency to rely on the more popular forces of the "new" Right. In the short run, however, the party's organizational limitations did not have a crippling effect on its parliamentary representation. The Federation could rarely conquer new territory, but it retained much of its traditional strength. The Catholic, conservative, and socially prominent deputies of the Federation were certain of the support of the Church, the landed and commercial interests, and in general the local *notables*. Since their electorate in many cases had been predisposed for generations to vote for a conservative Catholic, a candidate of the Republican Federation could often count on being elected even where the party's organization was weak or nonexistent. Particularly in the west many of the deputies had something approaching a hereditary right to their seats. As a result party headquarters sometimes expended more energy trying to rally already elected conservatives to the Federation than in assuring their election.

The obvious consequence was a high degree of independence among the Federation's deputies with respect to the party and to its *militants*. As the electoral statements of elected deputies (collected in the so-called *Barodet*) clearly revealed, candidates of the Republican Federation, unlike most other candidates, rarely referred to their party. Usually they preferred vague appellations like *union républicaine* or *union nationale*. Sometimes this ambiguity was deliberate. Identification with the Fed-

30. *Bulletin Mensuel de la Fédération Républicaine du Calaisis*, January, 1931.

eration, especially with Marin's right-wing nationalism, could be an electoral handicap. In 1932, particularly, candidates in the less secure constituencies sometimes went to ingenious lengths to obscure, and even to deny, their affiliation with the Republican Federation.[31] Even those deputies who were most solidly entrenched and most closely identified with the Federation rarely burdened their electors with reference to the party. Louis Marin himself saw no reason to mention the Federation in his election campaigns. Although probably everyone in his constituency in Nancy knew that Marin was president of something called the Republican Federation, they elected him because he was *notr' Louis*, who pedaled around the constituency for years and knew the name of every commune and mayor by heart.[32] Most deputies could define their particular brand of conservatism without reference to a party whose exact significance might be lost on provincial voters. In the few instances where a candidate did mention his membership in the Republican Federation, it was done as supplementary, and incidental, proof that he was what he claimed to be—a conservative, nationalistic Catholic. For most, the Republican Federation began only once one reached Paris.

This sense of supreme independence shaped the relationship of the deputies to the *militants*. Since they rarely owed their election to the work of the rank and file, the deputies were adamant against accepting orders from them or even taking their wishes very seriously. Even in the Rhône, the deputy François Peissel pointedly reminded the local *militants* that the Federation was not like the Socialist party, which held deputies responsible before their local federations and their party congresses.[33] As a former president of the Federation of the Rhône, Peissel

31. See for example *Le Petit Loir-et-Cher*, April 30, 1932; *L'Abeille Jurassienne*, April 9, 1932; *La Liberté de l'Ain*, April 17, 1932.
32. *L'Eclair de l'Est*, a major daily in Nancy, gives the flavor of Marin's electoral campaigns. On one occasion the mayor of a little village apologized to Marin that a local picnic had reduced the attendance of villagers at his rally but assured him that he would receive thirty-four of the village's thirty-seven votes. *L'Éclair de l'Est*, April 20, 1932.
33. *L'Union Républicaine du Rhône*, July 17, 1932.

had no objection to the existence of a propaganda and electoral organization, but he insisted that its members had no business restricting the liberty of a deputy.

Although no one in the Republican Federation ever advocated the kind of discipline practiced by the Socialists, it was galling for *militants* who were strongly attached to the party and its program to discover that many of its deputies were determined to act as free agents. They were further disturbed by the characteristic reflex of deputies, once safely in parliament, to drift toward the Left. In 1932, for example, Peissel and his fellow deputy from the Rhône, Antoine Sallès, joined a dissident parliamentary group in order to dissociate themselves from the more extreme nationalists in the main party. The devoted *militant* Bosse-Platière bitterly complained that by "independence" the typical deputy really meant a free hand to "join all the little cliques and muddle in all the little corridor intrigues, thanks to which, if he pinkens his political coloration a little, he can finally hope to get his hands on a portfolio." It was frustrating and disillusioning to be a *militant* in a party that formally excoriated the indiscipline and the opportunism of French conservatives only to watch one's deputies participate in the most sordid aspects of *la république des camarades.* In 1937 Octave Lavalette, propaganda delegate for the Federation of the Rhône, blamed the growing malaise among the party's *militants* and the consequent inroads made by the more popular Parti Social Français on the successive betrayals by the Federation's deputies. In a thinly veiled allusion to Sallès and Peissel, he complained to the annual departmental party congress about deputies who patronizingly contrasted their broader outlook and tactical flexibility with the narrow-minded intransigence of provincial *militants.* Behind this rhetoric, he asserted, lay a self-serving opportunism, which demoralized the party, robbed it of cohesion, and deprived it of "that intransigence which makes parties strong, makes them grow, and makes them prosper."[34] Bosse-Platière and Lavalette

34. *Ibid.*, July 1, 1934, April 7, 1937.

were party men par excellence; they were also perennially unsuccessful candidates in legislative elections. Treated cavalierly
by their deputies and made to feel like poor relations, such
militants vented a deep resentment.

Robert de Jouvenel's famous dictum that two deputies, one of
whom was a revolutionary, had more in common than did two
revolutionaries, one of whom was a deputy, found its reflection
on the extreme Right. At both ends of the political spectrum,
the lure of political power and the exigencies of parliamentary
politics pulled deputies toward the Center and away from their
respective parties. But unlike their counterparts on the Left,
the *militants* of the Republican Federation were helpless in the
face of the indiscipline of their deputies. The Federation of the
Rhône was outraged by the defection of Sallès and Peissel but
had to content itself with dyspeptic editorials. Any attempt to
discipline a securely entrenched conservative deputy would inevitably be futile. In 1936, for example, Victor Perret mounted
what he called a "punitive expedition" against Laurent Bonnevay, a deputy who had quit the Republican Federation in the
1920s for the more moderate Alliance Démocratique and who
now openly questioned the republicanism of the party of Louis
Marin. But Bonnevay had been a deputy from the archly conservative constituency of Villefranche since 1902, and despite
Perret's energetic rival candidacy, he was reelected on the first
ballot. Although occasionally a departmental organization chas-
tised an unfaithful deputy, the average *militant* of the Federation was unable to exercise much influence over the policy of the
party or any control over its deputies and was left with only a
sense of impotence.[35]

The Republican Federation was not unique in this respect.
The French electoral system militated against tightly disciplined

35. *Le Nouvelliste*, March 9, 1936; Léger, *Les Opinions politiques*, 140; Pressac,
Les Forces historiques, 107. When Louis Nicolle, deputy from the Nord, entered Albert
Sarraut's Center-Left government in early 1936, his local committee and several of the
party's other deputies openly censured his unprincipled opportunism. *Le Temps*, January 25, 26, 31, February 2, 3, 1936.

parties. The return to the system of single-member constituencies in 1927 strengthened the hold of a deputy over his relatively small *circonscription*, "stagnant ponds" as they were called by critics of the system. As one *militant* angrily observed, a deputy could now treat his seat as "a dynastic right" and was far less indebted to his party organization than he would be in the much larger constituencies of a system of proportional representation. The reintroduction of the single-member constituency had in fact caused at least six departmental federations to fold and accentuated the weakness of the party vis à vis its deputies.[36]

Similar problems beset the other major conservative party, the Alliance Démocratique. Like the Federation, the Alliance was descended from the *progressistes*, coming from the liberal rather than the conservative wing, and was primarily a collection of deputies supported by a handful of departmental committees. Despite periodic announcements that the Alliance was about to become a full-fledged, popular political party, until 1933 it was only "an organization of liaison between existing political parties." That year, under the leadership of the deputy from the Yonne, Pierre-Etienne Flandin, the Alliance announced its intention to transform itself into "a large, popular political party" characterized by tight discipline and a mass base. During the next several years the party generated an elaborate formal party apparatus, a youth organization, a women's group, and detailed disciplinary provisions. As with the Federation, however, an aura of unreality surrounded this proliferation of organizations and statutes. Attempts to impose discipline on the party's deputies failed utterly; and even President Flandin, notwithstanding his pleas for tactical unity, acted as a completely free agent.[37] If only because the proximity of the Alliance to ministerial posts

36. *L'Union Républicaine du Rhône*, June 26, July 17, 1932; Guiter to Marin, August 11, 1931, in Marin Papers, carton 73; *La Nation*, September 17, 24, 1927.

37. See the Alliance's *Correspondance politique et agricole*, March 10, 1910, July 5, 1911, for the projected creation of a *"parti du peuple."* *L'Alliance Démocratique*, October 4, 1935, March 6, June 26, 1936; Georges Lachapelle, *L'Alliance Démocratique* (Paris, 1935), 50. In the face of opposition from the party's executive and from many deputies, Flandin also entered the Sarraut government in January, 1936, which prompted a bitter debate in the executive but no disciplinary action.

prompted its members into indiscipline more readily than was the case with its right-wing neighbor, the Alliance never even attained the degree of cohesiveness reached by the Federation.

The exception to this pattern was the Parti Démocrate Populaire, which did create something approximating a democratic and mass political party. Founded in 1924 by Auguste Champetier de Ribes, Paul Simon, and Robert Cornilieu, the Parti Démocrate Populaire (PDP) was a Christian democratic party in the tradition of Marc Sangier's prewar liberal Christian Sillon.[38] Unlike the Federation, the PDP could not rely on a substantial traditional political power base, nor count on the automatic support of traditional elites and the adhesion of conservative Catholic deputies. Since its avowed purpose was to demonstrate the compatibility of Catholicism and liberal democracy, the party's style was self-consciously democratic. A relatively open, active, and popular political party suited both the objective needs of the PDP and its temperamental inclination.

To attract votes from the segment of French society that rejected ultranationalistic and conservative Catholicism without embracing anticlerical liberalism or socialism, the PDP needed an effective organization. In some areas of France, particularly the Catholic west, the local organizations of the party were models of political activity. In the Finistère, for example, the departmental federations of the PDP included a large number of local sections, which were proportionately represented at departmental meetings and which were systematically canvassed on local and national issues by the departmental executive. In contrast, the Federation's organization in that large department consisted of two isolated committees in Brest and Quimper, both of which disappeared by 1939.[39] Delegates to the PDP's national congresses were mandated by their local branches and

38. On the origins of the PDP see Jean Raymond-Laurent, *Le Parti Démocrate Populaire* (Le Mans, 1965); R. E. M. Irving, *Christian Democracy in France* (London, 1973); Mario Einaudi and François Goguel, *Christian Democracy in Italy and France* (Notre Dame, Ind., 1952).

39. *Le Petit Démocrate*, October 25, 1931; Raymond-Laurent, *Le Parti Démocrate Populaire*, 65–67; *Le Petit Breton*, February 9, 1936; *La Province*, June 10–17, 1931. See also Guiter's notes on the state of organization in Marin Papers, carton 75.

represented in proportion to the party's strength in each department. The party organized periodic *journées du militant* in Paris, where the executive and the deputies could exchange views with the rank and file. *Le Petit Démocrate*, the party's newspaper, regularly published information about the number of members in each department, organized recruitment drives, and elaborated upon the party's electoral strategy in every region of France. By attempting to secure the loyalty and muster the enthusiasm of a mass of adherents, the PDP sought to overcome the disability of being distrusted by both the anticlerical Left and the nationalist Catholic Right. Despite its efforts, however, the PDP never became a major party, electing only nineteen deputies in 1932 and eleven in 1936.

The paucity of the Republican Federation's organizational activity was paralleled by its persistent inability to form a cohesive parliamentary bloc. Dominated by highly independent deputies, the party never succeeded in imposing discipline, or even cohesion, upon its representatives in parliament. In the early 1930s a series of intestine personal quarrels led to the dispersal of many of the party's deputies. The public dissension profoundly demoralized the rank and file, exacerbated the latent tensions between deputies and the *militants*, and helped to isolate the party on the extreme Right.

The proliferation of parliamentary groups was one of the more scandalous features of political life in the Third Republic. Parliamentary groups, whose numbers increased with each successive legislature, were rarely related to any organized political party outside the Chamber. To the right of the Radicals there were as many as ten different groups, each one labeled with some ingenious combination of evocative words like *left, independent, republican, democratic,* or *social*. The more inconsequential the group, the more pretentious was its title. As commentators remarked, the Groupe des indépendants d'action économique, sociale et paysanne, formed in 1932, had more words in its title than it had deputies in the Chamber.[40] The ideological and pro-

40. *Politique*, July, 1932, p. 656.

grammatic differences among the various groups on the Right were usually a mystery to all but the best informed insiders; and, in fact, the differences were primarily personal and tactical ones. For those deputies who found membership in one of these groups too confining, there existed the group of Indépendants, which gathered together nonconformists of all political hues. The devotees of complete freedom could find refuge in a group that was quixotically known as "the group of deputies belonging to no group." The multiplication of tiny parliamentary groups (known to observers as the disease of *groupite*) enhanced the possibilities for complex bargaining during ministerial crises and facilitated the entrance of certain politicians into cabinets. It also confirmed the image of conservative politicians as members of a cozy club, more concerned with its arcane ritual than with furthering the conservative cause.[41]

During the 1920s the Republican Federation managed to avoid the worst ravages of *groupite*, gathering most, although not all, of its deputies into the Union Républicaine Démocratique. The Union was the semiofficial group of the Federation, and the name Union Républicaine Démocratique was often used interchangeably with that of Republican Federation even after the former ceased to exist in 1932. But between 1929 and 1932 a complex of internal squabbles scattered the party's deputies throughout parliament and ultimately prompted a serious rupture in the Federation.

The Federation's feuds are intriguing to explore but tedious to relate. The critical factors, however, were tactical disagreements over foreign policy, the overbearing manner of Louis Marin and his principal lieutenants, and above all the craving after independence on the part of many conservative deputies. The tactical differences stemmed from the problem of reconciling the party's traditional nationalistic stance on foreign policy with the realities of international and domestic politics. The related issues of the interallied debts and the German reparations brought the problem to a head. Although the Mellon-Béranger and

41. For a good discussion of this problem see *Le Temps*, April 21, 1932.

Caillaux-Churchill agreements of 1926 had formally settled the war debts issue, the agreements were unpopular in France and had not yet been ratified by parliament. In principle the Federation adamantly opposed the war debts settlement. It considered the United States to be both crassly immoral and illogical for insisting upon treating as ordinary commercial debts money that had been borrowed for the purpose of fighting a common enemy. France, the party reasoned, had amply paid her debts in human lives.[42]

The debts issue was connected to that of war reparations. An international committee of experts, headed by Owen D. Young, recommended a settlement guaranteeing that German payments to France would exceed French debts payments to Great Britain and the United States. To encourage the Germans to accept the Young Plan, Aristide Briand, the French foreign minister, was prepared to evacuate the left bank of the Rhine by 1930, or four and one-half years earlier than provided for by the Treaty of Versailles. The Republican Federation was even more hostile to the Young Plan, for it had never been content with the size of German reparations; and the further reductions of the Young Plan appeared to be yet another unnecessary concession to Germany. The withdrawal of French troops from the Rhineland meant abandoning the last vestiges of security granted by the Treaty of Versailles and marked the last of a string of unilateral surrenders that characterized the naïve and dangerously indulgent foreign policy of Briand.

The attitude of the Federation was important because after the conservative electoral victory of 1928 the party was part of a governmental coalition headed by Raymond Poincaré. Poincaré recognized that the debts-reparations settlement was less than ideal but realized that it was the best settlement France was likely to obtain. Furthermore, he was alert to the grave financial and diplomatic consequences of a failure to ratify the interallied debts settlement. Despite Louis Marin's strenuous pleadings,

42. *La Nation*, February 2, 16, 1929.

by 1929 Poincaré's realism began to spread to many members of the Federation, who reluctantly conceded the need to bow before concrete political and financial realities and who recognized that opposition to Poincaré would only bring to power a more left-oriented government that would almost certainly retain Briand at the Quai d'Orsay. Whereas Marin argued that the Federation's duty as the right flank of Poincaré's government was to force it to adopt a firmer posture, the bulk of the deputies insisted on loyally supporting the government in its unpleasant but unavoidable policy. The Federation's congress at Rouen in June failed to resolve the conflict between principle and tactics, while Poincaré's eloquent persuasion and subtle ministerial pressures reduced Marin's supporters to a handful. When the war debts question was voted upon in July, a mere fifteen deputies supported Marin in voting against the government.[43] Early in 1930 the majority of the party's deputies also voted for the Young Plan.

Marin did not take his defeat gracefully. *La Nation* caustically abused Poincaré's government and the similar governments of his successors, Briand and André Tardieu. Moreover, it abounded with attacks on the majority of the party's deputies, whom Marin persisted in calling dissidents. He continued to vote against the conservative governments of the day; and in October, 1929, he and fourteen of his supporters, voting with the Left, succeeded in defeating the Briand government. The result was a two-week ministerial crisis, which was finally resolved

43. *L'Echo de Paris*, June 3, 1929; *Le Journal de Rouen*, June 9, 13, 1929. Marin's supporters included Edouard de Warren, François de Wendel, Joseph Denais, Victor Perret, Charles Maurice-Bellet, president of the federation of the Seine, and Jean Baudouin from the Seine-Inférieure. Advocates of a more supple foreign policy were led by Henri de Kerillis, Georges Pernot, Charles de Lasteyrie, and later Edouard Soulier, Pierre Taittinger, and Jean Ybarnegaray. Gaetan Sanvoisin, "La responsabilité presente des modérés: histoire des deux mois," *La Revue Hebdomadaire*, August 17, 1929, pp. 351–60. Sanvoisin, a right-wing critic of the government, detailed examples of ministerial patronage, offers of future portfolios, and promises of future electoral support designed to win over some of the URD deputies. Those voting with Marin included Blaisot, de Wendel, de Warren, Gustave Guerin, and Louis Dubois. All fifteen deputies came from conservative and nationalistic constituencies but no more so than most of the deputies who voted with the government.

when Marin and his faction, somewhat inconsistently, now voted for a Tardieu government that was virtually identical to that
of Briand.[44]

To most members of the Federation, Marin's stubborn fidelity
to what he believed to be the sacred core of the party's doctrine
represented the *politique du pire* and would benefit only the
Left. François Peissel and Georges Pernot privately complained
that Marin's tactics would isolate moderate conservatives on the
extreme Right. Publicly Pernot and about fifty deputies attempted to force Marin to accept tighter and more democratic control over the voting within the Union Républicaine Démocratique (URD), with the party voting as a bloc on critical issues.
The internal tensions became increasingly public as competing
elements within the URD leaked information to their respective
champions in the Parisian press. Naturally, both sides posed as
partisans of discipline. The majority in the URD insisted that
Marin and his coterie ought to abide by the decisions of the
parliamentary caucus; Marin countered that all deputies were
bound by the program and the formal resolutions of the Republican Federation.[45] Conveniently forgotten was the fact that the
right of indiscipline was in practice, if not in theory, the most
cherished of all principles in the Republican Federation. For
many deputies the instinctive response to the conflict was simply to leave the URD. Although the formation of a rival group
was rumored, individual deputies merely drifted into neighboring and more congenial formations. A total of seventeen left the
URD, motivated by unhappiness with Marin's attitude, anxiety
about their home constituencies, and occasionally personal antagonism to fellow URD deputies. Well into 1930 the public
difficulties of the URD remained a source of regret for conser-

44. *Le Journal des Débats*, October 24, 1929; *Le Temps*, October 25, 1929. On the
confusion created by Marin and his coterie, see *La Nation*, November 28, 1929; *L'Echo
de Paris*, November 10, 1929; *Le Charivari*, November 16, 1929.

45. François Peissel to Guiter, September 6, 1929, Georges Pernot to Guiter, September 14, 1929, both in Marin Papers, carton 73; *Le Temps*, November 15, 20, 1929;
Le Matin, November 15, 1929; *L'Echo de Paris*, November 18, 20, 22, December 17, 1929;
Aux Ecoutes, November 30, 1929; *Le Petit Bleu*, November 16, 20, 1929; *Le Journal
des Débats*, December 4, 1929; Louis Marin in the *Journal Officiel*, March 29, 1930,
p. 1411.

vatives and the subject of unabashed amusement on the Left.[46]

Throughout, Marin posed as the defender of the party's nationalistic principles and of the wishes of the rank and file against the opportunism of most deputies. To some extent he was right. The Federation of the Seine vigorously supported him and reviled the majority of the party's deputies. Many individual party members wrote Marin congratulating him on his resistance.[47] Most *militants*, however, were aghast at the havoc that Marin and his faction seemed to be wreaking among conservatives. They noted the unwelcome support that Marin's extreme nationalism was receiving from the Action Française and complained that the party was losing members to the more moderate Alliance Démocratique and the Parti Démocrate Populaire. A substantial number of departmental organizations either disavowed Marin's position or admitted that it provoked severe internal problems among them. Jean Guiter received a number of resignations and the expression of disaffection from some prominent financial supporters. Auguste Isaac, Marin's predecessor as president, resigned in disgust; and even such staunch allies as Victor Perret and Jean Baudouin, alluding to difficulties in their respective federations, timidly suggested a more flexible stance. Although Jean Guiter complained that the crisis had "dangerously compromised" all his organizational efforts since 1925, Marin still remained unmoved.[48]

46. For the motives of departing deputies see the letters to Marin from Camille Cautru, Ernest Flandin, Louis Nicolle, Henri Auriol, Henry Cravoisier, Joseph Mathieu, and Amidieu du Clos, all in the Marin Papers, carton 73. See also *L'Echo de Paris*, November 28, 1929, January 31, 1930. *Le Populaire*, October 23, 1929; *L'Ere Nouvelle*, February 17, 25, March 7, 1930.

47. Minutes of the Republican Federation of the Seine, November 12, 1929, February 5, 1930, in Marin Papers, carton 82; Guiter to Marin, February 14, 1930, in Marin Papers, carton 73; *L'Action Sociale et Nationale*, May 15, 1930. About one hundred of these letters—mostly from individuals—are preserved in the Marin Papers, carton 73.

48. Guiter to Marin, November 14, 18, 19, 20, December 21, 24, 28, 1929, January 3, 6, 31, March 26, September 8, 1930, Emmanuel Prunet (president of the National Republican Union of the Tarn-et-Garonne) to Guiter, November 11, 1929, January 11, 1930, René Durant (president of the party's branch in the Haute-Marne) to Guiter, November 16, 1929, the secretary-general of the Republican Federation of the Eure-et-Loire to Guiter, April 17, 1930, Aimé Bourreau (president of the Republican Federation of the Alpes-Maritimes) to Guiter, January 11, 1930, Auguste Isaac to Guiter, April 19, 1930, Victor Perret to Marin, December 23, 1929, January 9, 30, 1930, Marin to Guiter, April 19, 1930, all in Marin Papers, carton 73.

In another party the internecine warfare of 1929–1930 would have led to some kind of *reglement des comptes* in the 1930 congress. Indeed, some local sections feared that it might. Aside from scattered unpleasantries, however, no one at the May congress confronted the issue squarely or attempted to resolve it. All sides contented themselves with pious hopes for future reconciliation.[49]

After the ratification of the war debts settlement and the Young Plan, there was in fact little of substance to divide the Federation. Personal antagonisms remained, however, which Marin exacerbated in the summer of 1931 with an ill-advised attempt to expel Henri de Kerillis from the National Council of the party. Kerillis had long been a trenchant critic of the stagnation of the *modérés*, and he amused himself in June, 1931, with a series of caustic (and accurate) articles about the flabbiness of the Republican Federation. Marin's attempt to punish Kerillis by expelling him infuriated many of the party's leading deputies and senators. Kerillis had been their very vocal ally in 1929, and they shared his irritation with Louis Marin, if not his ideas on modernizing conservative politics. Incensed by Marin's unilateral action, they protested his attempt to stifle free criticism and pointed to the invaluable electoral assistance of Kerillis' Centre de propagande des républicains nationaux. Marin had the support of some of his traditional allies from the departmental federations, although not that of most rank and file. Some *militants* did share Marin's distrust for clever and ambitious young men like Kerillis, but most were bewildered and angered by what appeared to be a perverse attempt to alienate a useful ally.[50] The expulsion session turned into a fiasco, and Marin barely escaped with a vote of confidence. Although vindi-

49. *Bulletin Mensuel de la Fédération Républicaine du Calaisis*, June, 1930; *Le Temps*, May 19, 1930.

50. *L'Echo de Paris*, May 23, July 4, 5, 6, 7, 8, 9, 1931; *L'Ordre*, July 9, 1931; Guiter to Marin, August 11, December 15, 1931, in Marin Papers, carton 73. On the bewilderment of the *militants* in the Seine-Inférieure and the Maine-et-Loire, see *Le Journal de Rouen*, July 5, 1931, and *Le Petit Courrier* (Angers), June 1, 16, 1931. For an example of the long-standing distrust of Kerillis in the Republican Federation of the Seine, see the minutes for May 27, October 27, 1926, in Marin Papers, carton 82.

cated, Kerillis gradually withdrew from an active role in the party.

The internal rifts within the Federation also served to shift its political center of gravity toward the Right. The intransigence of the Marin faction earned the party the support of the Action Française but disrupted relations with its Center-Right neighbors, most notably the Parti Démocrate Populaire. Always anxious to emphasize the gap that separated liberal Catholicism from the ultranationalistic and socially reactionary Catholic Right, the PDP took advantage of the divisions within the Federation to accentuate these differences. Charging that the Federation had broken with its former tradition of moderate Republicanism and was now a party of the extreme Right, the PDP suggested that the party of Louis Marin could more appropriately march under the banner of the Action Française.[51] While conceding that there was still a republican wing of the Federation, the PDP concentrated its ire on the refractory wing of Louis Marin and his friends Edouard de Warren, François de Wendel, Victor Perret, and Philippe Henriot. For the sake of polemical effectiveness the PDP ignored the presence of truly dubious republicans like Pierre Taittinger in the ranks of those who opposed Marin's foreign policy.

La Nation sneered at the naïve Briandism of the PDP and wondered aloud about the need for another Catholic party in France. The "eternally revolutionary ferment of the gospels," of which the PDP so fondly spoke, impressed the Federation as resembling the "blasphemous rapprochement between the gospels and Revolution" recently condemned by Pius X. Some branches of the Federation, in imitation of the Action Française, began to refer to the PDP as the Parti des Poires or even the Pédés.[52] In turn, the PDP, which usually allied with the Federation in electoral campaigns, now singled out candidates of the Marin wing for attack. It successfully opposed Edouard de War-

51. *Le Petit Démocrate*, June 7, November 8, 1931.
52. *La Nation*, January 3, 1931, January 30, 1932; *L'Entente Républicaine Démocratique de Hazebrouck*, January, 1933.

ren in the 1931 cantonal elections and the 1932 legislative elections. In 1932 the PDP ran candidates against Philippe Henriot in the Gironde and Roger Fulchiron (Victor Perret's lieutenant) in the Loire, giving as its reasons their prominence in the reactionary wing of the Federation.[53]

By 1932 Louis Marin must have recognized that the legacy of bitterness threatened to rupture the party because during the elections he behaved in an uncharacteristically conciliatory manner. Under pressure from the majority of the party's Parisian deputies, Marin supported the candidacies of Henri de Kerillis and a vice-president of the PDP against right-wing nationalists, whose position was close to his own. Indeed, his concessions earned him harsh words from the usually sympathetic extreme Right.[54]

The 1932 election resulted in a general shift toward the Left, and the Federation lost about twenty seats. It nonetheless counted eighty elected deputies, and *La Nation* cheered discouraged *militants* by noting that, as a result of a resolution passed at the February, 1932, congress of the party, all elected deputies were now pledged to sit in one united parliamentary group bearing the Federation's name. When the new Chamber reconvened, however, it became apparent that only forty, or half of the expected deputies, actually intended to join the new group of the Republican Federation. The rest sat in no less than eight other groups.[55] Some of these deputies, like Henri Auriol, Désiré Ferry, or Robert Schumann, had, notwithstanding their continued formal membership in the Federation, long since migrated to the political center. But sixteen of the Federation's

53. *Le Petit Démocrate*, April 17, 1932.
54. *L'Echo de Paris*, May 6, 1932; Georges Dovine, "Philosophie d'un scrutin: le suicide des partis nationaux," *La Revue Hebdomadaire*, June 4, 1932, pp. 84–104.
55. *La Nation*, May 26, June 25, 1932. Those sitting elsewhere included sixteen in the Groupe des indépendants républicains et sociaux led by Georges Pernot, twelve in the Centre républicain led by André Tardieu, five in P.-E. Flandin's Républicains de gauche, three as independents, and one each in the Parti Démocrate Populaire, the Républicains du centre, the Indépendants d'action économique et paysanne, and the group of deputies belonging to no group. An independent calculation based on Jean Guiter's notes yielded virtually identical figures.

deputies, including some of the most prominent, founded a separate group, the Indépendants républicains et sociaux. Georges Pernot, still a vice-president of the Federation, presided over the new group, whose membership included such leading party figures as François Peissel, Antoine Sallès, Robert Serot, Camille Cautru, Jean de Tinguy du Pouët, and Etienne d'Audiffret-Pasquier. The division had been rumored for some time and effectively shattered any illusions about the unity and the authority of the Republican Federation.

Although the dispersal of the Federation's deputies obviously reflected the internal conflicts of the previous three years, there are no profound reasons why some deputies chose to leave and some did not. No one in the Third Republic founded a splinter group without doing so in the name of unity, and the Indépendants républicains et sociaux were no exception, giving as their goal the reconciliation of diverse conservatives. Pernot's hopes of creating a large swing group of moderate conservative deputies were disappointed, however, since the groupe Pernot attracted only two deputies not previously in the Union Républicaine Démocratique. Due to the curious workings of the Chamber, moreover, his group was assigned seats to the right of the Republican Federation.[56]

Equally predictable was the groupe Pernot's insistence that it stood for a more enlightened social policy and a more flexible foreign policy than did the main body of the Federation. To be sure, Pernot, Sallès, and Peissel were known as social Catholics, several members of the new group had openly criticized Marin's foreign policy, and the group enjoyed the formal blessing of liberal Catholics. Yet taken as a whole, the voting record of the groupe Pernot was no more progressive than that of the main party. Some had been among the small minority of the Federation to oppose the 1931 Social Insurance Act; others had voted

56. *Le Matin*, May 15, 1932; *Le Courrier de la Montagne*, June 18, 1932; *Le Temps*, June 26, 1932. Since the more established groups received priority in the distribution of seats, the official group of the Federation was permitted to choose seats to the left of the groupe Pernot.

with Louis Marin in 1929. Nothing in the social composition of the group, including as it did a prince, a duke, a baron, and three counts as well as two of the largest industrialists in the Chamber (Jean Plichon and Louis Nicolle), would have rendered its members ill at ease among the deputies of the Federation.[57] Similarly, among deputies sitting in other splinter groups there were nearly as many former supporters of Marin as former dissidents.

Ministerial ambition generated many new groups in the Third Republic, and some of the dispersed deputies were *ministrables*, potential cabinet material.[58] Given the composition of the 1932 Chamber, however, a shift from the Federation to one of the groups on its left flank would not greatly enhance the likelihood of entering a government, and only Georges Pernot and, very briefly, Louis Nicolle ever did. Nor did electoral considerations determine the deputies' actions. Although one deputy alluded to pressure from his electoral committee, deputies generally did not discuss their postelection plans with their electors.[59] The electoral declarations of the deputies reveal nothing. Typically, in the Moselle all five of the Federation's deputies presented virtually identical statements but ended up sitting in five different groups. Neither geographical distribution nor the attitude of local branches of the Federation provides a clue to the dispersal of the deputies. Even the timing is perplexing, since in 1932 Marin had acted with uncharacteristic restraint. Moreover, given the electoral victory of the Left, the Federation was back in the opposition, where Marin's intransigence was more appropriate.

If the deputies of the Republican Federation were not driven apart by fundamental causes, it was because they had been held together by such fragile ties. The attachment of many of them to

57. *L'Aube*, June 11, 1932. The Federation's supporters ironically noted the prevalence of "fin de race" aristocrats among the *mal à droites* in the groupe Pernot. *Le Charivari*, June 11, 1932; *Le Journal de Rouen*, June 5, 1932; *L'Action Française*, June 3, 1932.

58. Including Camille Cautru, Robert Serot, Georges Pernot, Etienne d'Audiffret-Pasquier, and Louis Nicolle.

59. Jules Appourchaux to Guiter, June 2, 1932, in Marin Papers, carton 85.

the party was remarkably cavalier. Georges Bret, deputy from the Ille-et-Vilaine and hitherto a staunch Marin loyalist, assured Jean Guiter that his decision to sit in another group and subsequently to resign from the Federation represented "no change of political views," only a desire to regain his "political independence."[60] A congress of the Federation might have passed some well-intentioned resolution about groups within the Chamber, but most deputies did not believe that this altered their right to do as they pleased once inside parliament. Characteristically, none of those who joined the groupe Pernot felt that his actions were sufficiently momentous to resign from the Federation.

Marin and his followers were nonetheless outraged at this flagrant violation of party discipline and insisted upon punitive action. This time they had the general support of the rank and file. A number of departmental federations issued statements protesting the indiscipline among the deputies and demanding enforcement of the congress' resolution. The most indignant federation, that of the Seine, angrily expelled one erring deputy, Julien Tardieu, from its midst. Led by its vice-president and future deputy, Georges Cousin, the federation formally demanded the expulsion from the party's governing bodies of all deputies who had not rejoined the Federation's parliamentary group before the fall session of parliament. Still, some *militants* urged caution, observing that expulsion might have more severe consequences for the party than for the deputies. And many deputies, traditionally distrustful of the disciplinary initiatives of the Marin faction, opposed any drastic measures. Charles de Lasteyrie, deputy from Paris, reminded Marin that the Alliance Démocratique, in an effort to unite its traditionally dispersed deputies, had similarly obliged all its candidates to sit in a single parliamentary group in 1932. Although the formal resolution of the Alliance had no visible effect on its deputies, Lasteyrie noted, the Alliance was not threatening expulsion. Marin and

60. Georges Bret to Guiter, July 21, 1932, Jean Thureaux-Dangin to Guiter, July 21, 1932, in Marin Papers, carton 82.

his nonparliamentary lieutenants, however, were determined to carry out what one of them later called the "sanitary operation" and, after energetic last-minute maneuvering, managed to gain a majority in the National Council. After a prolonged and bitter discussion, on July 7 the Council voted 61 to 39 to expel the defecting deputies from executive office. Those deputies who were affected subsequently resigned from the Federation. Three deputies and two senators, although remaining in the Federation and the parliamentary group, resigned as vice-presidents in protest against the action of the Council.[61]

This disciplinary action, unique in the history of the Federation, reflected the party's weakness not its strength. The party leadership and the rank and file had an airtight case against the rebels but one that ignored the elementary realities of conservative politics in France. They were correct to lament the demoralizing effects on the *militants* of such indiscipline,[62] but the fact remained that these *militants* had rarely contributed decisively to the reelection of the deputies concerned. Most of the deputies of the groupe Pernot, for example, had been elected easily in 1932, usually on the first ballot. And they would be elected again in 1936. In a party whose organization carried electoral clout, expulsion or the threat of it could be an effective weapon. In a party like the Republican Federation, it was only a gesture of despair.[63]

61. The *ordre du jour* of the Republican Federation of the Alpes-Maritimes, May 31, 1932, the Republican Federation of the Bouches-du-Rhône, June 6, 1932, in Marin Papers, carton 73; the *ordre du jour* of the Republican Union of the Var, June 26, 1932, and Guiter to Marin, July 13, 1932, in Marin Papers, carton 82; Perret to Marin, June 10, 1932, in Marin Papers, carton 79; minutes of the Republican Federation of the Seine, June 21, 1932, in Marin Papers, carton 82 (the motion was reproduced in *Le Charivari*, June 25, 1932); two letters to Guiter, no date but late in June, 1932, in Marin Papers, cartons 73 and 82; *L'Echo de Paris*, March 19, 1932; Charles de Lasteyrie to Marin, August 6, 1932, in Marin Papers, carton 73; Jean Baudouin to Guiter, February 12, 1933, Guiter to Marin, June 28, 1932, in Marin Papers, carton 82. For the final vote, see *La Nation*, July 9, 1932. (How individual members voted was not recorded.) Those who resigned in protest were Charles de Lasteyrie, Edouard Soulier, Paul Chassaigne-Goyon, and Senators Manuel Fourcade and Maurice Hervey.

62. For example, *Le Journal de Rouen*, June 5, 1932; *La Nation*, June 25, 1932.

63. The experience of the Republican Federation contrasts strikingly with that of its approximate German equivalent, the Deutschnationale Volkspartei. The latter was an

Reflecting on what it meant to be a *militant* in the Republican Federation, one is tempted to ask not why there were so few but why there were any at all. What, after all, would motivate a man to become a *militant* in the Republican Federation? For some the answer was undoubtedly ambition. Local committees were often springboards to departmental or national politics. Although the party relied heavily on relatively independent *notables* for its deputies, a substantial number of its parliamentary representatives, and even more of its aspirants, had previously been active in local organizations. There were also other benefits that might accrue to prominent *militants*. In 1934 Etienne Peille, twice unsuccessful candidate for the Chamber and principal inspiration behind the Federation's branch in the Haute-Garonne, revealed one of the reasons for his organizational zeal. Sensing that the Republican Federation would soon be represented in a governmental coalition, he wrote Marin suggesting a future appointment as a *chef du cabinet*, both as a reward for his efforts and as a means for improving the Federation's political influence in his relatively barren department.[64] In general, however, the prospect of patronage would have moved few to join a party that in the best of times controlled only one or two minor portfolios.

Modérés, by and large, made poor *militants*. The term *modéré* implied more than just a location on the political spectrum; it also suggested an attitude toward politics. Conservatives felt ill at ease in mass politics, rarely showed passion for political activity, and preferred a quiet approach to politics over active and intense grass roots campaigning. The *modérés* were essentially content with the social and political structure of France and desired no fundamental transformation of society. A *modéré* might well have been disturbed by the errors of the dominant

elaborate mass party, in which the local conservative organizations had a powerful influence. When in the early 1930s some moderate deputies of the DNVP attempted a secession, they were crushed in subsequent elections by the potent electoral organization of the main party. Erasmus Jonas, *Die Volkskonservativen, 1928–1933* (Dusseldorf, 1965).

64. Etienne Peille to Marin, January 21, 1934, in Marin Papers, carton 79.

political elite or by the general direction in which modern society seemed to be moving, but his discontent rarely was great enough to stimulate him to make personal sacrifices to alter the situation. The *modérés* turned to politics reluctantly, often as a last resort, and usually during crises. When they did, they were likely to turn elsewhere, rather than to the Republican Federation.

The diagnoses of the leaders of the Federation themselves confirm the thesis that *militant* and *modéré* did not go well together. In 1934 Victor Perret complained: "The elites often disinterest themselves in politics, about which they pretend to know nothing, restricting themselves to their family life and their business interests."[65] Reflecting on the experience of the Federation from the perspective of the early 1940s, Joseph Denais concurred with Perret's assessment. He recalled:

> In the ranks of our party, I rarely met men who, on account of some joyful urge, were dedicated to political action. I met even fewer who were driven by ambition or appetite. Even the most ardent gave their support with resignation, lacked faith in the possibility of success, expected no personal gain, and often observed bitterly that the fulfillment of their duty was detrimental to them because it forced them to sacrifice their professional career, their fortune and above all their family life. . . . We never had enough *militants* because we would have had to demand total abnegation from them. As it was, even those who did work for us did not devote themselves totally to the cause.[66]

Yet the Republican Federation could hardly inspire devotion in its *militants*. An elitist, cadre party, it denied the rank and file any substantial influence in its affairs. The party's aspirations appeared, at times, to be limited to forming a government of national union with Marin or Blaisot in a minor post. The restless and frustrated youth of the 1930s could find little scope for venting their energies in the carefully supervised Jeunesse de la

65. *Rapport sur la politique générale fait au congrès de la fédération républicaine, 1934*, in Marin Papers, carton 82.
66. *La Renaissance Nationale*, November 30, 1941.

Fédération Républicaine. The party's deputies often epitomized the worst faults of *la république des camarades*.

During periods of relative social and political stability most *modérés* remained complacent and substantially content with the existing style of politics. In times of actual or impending social upheaval, on the other hand, the *modérés* lost their moderation. Frightened at last out of their lethargy, they were unlikely to turn to a Republican Federation which, by comparison with the new movements on the Right, seemed utterly colorless and ineffective. Its members could look forward neither to the revolution about which the Communists still dreamed, nor to the mysterious H-hour for which the Croix de Feu prepared. A member of the Croix de Feu enjoyed a sense of active participation in a dynamic and growing movement, whereas a member of the Federation was doomed to a limited and passive role in a stagnant political party. A right-wing activist in search of something new and potent would not find it in the Republican Federation.

III. *The Popular Front*

The year 1933 marked the end of the internal crises of the Republican Federation. The death of Briand and the rise of Hitler eliminated *Briandisme* as an issue, and Marin's Germanophobia seemed neither so outrageous nor so likely to disrupt a conservative coalition. Except during the truce of 1934–1935, the Republican Federation remained in the opposition and was never again forced to weigh party principles against parliamentary expediency. Occasional differences of opinion arose within the party, notably over the Parti Social Français and the appropriate response to the Nazi menace, but the open feuds of the 1929–1932 period were never repeated. Indeed, faced with the aggressive "new" Right, the leadership of the Federation demonstrated surprising cohesiveness and solidarity.

The problems facing the Federation after 1933 stemmed not from internal difficulties, but from a threefold set of external threats. Domestically, France seemed threatened by economic crisis, social upheaval, and growing political radicalism. At the same time, powerful new right-wing movements arose to challenge not only the existing political system, but also the Federation's place on the French Right. From the outside, Nazi Germany threatened the peace of Europe and in particular France's postwar security system. The reaction of the Republican Federation to the last two issues was governed by its perception of the first. It was the sense of a radically changing France, the loss of political and social stability, that sapped the Republican Federation's confidence and drove it both to alter radically its views on foreign policy and to cooperate with the least reputable elements on the extreme Right.

One critical factor that colored the Federation's perception of the later 1930s was the sense of being politically isolated on the Right. The reflex of parties like the Parti Démocrate Populaire and the Alliance Démocratique was to identify with the political Center and to fight against political polarization. Faithful to Adolphe Thiers's adage that "France is Center-Left," they sought to avoid at all costs what they called "the politics of two blocs" or, as the Parti Démocrate Populaire put it, to assure that the country "not be forced to choose between the politics of M. Marin and those of M. Blum."[1] Particularly when the political balance was tilted toward the Left, the Center parties strove to cooperate with the more tractable Radicals and with those moderate leftists who had severed their ties with the Socialists. This cooperation usually took the form of so-called governments of republican concentration, governmental coalitions that drew on all the formations of the Center, including the Radicals and the independent socialists, but which excluded both the Socialists and the Communists on the Left and the Republican Federation on the Right. Governments of republican concentration were unstable, for they rested on a narrow base and were at the mercy of any one of a number of groups whose defection could bring them down. Nonetheless, after the victory of the Left in 1932, concentration became a strong temptation for the parties of the Center because it offered them the sole possibility of attracting the Radicals away from the Socialists and of forming a centrist government.

The Republican Federation denied that the French political spectrum was divided into a Right, a Left, and a Center. The idea of the Center had been a useful one, the party maintained, at the beginning of the century when the Right had consisted of the monarchists, nationalists, and Bonapartists and the Center had included the moderate Republicans like those in the Republican Federation. But in the intervening years, the antirepublican forces had virtually disappeared, and what was once the

1. *Le Petit Démocrate*, January 4, 1931.

Center was now the Right. What separated the right-wing Federation from the groups that pretended to be in the Center were not the fundamental differences of the early twentieth century but nuances of tone and different tactics. The differences between the Federation, on the one hand, and the Alliance and the Parti Démocrate Populaire were minimal compared to the vast gulf that separated them all from the Left. The political map of France was divided into two separate spheres, which did not admit a middle ground. A *militant* in Hazebrouck gave the classic formulation of this thesis: "There will always be a Right and a Left, just as we will always be able to tell good from bad and true from false." "Centrism," Marin sarcastically observed, meant little more than the worship of "Sainte Opportune."[2]

Governments of republican concentration were anathema to the Federation because they represented the worst features of centrist politics and, just as surely, because they excluded the Federation from office. Such governments ignored the elementary principles of parliamentary mathematics and drove a wedge between the Federation and its political neighbors. The Federation wished to form the right flank of a broad coalition of the *modérés*—the so-called governments of National Union. Ideally the sectarian and opportunistic Radicals could be excluded, but if necessary the government could be extended to include the less doctrinaire of their number. Unfortunately for the Federation, the left-wing victories of 1932 and 1936 rendered a government of National Union unlikely.[3] After 1932 the real choice lay between a left-wing coalition of the Cartel des Gauches or the Front Populaire and the centrist coalition of republican concentration. Recognizing this, the center parties drew away from the Federation.

The Parti Démocrate Populaire had already broken with the Federation in the early 1930s and had campaigned against some of the party's more conservative candidates in 1932. By 1933

2. *L'Entente Républicaine Démocratique de Hazebrouck*, September, 1934; *La Nation*, August 5, 1933. Marin cited LaFontaine: "I am a bird, see my wings; I am a mouse; long live rats" in reference to the Center parties and their pretensions.

3. Except in the unusual truce situation prevailing after the events of February 6, 1934.

the Alliance Démocratique too began to look toward its Left. From its origins as the left flank of the *progressistes*, the leaders of the Alliance had been more open to cooperation with the Radicals than their counterparts in the Federation. True to its favorite slogan, *ni réaction, ni révolution*, the Alliance hovered between the Federation and the Radicals, with a distinct preference for the latter. A centrist orientation offered greater possibilities of exercising real political power and also corresponded to the Alliance's electoral situation. A laic party, the Alliance had little appeal in the Catholic west and east but was relatively well represented in the center and the Ile de France.[4] In these anticlerical and traditionally left-leaning areas, a conservative had a better chance if he appeared to blend into the right wing of the Radicals.

When Pierre-Etienne Flandin became president of the Alliance in March, 1933, he and his two vice-presidents (André de Fels and Léon Barety[5]) began to make overtures to the Radicals, emphasizing the differences that separated the Alliance from the Right. In his inaugural address Flandin condemned the Right for seeking to "retain the existing social system with all its excesses and abuses." An outraged Federation indignantly rebutted the "excesses and abuses" speech, demonstrating rather plausibly that the Alliance's record on social questions was no more progressive than its neighbor. Nonetheless, in spite of the protests of members like Paul Reynaud, André Tardieu (who resigned in 1935), and Charles Reibel, the Alliance persisted in its new orientation and continued to stress its differences from the Republican Federation. While never formally renouncing cooperation with the Federation, the Alliance resisted any suggestion of a Cartel des Droites and devoted its energies to wooing the Radicals.[6]

4. One of the Alliance's favorite watchwords was "anti-clerical but not anti-religious." Georges Lachapelle, *L'Alliance Démocratique* (Paris, 1935), 19.
5. De Fels was former deputy from the Seine-et-Oise; Barety was deputy from the Alpes-Maritimes.
6. *La Nation*, July 1, December 2, 23, 1933, November 10, 1934; *L'Alliance Démocratique*, May 10, 1935; Emile Roche quoted in Georges Suarez, *Pour un parti central* (Paris, 1936), 60–61.

In bitter reaction the Republican Federation warned its neighbor that, since many of the deputies of the Alliance owed their election to the "disinterested support" of the Federation, a rupture "would amount to electoral suicide." Although such claims were largely bravado, at least one member of the executive of the Alliance recognized that his party's electoral organization was inferior even to that of the Federation. Unlike the Parti Démocrate Populaire, the Alliance usually continued to cooperate electorally with the Federation, but its leaders repeatedly proclaimed their discomfort with the "nationalism and egotism of the Right."[7] The increasing isolation of the Federation accentuated its sense of insecurity in the face of the severe social and political shocks of the decade and pushed it toward the extreme Right during the latter part of the 1930s.

A conservative party, the Republican Federation wanted to preserve the existing social order. Although conceding the need for change and for social legislation, it sought to limit the scope of these changes and to cushion their impact. The party was deeply hostile not only to revolution, but also to any modification of the existing social system that would significantly alter the distribution of economic and social power. The severe economic crisis of the 1930s and the emergence of the Popular Front profoundly challenged that distribution and threatened to bring about a dramatic change in French society if not, as many conservatives feared, a Red revolution. The Federation was ill prepared to deal with such changes. Despite its claims to a modern social program, the Federation represented an old order, which could neither understand nor meet the economic and so-

7. *La Nation*, November 10, 1934; *L'Union Républicaine du Rhône*, August 23, 1933; *L'Alliance Démocratique*, March 6, 1936; Suarez, *Pour un parti central*, 86. The parliamentary strength of the Alliance declined somewhat in the 1930s but not because of the actions of the Federation. Prior to the 1936 election the Alliance reportedly had fifty-seven deputies (*Le Temps*, May 30, 1936); by 1938, it had forty-seven deputies (*La Liberté*, November 12, 1938). But these were at best guesses, since deputies of the Alliance were dispersed among a half-dozen parliamentary groups and were often indistinguishable from dissident Radicals. Even the party's leaders were vague on this point; see Emmanuel Beau de Loménie's interview with André de Fels in 1935, "Verrons nous se faire un regroupement national: L'Alliance Démocratique," *La Revue Hebdomadaire*, November 9, 1935, pp. 222–33.

cial crises of the 1930s. The Federation's response was that of a threatened and frightened elite, searching desperately for some way to restore social and political stability.

The Republican Federation unabashedly defended the social status quo, but it denied being insensitive to social problems. Spokesmen for the party professed a deep concern for the social and economic conditions of the lower orders of society, asserting that one could have a social conscience without embracing socialism. One member of the party affirmed that on some questions he was in accord with the Socialists and could "agree . . . and desire . . . that limits should be placed on the excessive abusive powers of money, that the weak should be able to band together against the strong and that workers should enjoy rights and guarantees which have not, up until now, been sufficiently recognized." In so far as socialism represented a general sympathy for the weak, an unspecified recognition of their rights, and a vague antagonism to extremes of wealth, it did not seem unacceptable. Unfortunately, socialism represented other things as well, such as "the weakening of the idea of the motherland, the disruption of the idea of property, the suppression of the notion of self-interest which is the principal motor behind human actions . . . the diminution of the authority without which no society can live, the horrible principle of the class struggle, the dictatorship of the proletariat which would have as consequence the predominance of number over value, of matter over spirit, and force over law."[8] Insofar as the Federation accepted the principle of social reform, it did so on the condition that the social system in no way be altered and that the traditional social values and social hierarchy remain untouched.

Agreed on the need to preserve the existing social order, members of the Federation sometimes differed about the merits of liberal capitalism. Although the Federation included a number of leading French capitalists, an anticapitalist strain nevertheless ran through the party's discussion of social problems.

8. J. Grzmbowski of the Republican Federation of the Aude in *La Liberté de l'Aude*, July 18, 1926.

Many rank-and-file members felt a deep resentment against the liberal economic order and those who controlled it. Perhaps the best expression of what was essentially a Legitimist hostility toward the *grande bourgeoisie* was the impassioned speech of a retired colonel at the Federation's 1932 congress, who argued that 1789 had represented the replacement of "an aristocracy of birth by an aristocracy of money and interest." Subsequently, France had been dominated by a "new plutocracy," which "filled its pockets at the expense of others." Members of the party often attacked materialism and greed, which they perceived to characterize liberal capitalism, and lamented the unstable society that it created. A *militant* from Hazebrouck indicted the irresponsible capitalist bourgeoisie, whose "lust for gain and repudiation of their social duties prevented them from instituting a stable social order." Economic liberalism, Xavier Vallat noted, had weakened the social fabric, then provoked a reaction in the form of revolutionary socialism. "The first," he wrote, "is the elder son, the second, the younger son of the same father—revolutionary individualism. The whole family is very sick."[9]

Usually, however, the attacks on liberal capitalism were little more than rhetorical flourishes designed to attract the sympathy of middle-class voters. Xavier Vallat's primitive anticapitalism nicely complemented his equally primitive anti-Semitism. He amused *militants* at a rally in Beauvais by calling for strict laws against usury and complaining of the excessive personal fortune of his fellow deputy, Louis Louis-Dreyfus. He proposed confiscating all personal incomes in excess of one million francs a year in return for titles of nobility.[10] Vallat's tongue was obviously in his cheek; he was far less concerned with redistributing wealth than with restricting the financial power of a Radical Jew.

9. *Compte rendu des congrès de la Fédération républicaine*, II, 155. (A stenographic record of *some* of the proceedings of the Federation's congresses is presently in the possession of Mme. Louis Marin.) It is appropriate that the Legitimist historian, Emmanuel Beau de Loménie should have been briefly attracted to the Federation in the 1930s because it seemed the best vehicle for his conservative anticapitalist sentiments. See Emmanuel Beau de Loménie, *Les Responsabilités des dynasties bourgeoises* (5 vols.; Paris, 1943–74), V, *De Hitler à Pétain* (1973), 246–49. *L'Entente Républicaine Démocratique de Hazebrouck*, April, 1934; *La Gazette d'Annonay*, December 22, 1934.

10. *L'Oise Nationale*, February, 1936.

Louis Marin periodically denounced "international finance" for being "egotistic, grasping and domineering" and complained that "the constant and dominating intervention of financial . . . and banking elements in politics" had made these latter "insolent and criminal."[11] These remarks, coming as they did from the man who sat in the Chamber between Messieurs de Wendel and de Warren, usually provoked howls of laughter from the benches of the Left. When Louis Marin denounced the collusion between finance and politics, he was referring only to international, American, or German finance; and the kind of grasping financier whom he distrusted was not François de Wendel but Owen D. Young. By focusing on foreign, international, and Jewish big business, the Federation could appeal to the latent antagonisms of its middle-class electoral clientele without disquieting the French business elite or the financial supporters of the party.

The Federation recognized that the comparative social stability of France was due to the relatively gradual nature of her industrial revolution and to the fact that she was not polarized between large-scale industry and organized labor. Reflecting on the social instability of her European neighbors, Louis Marin praised "fortunate France which has founded its secular social structure on small and medium landed property and on the regime of small commerce and the artisans."[12] The party's discussions of social questions carefully emphasized that the peasants, the artisans, the *petit commercants* were far more numerous than the industrial working class and formed the real basis of French society. These classes possessed property and had a stake in the continuation of a stable and ordered society.

The peasantry, relatively immune to the corrosive forces of modernism, seemed to be an especially stable element. Minimizing class differences within the rural population, spokesmen for the Federation, in common with most politicians in the Third Republic, glorified the peasant producers. The party noted uneasily the rural exodus of the interwar years and deplored the

11. *Journal Officiel*, March 27, 1931, p. 1321, June 26, 1931, p. 3389.
12. *La Nation*, September 5, 1936.

resulting depopulation of the French countryside. The Federation also realized that the new social and political currents of the period threatened to disrupt the tranquility of the rural countryside. Even rural electrification and its social consequences caused some anxiety. Pierre de Monicault, deputy from the Ain and a large-scale agricultural producer, feared that the advent of electric lighting would likely encourage rural workers to stay up late carousing. The result would be less work the next day and the gradual decline of the traditional industriousness of the rural population.[13]

The Federation had an obvious fondness for the artisans, that class of workers who could serve as a link between the industrial proletariat and the bourgeoisie. By permitting the gradual rise of one class toward the condition of the other, this intermediary stratum would contribute to class harmony and help discredit the Socialist notion of an irreducible antagonism between the proletariat and their employers. To the Federation, the artisans demonstrated the possibility of "the continuous ascension of an elite" from among the working class "towards those goods that are considered the privileges of the bourgeoisie: property, inheritance, higher intellectual culture." Furthermore, the traditional social harmony that was impossible in the sterile and impersonal factory could be achieved in the smaller, more intimate atmosphere of the workshop. Some members viewed the gradual passing of the artisan and his milieu with a sadness that reflected aesthetic sensibilities, concern for social stability, and occasionally economic self-interest. Victor Perret, a manufacturer of handmade fancy silk products, complained: "The factory has killed the artisanal industry, and the taste for better things, that only . . . artisans know how to make, has disappeared." He urged the vigorous defense of the artisan class, which would thereby "contribute to the social reconstruction of the family and to social peace."[14]

13. *Ibid.*, October 25, 1925.
14. Louis Duval-Arnould, *La Nation*, November 10, 1925; *L'Union Républicaine du Rhône*, February 5, 1933.

The leaders of the Republican Federation also praised and defended the small businessmen as the backbone of France. During the interwar years French small businessmen worried increasingly about the growth of cooperatives and large department stores like the Prisunic and the Uniprix. At the 1928 congress, Pierre de Monicault, presenting the party's report on social policy, registered the plight of the *"petit commercant* who is being crushed between the department store and the cooperatives." Etienne Peille, president of the local committee in Toulouse, insisted that "every branch of commerce touched by the Prix Unique is a branch condemned to death."[15] By ruthless competition, the new department stores forced their smaller competitors out of business, bought up the remaining stock, and began to charge monopoly prices. Some two million small businessmen were thus threatened. Yet no one in the Federation analyzed this problem very deeply. De Monicault merely summarized the problem as "very complex" and Peille, taking advantage of the fact that the new stores were often backed by German capital, simply denounced them as "a dangerous emanation of International Capitalism." As with finance capitalism, commercial capitalism could only be condemned if it were foreign.

It was with the working class that the Republican Federation felt least at ease. Officially, the Federation professed allegiance to the social teachings of Pope Leo XIII and the Catholic corporatist doctrines of Albert de Mun, René de la Tour du Pin, and Hyacinthe de Gailhard-Bancel. Although elaborating no specific model for French society, the party extracted from the corporatist theorists certain fundamental ideas. The most important was that industrial production should take place, not in an atmosphere of class antagonism and social irresponsibility, but in one of social harmony where class peace and cooperation would replace class struggle. Employers would eschew outdated liberal economic doctrines and assume their moral and social

15. *La Nation*, December 22, 1928; *Le Sud-Est républicain de Toulouse*, March 12, 1934.

responsibilities toward their employees. These latter would abandon all ideas of class hatred and prepare for loyal collaboration with their employers. The debilitating struggle between labor and capital would come to an end, and the various productive elements within a profession would collectively determine wages, prices, and working conditions. Instead of fighting one another, Frenchmen of different classes would cooperate harmoniously to the advantage of all.

Yet there were to be strictly defined limits to the fraternal cooperation between capital and labor. The collaboration of the two productive forces did not mean that the rights and prerogatives of the employer could be infringed upon, nor was the working class to take advantage of this collaboration to make a nuisance of itself. One of the leading exponents of "social capitalism" was Emile Romanet, a director of the metallurgical firm Maison Joya and the vice-president of the Republican Federation of the Isère. He was one of the first major French employers to establish a profit-sharing system within his firm. He also organized a system of family allocations for employees with large families.[16] In 1932 he presented a report revealing what he meant by class collaboration. In describing the ideal conditions for contact between employer and employee, he observed:

> It is desirable that the meetings which unite the management with the staff or their representatives take place with the goals clearly defined, by arranging well in advance the questions to be discussed and by avoiding anything that could embarrass or weaken the authority of the management or the administration of the enterprise. It is important that the employees not remain unaware of the problems and responsibilities of the management. One must neutralize the errors and the lies as they arise so that the workers not follow the well-paid leaders of occult or foreign organizations.
>
> One must show the workers that far from being enemies, capital and manual labor have common interests and that the prosperity of the enterprise benefits everyone.[17]

16. Pierre Barral. *Le Département de l'Isère sous la IIIe République, 1870–1940* (Paris, 1962), 324.
17. *L'Union Républicaine du Rhône*, August 21, 1932.

Beneath the language of professional collaboration there lay the very real desire to limit the power of working-class organizations. The Federation did not condemn labor unions because they artificially interfered with the supply of labor and violated immutable economic laws. Rather it denounced them for being under the control of occult and foreign influences, false shepherds who led the French working class astray and who were intent, not to improve the conditions of the working class, but to lay the groundwork for revolution and the destruction of the social fabric of the nation.

The Republican Federation differed from other parties, its spokesmen argued, not because of the class interests it defended, but because its social doctrine was founded on a "spiritual, moral and . . . religious ideal" rather than on "the satisfaction of appetites and desires which are limited to terrestrial life." It was not enough to cater to the material wants of the working classes; one also had to minister to their spiritual needs. Louis Duval-Arnould, a Parisian deputy, defended the Federation from the charge of being "a bourgeois party." Whereas the Left had "been able to gain the votes of the working classes with purely material and demagogic promises," the Federation had attempted to "win their hearts by giving them an idea."[18] The Federation habitually reminded the working classes that man did not live by bread alone and that spiritual harmony was a necessary condition for social harmony.

The religiosity with which the social thought of the Federation was larded stemmed in part from the official Catholicism of the party and in part from baser considerations. A report on social policy given at the 1937 congress of the Federation of the Rhône revealed what the party considered to be the social function of religion. The report concluded: "Finally, and most important, we must never forget the essential primacy of the spiritual over the economic and the material. Only the profound idea of that superiority can render acceptable the inevitable in-

18. Xavier Vallat, *La Nation*, September 29, 1932; *L'Entente républicaine démocratique de Hazebrouck*, March, 1934.

equality of condition without which a society can neither exist nor be conceived of. Man must accept the fact that his very nature makes it impossible to raise everybody to the same level."[19] In short, the Federation regarded the poor as a permanent feature of French society and sought to persuade the working classes to accept that fact. Given these attitudes, the Federation would be severely shaken when, in the middle 1930s, the working class began to make extensive demands on French society.

The Republican Federation did not object in principle to social legislation. Indeed, it frequently insisted that all the major and lasting pieces of social legislation in the Third Republic had been the work of *modérés*. But it opposed the excessive statism that it claimed so often accompanied proposals for social legislation—particularly when those proposals emanated from the Left. State intrusion into that sphere of activities that properly concerned only the individual undermined existing social bonds and tended to leave the individual at the mercy of the omnipotent state. Furthermore, the state rarely administered social legislation as effectively or as efficiently as could private and regional organizations. The state, according to the Federation, did little more than increase the cost of any given piece of social legislation through red tape, unnecessary paperwork, and vastly increased numbers of parasitical civil servants.[20]

The Federation approached uneasily even very moderate and long overdue pieces of social legislation, particularly if it feared that such reforms would weaken the influence of traditional social and local elites. The Social Insurance Act, passed in 1928 and amended in 1930, marked the most important piece of social legislation between the end of the Cartel des Gauches and the coming of the Popular Front. The Republican Federation never openly challenged the principle of the Social Insurance Act, and almost all of its deputies voted for both the 1928 law and its 1930 modification. Nevertheless, the party distrusted the

19. *L'Union Républicaine du Rhône*, August 24, 1937.
20. Gustave Gautherot, *La Nation*, February 4, 1939.

specific form of the act. Instead of being administered by the
state, the Federation argued, the new law should have been implemented by "the guild unions, professional groups, credit
unions and diverse corporative and mutualist associations." In
the Chamber, Gustave Guerin cited de Mun, de la Tour du Pin,
and Gailhard-Bancel to prove that mutual aid societies could
administer the law more cheaply, more effectively, and without
unduly worrying either employers or employees. He also objected to the compulsory contributions provided for in the act
and contrasted "forced savings" with "free savings . . . willingly
and joyously accepted." He concluded that "obligation is not
part of the French character." Charles de Lasteyrie, speaking on
behalf of the Federation, objected that the law would burden
France with civil servants, would strike at the family by putting
a premium on bachelorhood, and would handicap industry by
imposing premiums it could not afford.[21] While recognizing that
France was behind other nations in its social legislation, he
nonetheless argued that changes be introduced slowly and by
easy stages.

The Federation's objections to the statist aspects of the Social
Insurance Act may have reflected the desire "to maintain a logical demarcation between the role of the citizen and that of the
state." But it also reflected the wish to limit the scope and effectiveness of a measure the party dared not oppose. Throughout
the 1930s the Federation continued to call for modification of
the Social Insurance Act, asserting that it should be administered privately. A minority in the party, led by Charles de Lasteyrie, director of a major insurance company, wanted to go further and render the plan optional both for employees and for
employers. Even at the end of the decade the party still insisted
that private control of social insurance would "offer its members
a better management and firmer guarantees" and would "restore

21. Edouard de Warren, "La République des Modérés," *La Revue de Paris*, February 15, 1929, p. 247; *Journal Officiel*, February 7, 1930, pp. 535–38, 551–54. Under
the proposed legislation employers were obliged to make a heavier contribution for
married men than for bachelors.

the notion of foresight and of savings, a notion that would end the habit of always relying on the providential state."[22]

The economic crisis came later to France than to the rest of Europe, and its impact was less severe. Nonetheless, by 1935 there were over 800,000 unemployed, where there had been virtually none five years earlier. The depressed economic conditions began to squeeze important segments of the working class—the peasantry, salaried workers, and small businessmen. The mounting unemployment and the declining standard of living of many Frenchmen heightened social tensions and gave an impetus to the Left. Few politicians in France understood the economic crisis, but the Socialists and Communists could blame it on the capitalist system and offer radical, if usually vague, alternatives. The modérés, with few exceptions, could offer only conventional and unappealing solutions to the depression. In common with most conservatives the Republican Federation attributed the depression to the disorder in public finances and to the excessive interference of the state in the economy. Devaluation, the remedy so forcefully championed by the conservative Paul Reynaud, found no support in a party that distrusted any tinkering with the franc. It preferred the time-worn recourse to deflation. By depriving deputies of the right to initiate money bills, reducing the number of civil servants and cutting their salaries, and abandoning costly state monopolies, the government could drastically reduce its budgetary expenditures. Having reduced spending, the government could then alleviate the tax burden, which crushed the average Frenchman and discouraged private initiative. The Federation advocated, for example, abolishing succession duties on inheritances of up to 500,000 francs in order to preserve the sanctity of the family and to encourage the traditional French virtues of saving and entrepreneurship. The party also sought an end to the inquisitorial aspects of the tax system, "the constant interference by treasury agents in our personal affairs." Removing the stifling effects of

22. De Warren, "La République des Modérés," 247; La Nation, February 4, 1939.

government fiscality would, the Federation hoped, revive the national economy.

The Federation did not, however, consistently demand the withdrawal of the state from the economy. Joseph Denais, for example, argued that "private initiative alone can restore the country to economic activity," but he also believed that the government ought to encourage the initiatives of private industry. He thought that the housing problem could be solved and a good deal of unemployment alleviated if the government assisted those firms that specialized in low-cost housing. Denais, who was a director of a Société de Logement Bon Marché, concluded that private enterprise, with the aid and encouragement of the government, could solve both the economic and the social problems of the depression. Similarly, the Federation asserted that the government could greatly accelerate economic recovery by raising both industrial and agricultural tariffs and by encouraging the exploitation of colonial wealth.

Although the Federation conceded that unemployment and the resulting impoverishment of the working classes were serious problems, virtually its only solution was to deport foreign workers and to initiate stricter controls against the professional unemployed. Even when attempting to express their concern for the laboring masses, spokesmen for the Federation sounded as if they could not quite believe that conditions were as bad as people claimed. On the eve of the Popular Front, the Republican Federation offered little in the way of a solution except its faith in financial orthodoxy, its trust in private enterprise, and its belief that many social evils could be attributed to foreigners and to the indolent poor.

In such circumstances, the Popular Front seemed to be the cardinal menace to French society. In a period of economic depression, acute social crisis, and mounting international tension, an electoral alliance of the parties of the Left, including the Communists, inevitably frightened the representatives of the party of order. At a minimum the Popular Front threatened to repeat what, from the perspective of the Federation, had been the disastrous experience of the 1924–1926 Cartel des Gauches. More seriously, the presence of the Communists in the Popular Front convinced many in the Federation that the new alliance was a prelude to a revolutionary seizure of power. The Republican Federation could not conceive of the Popular Front as an alliance for limited ends in which the Radicals would act as an effective brake on the ambitions of the extreme Left. Nor did it recognize that the Communists were willing to forego temporarily the possibility of revolution in order to resist the growing menace of fascism. The Federation interpreted the Popular Front as an unholy and unnatural alliance. It frequently warned the Radicals that they had no place in an alliance with the Communists, whose change of tactics was a mere subterfuge. Louis Marin argued: "All the groups of the Left are . . . despite their diverse labels . . . the forward agents and conquering troops of the Communists." "Once having taken power by legal means," announced Gustave Gautherot, senator from the Loire-Inférieure and member of the executive committee, "the Communist party will sacrifice its electoral allies and establish, for its exclusive benefit, a dictatorship of the proletariat." The violent disorders provoked by the victory of the Spanish Popular Front served as an object lesson for those who retained illusions about the fate of France in the event of a victory of the left-wing coalition. The party also alluded to the Russian Revolution and particularly to the role they felt the liberals had played in bringing the Bolsheviks to power. Thus, Victor Perret labeled the Radical leader, Edouard Daladier, "the French Kerensky." The Federation rarely analyzed the exact way in which the Communists would exploit their allies to promote revolution, but it assumed that a government of the Left would be unable or unwilling to preserve order at home and inclined to push France into a foreign war. Both circumstances would play into the hands of the Communists. Gustave Gautherot summed up the anxieties of the Federation when he predicted: "With the coming of the Popular Front there will be an era of social revolution, civil war and international war."

The Federation's dismal predictions cannot always be taken at their face value. It was electorally expedient to predict war and revolution, and the Federation was not above capitalizing on the Red menace to prevent a moderately reformist government from coming to power. The rhetoric of the 1936 campaign, much of which resembled that of earlier campaigns against the Cartel, revealed that the party was often as frightened of a Left-liberal coalition as of a Communist coup. As often as its speakers predicted a Spanish-style bloodbath, they also foresaw a return to the financial incompetence of the 1924–1926 experience or to the corrupt, unstable governments of the period from 1932 to 1934. Even Gustave Gautherot, the Federation's most accomplished Red-baiter, alternated his ravings about the "dictatorship of the proletariat" and the "red dictatorship" with prognostications about the imminent "sterile" and "bureaucratic" statism and "the governmental impotence and ministerial cascades analogous to those of 1932–1934."[23]

Yet the extreme fears expressed by the Federation cannot simply be discounted as insincere fabrications. To a party as wedded to the traditional social order and as suspicious of change as the Federation, even the moderate reforms of the Popular Front may have seemed revolutionary. The bewildering experiences of the 1930s may well have induced a kind of social myopia which made massive but relatively peaceful sit-in strikes resemble a revolutionary seizure of power. Furthermore, the Federation's anxieties about revolution were sufficiently genuine to cause radical modifications in its orientation on foreign policy and to subtly alter its attitude toward the extraparliamentary Right.

The electoral victory of the Popular Front appeared to bear out the worst fears of the party of order. Although the overall shift in votes from the Right to the Left was slight, the Popular Front gained a clear majority in parliament. Within the left-wing coalition, the Socialists and especially the Communists

23. *La Nation*, February 8, April 4, 18, 25, May 2, 23, September 19, 1936.

gained at the expense of the Radicals. The Communists were the true winners, nearly doubling their popular vote and gaining seventy seats, which made them for the first time a major force in the French parliament. The advances of the Communists tended to confirm conservative suspicions that the Popular Front had served as a cover for Communist subversion with the other parties playing, wittingly or unwittingly, the role of dupes. Although the more than one hundred Radical deputies constituted an obvious counterbalance to the revolutionaries, conservatives initially concentrated on the prospect of seventy Communist deputies and the fact that the Socialists, now the largest single party in parliament, would for the first time form the government.

Anxieties prompted by the electoral victory were greatly magnified by events outside the Chamber. In late May and early June, 1936, a wave of sit-in strikes swept France; and more than one million factory workers, spurred on by the election results, occupied their places of work and demanded immediate wage increases and social reforms. The sit-in strikes were spontaneous; the leaders of the Popular Front and the trade union officials merely followed, sometimes reluctantly. Contemporary observers often interpreted the factory occupations of June, 1936, as manifestations of the revolutionary spontaneity of the working class, a popular upsurge intent on fundamental transformation of French society. Subsequently, scholars have questioned this assessment, pointing to the apparent absence of any clear revolutionary consciousness among the striking workers.[24] Yet, even if the rank and file of the working class, as well as their leaders, sought essentially limited gains and not a revolution, the sit-in strikes were still in some senses revolutionary. The actions of the working class represented a massive defiance of bourgeois society, an important if temporary act of liberation from the social, economic, and moral hegemony of their social

24. See for example Antoine Prost, "Les grèves de juin 1936, Essai d'interprétation," in René Rémond, et al. (eds.), Léon Blum, Chef du gouvernement, 1936–1937, Actes du colloque (Paris, 1967), 69–87.

superiors. The workers could snub their employers with impunity, ignore their foreman, exercise control over what was formally the property of the *patron*, and not incidentally escape from the drudgery of industrial labor. In retrospect these do not appear to be revolutionary actions, but for a while, both workers and their social antagonists believed that the factory occupations portended dramatic, indeed revolutionary, changes in French society. The strikes of June, 1936, may well have been (as Antoine Prost suggests) largely symbolic gestures, escapist Saturnalia. But for critical segments of the bourgeoisie these gestures constituted an overt defiance of law, order, and the right of private property. Although the events of June did not lead to revolution and although most workers probably did not expect them to, the possessing classes were no less frightened.

The experience of the first months of the Popular Front had other frightening ramifications for conservatives. As a result of the social and political excitement, previously quiescent elements in French society were politicized for the first time. The Socialist party doubled its membership in 1936; the Communists more than tripled theirs. The Socialist- and Communist-dominated labor union, the Confédération Générale du Travail, grew from less than 800,000 members at the beginning of 1936 to more than 4 million by the end of the year—a fivefold increase. Consequently, in spite of the moderate demeanor of the Popular Front government and its cautious policies, French conservatives, sensing a mass political mobilization, felt political and social power slipping from their hands.

As he watched law and order being replaced by force and brutality, Louis Marin's indignation knew no bounds. To the Parisian newspapers, which reported that the strikers had done little damage, Marin retorted that "there was, on the contrary, an unheard of moral damage; brutal force reigns over justice and law." The fledgling Socialist government was understandably reluctant to expel the strikers and chose to negotiate with those whom conservatives deemed to be simply lawbreakers. Louis Marin, who now wondered if he were still living in "a legal regime," fulminated during the first session of parliament against the "state of insurrection" prevailing in France. The legions of the Confédération Générale du Travail had trampled on the principle of private property, as well as on the liberties of "the factory managers, the engineers, the supervisors and the workers."[25] This seemingly unchecked sway of the Confédération persuaded some members of the Federation that France was facing a revolution. Fifteen years later, François Martin reflected on the events he experienced as the newly elected deputy from the Aveyron. Martin argued that a revolutionary situation exists whenever "legitimate institutions are overrun by a power, exercised illegally, which succeeds in seizing control of national sovereignty." From his perspective "in 1936 and 1937 the authority of the state was held in check by the formidable power of labor unions overflowing their true functions. In the end the law could do no more than sanction the *de facto* creations of the labor unions. And that is a situation which we must recognize as revolution."[26]

During June and July, spokesmen for the Federation strenuously complained about the revolutionary disorders that abounded in the country. André Daher, the newly elected deputy from Marseilles, recounted to the great amusement of the Left his difficulties in finding food and lodging in strike-ridden France. François de Saint-Just, deputy from the heavily struck region of the Nord, told of unemployed urban agitators, who bicycled around the peaceful countryside stirring up the otherwise contented rural laborers and in some cases forcing them to strike. A party that feared the consequences of rural electrification could only be aghast at the prospect of agricultural laborers organizing and becoming radicalized.[27]

As disquieting as the actions of urban and rural strikers was the passivity of the police. The Federation repeatedly protested that the police, far from protecting private property, appeared

25. *La Nation*, June 6, 1936; *Journal Officiel*, June 6, 1936, p. 1332.

26. Cited in the Hoover Institution, *France During the German Occupation* (3 vols.; Stanford, 1957), I, 414–15.

27. *Journal Officiel*, June 11, 1936, pp. 1378–79, July 3, 1936, pp. 1726–27.

to condone the multiple acts of illegality that occurred under their noses. Charles des Isnards, deputy from Paris, described an attack by the police on an automobile on the Champs-Elysees, which had the temerity to display the tricolor flag. Moments later these same police allegedly saluted a car flying the red flag.[28] Such charges were absurd, but they indicate how disturbing it could be for those who had always assumed that the repressive mechanism of the state was on their side to find the police far less responsive to their needs. The evident un-willingness of the government to repress the unlawful actions of the workers suggested to them that France could easily fall vic-tim to a well-directed revolutionary plot.

The wave of strikes in the summer of 1936 and the rapid growth of the hitherto weak labor movement appeared to the Federation to be the work of a noisy minority who took orders from Moscow and cowed a docile majority into following it. Pierre Vallette-Viallard, deputy from the Ardèche and a build-ing contractor who had recently experienced a strike, com-plained that the Communist-infiltrated Confédération Générale du Travail sought not social justice but a dictatorial monopoly over labor. The Confédération had struck his plant, he claimed, primarily to obtain the dismissal of a fellow worker, who be-longed to the moderate Confédération française des travailleurs chrétiens. Edouard Soulier, who admitted that the fate of the employers concerned him as much as that of the workers, re-counted the story of a good employer, who had been forced out of business by the foolish demands of his workers. Having been misled by outside agitators, these workers now had nothing to show for their militancy but the prospect of unemployment. The parable of the honest employer plagued by the extreme and un-reasonable demands of his misguided workers was a favorite theme of the Federation. So was the warning that a government too weak or too partisan to stop such patent illegality could hard-ly protect France from revolution. The issue, as Edouard Soulier saw it, was: "Social justice, yes! Dictatorship of the proletariat,

28. *Ibid.*, June 30, 1936, p. 1642.

no!" Illegal strikes led by the Communist-dominated Confédération could never result in the former and could very possibly lead to the latter.[29]

Even if the nation escaped a revolution, the Federation insisted that the policies of the Popular Front would shortly ruin France. The Federation's root and branch opposition to the program of the Popular Front distinguished it from the Center parties. Although Jean Montigny, speaking for a group of deputies of the Alliance Démocratique, expressed grave reservations about the program of the new government, he declared, "You will never find a spirit of systematic hostility on these benches." Similarly, Pierre Trémintin, representing the Parti Démocrate Populaire, promised, "Our votes will often be mixed with yours." By contrast, Marin assured Blum that he did not share the conciliatory attitude of the Center and would not allow the Socialist experiment to go unchallenged. "We are determined," he declared, "to oppose that experience as much as possible. We will not let it pass." In his estimation, there was little point in giving the Socialists a chance, for they had already demonstrated their incapacity. "Every time, in whatever country, the Socialist party has been in power for any length of time, it has led . . . to ruin and disaster." France could expect no better luck.[30]

Whereas *La Nation* poured forth savage diatribes directed to the Left, both the Alliance and the Parti Démocrate Populaire sought to moderate their opposition to the "Blum experience." The PDP, although basically sceptical about the social policy of the Popular Front, nevertheless expressed the hope that it would end the social and economic crisis. Anticipating an eventual disillusionment with the Popular Front among the Radicals and the reformist socialist splinter groups, the PDP talked hopefully throughout 1937 of a possible union *à la Van Zeeland*, a reference to the coalition of Christian socialists and reformist socialists in Belgium. To the intense exasperation of the Federation, the Alliance also concentrated on the possibility of a government of republican concentration, asserting that its differ-

29. *Ibid.*, August 6, 1936, p. 2473; *La Nation*, June 20, 1936.
30. *Journal Officiel*, June 6, 1936, pp. 1330, 1344, July 24, 1936, p. 2125.

ences with the Radicals were mostly "sentimental," and "only the thickness of an onion skin" now separated the two parties. Like the PDP, the Alliance ignored the Republican Federation, except to identify it with "a reactionary conservatism that is incompatible with the development of modern society." Louis Marin's repeated attempts to form a parliamentary intergroup among the parties of the opposition were rebuffed by both the PDP and the Alliance.[31]

Although the opposition parties differed in their assessment of the Popular Front, in parliament their votes usually coincided. In spite of its verbal ferocity, the Federation did not oppose all the social legislation of the Popular Front government. As early as 1931 the Federation had voted for a measure that granted workers a one-week paid vacation. After passing in the Chamber, the law died in the Senate. In 1936 neither the Republican Federation nor anyone else voted against the proposal of a two-week paid vacation. The Federation also accepted, albeit reluctantly, the principle of collective bargaining. Although its spokesmen regretted that the Chamber was voting under duress and quibbled that the leftist Confédération Générale du Travail had been treated as the sole representative of the working class, only two deputies of the party (Gustave Guerin and Félix Grat) voted against the measure, twenty-three members abstained, and the rest voted in favor.

On two major pieces of legislation, the forty-hour week and the Wheat Board, the Federation and most of the other opposition deputies stood firm.[32] Xavier Vallat, Henri Becquart, and Pierre Vallette-Viallard claimed that they saw no objection to the forty-hour week as a social measure, but they rejected the government's contention that the shortened workweek would absorb unemployment and stimulate the economy. The forty-

31. Le Petit Démocrate, July 14, 1936, August 8, 22, 1937; L'Alliance Démocratique, June 26, 1936, April 23, November 5, 1937; Léon Barety to Marin, July 15, 1937, François-Xavier de Reille-Soult to Marin, July 7, 1937, in Marin Papers, carton 85. Reille-Soult, speaking for the PDP, asserted that it was not in the interests of the nation "to oppose one bloc against another"; his party preferred "to prepare rapprochements between various elements which today are antagonistic to one another."

32. Journal Officiel, June 3, 1936, pp. 1722–30, June 12, 1936, pp. 1423–41.

hour week, on the contrary, would raise production costs to a prohibitive level and drive France from the international market. It would destroy the small and medium firms, increasing rather than decreasing the number of unemployed. Henri Becquart, speaking on behalf of the textile industry of the Nord, argued that such legislation would give France the shortest workweek in Europe and make it impossible for the textile industry to compete in foreign markets. Vallat feared that the law would contribute to the depopulation of the countryside as the rural population, attracted by the shorter hours of the urban workers, abandoned their fields. Alfred Oberkirch, deputy from the Haut-Rhin, insisted that he favored the forty-hour week in principle but would vote against it because its application in the midst of a depression would be economically disastrous. When the vote was taken, the entire Republican Federation and one hundred other opposition deputies voted against the law.

The establishment of the Wheat Board, the principal agricultural legislation of the Popular Front, provoked similar opposition. From the early 1930s French agriculture had been plagued by crop surpluses and sharply declining commodity prices. Since there was no agency for market regulation, prices fluctuated widely, and speculation became rife. This tendency worked to the advantage of large producers, who could afford to wait for higher prices before selling; small producers, on the other hand, were forced to sell as soon as their crops were in, when prices were usually low. Georges Monnet, the new minister of agriculture, introduced a Wheat Board to raise agricultural prices and end the current crisis. The Wheat Board, a favorite socialist proposal, was empowered to buy, store, price, and market wheat. A central council, consisting of representatives of producers, of consumers, and of the government administered the board. Although the government had only minority representation on the council, decisions were to be unanimous, thus giving the government an effective veto over the producers. The actual marketing of the wheat was to be done by cooperatives, and the cost of administering the board would be met by a progressive tax to be levied on large producers (those growing more than a hundred *quintaux* of wheat a year).

The Republican Federation favored some kind of regulatory mechanism but insisted that its organization be exclusively professional, by which it meant that there be no government interference. According to Félix Grat, deputy from the Mayenne, government domination of the Wheat Board represented "the socialization of the means of production and exchange." Furthermore, by giving cooperatives a monopoly over marketing, the new bill would destroy all grain merchants, large and small. While pretending to strike at monopolists and speculators, the government would in fact hit thousands of small and extremely poor wheat dealers. The Wheat Board, like all state ventures into the economic and social life of the country, would be replete with *paperasserie*, drawing heavily on the national budget to pay for multitudes of bureaucrats. Financing the board by a tax on larger producers would only encourage fraud, for no one would willingly admit to producing more than a hundred *quintaux*. The inevitable probings by the state into the private affairs of the nation's wheat farmers would be ill received in a country where "one laughs when one sees Guignol whack the policeman." In short, the project was expensive, ineffective, and inquisitorial.

André Parmentier, Alexandre Duval, François de Saint-Just, Henri de Saint-Pern, Gustave Guerin, and Camille Blaisot all seconded Grat's attack. Parmentier, deputy from the Pas-de-Calais, an area dominated by large producers, made a strong plea for professional organization, which would in effect allow the producers to control the central council of the Wheat Board. The graduated tax on large-scale production struck him as particularly unjust; the wealth of the large producers was "the fruit of the labors of all the generations which have preceded them as well as of their personal labor," and no one, he concluded should be penalized for his labor. Ultimately, the entire French Right joined the Republican Federation to vote against the board.

On some issues, however, virtually the only opposition to the government came from the Republican Federation. Only the deputies of the Federation and a few former party members rejected Jean Zay's proposal to extend the school-leaving age to fourteen. The Federation distrusted any measure that increased the influence of the leftist corporation of teachers and despised the snide critic of the French flag who had become the minister of education.[33] Louis Marin argued that such an extension would also deprive the rural population of critically needed labor and, until adequate vocational programs were introduced, would only turn rural youth away from careers in farming and accentuate the already disturbing rural depopulation.[34]

Of the seventy-seven deputies who opposed the nationalization of the Bank of France, fifty-five sat in the ranks of the Republican Federation. The party rejected nationalization because it meant replacing "competent, honorable and independent men by a certain number of civil servants and politicians who are perhaps also honorable but are certainly less independent." François de Wendel, a regent of the bank who stood to lose his job if it were nationalized, assured the Senate that turning the bank over to politically manipulatable civil servants would deprive the bank of its "independence" and would ruin the franc and French credit.[35] The Popular Front also proposed to nationalize the war industries, the politically sensitive symbol of the "Gun Merchants," who were widely suspected of being the source of modern war. Only eighty-five deputies, including the entire Republican Federation, opposed this largely symbolic gesture. While admitting a preference for free enterprise, the Federation based its objection to nationalization on the pragmatic grounds that government-owned firms would be less efficient in wartime than private firms working under government stat-

33. In his early political career, Zay had bitterly decried the fact that 1,500,000 Frenchmen had died in the First World War for nothing more than the meaningless rag that was the French flag. His speech was often reproduced by the French Right in the 1930s.

34. *Journal Officiel*, July 2, 1936, p. 1677.

35. Joseph Denais, *La Nation*, May 2, 1936; *Journal Officiel, Sénat*, July 23, 1936, p. 808.

utes. Although some form of control over war industries was necessary, the Federation felt nationalization to be excessive and potentially harmful.[36] In rejecting these measures, the Federation reaffirmed its unbending opposition to the Popular Front. The irreducible bloc of opponents of the Popular Front centered around the Republican Federation.

Attacks by the Republican Federation against the government of the Popular Front often resembled those of the overtly anti-parliamentary Right. *La Nation* was far more restrained than newspapers like *Je Suis Partout*, *Candide*, or *Gringoire*; but individual deputies engaged in venomous personal attacks against leaders of the Popular Front, verbal assaults that were not free of the taint of anti-Semitism. The Federation was not officially anti-Semitic and announced on several occasions that it was open to Jews. The Marin Papers for the late 1930s even contain a few letters protesting his failure to speak out against the Jewish menace. There was, nonetheless, an undercurrent of anti-Semitism and racist sentiment in the party which often appeared in the guise of opposition to further immigration from eastern Europe. Jean Duquaire, president of a cantonal committee in the Rhône, for example, while disclaiming any "Hitlerian racism," complained that "the sky is already invaded by a growing crowd of dangerous insects from abroad." "The elected race," he grumbled, "wants France to be the Christ of nations." When Léon Blum presented his government in June, 1936, the Federation's most notorious anti-Semite, Xavier Vallat, pointedly remarked that for the first time in history his great Gallo-Roman nation would be governed by a Jew. The remark caused a major uproar in the Chamber and scandalized many observers. While Louis Marin preferred to observe a discreet silence, Victor Perret firmly defended Vallat's "courageous" actions and asserted that the controversial deputy had simply spoken what most Frenchmen felt in their hearts. At the same time, however, he admitted that Blum was not typical of all Jews and that many

36. *Journal Officiel*, July 17, 1932, p. 2000, July 16, 1936, p. 1942.

French Jews shared the conservative sentiments of the Republican Federation.[37] The Federation's anti-Semitism was moderate, "genteel," and (like most French anti-Semitism) neither racial nor political. Men like Perret, or even Vallat, subordinated anti-Semitism to their political concerns. They despised *"Je Vous Haïs"* Blum, the slave of Moscow, much more than Blum the Jew.[38] But their hatred of the Popular Front was such that members of the party were willing to use or to defend the use of racial slurs as a weapon against the government.

Henri Becquart followed Vallat's attack on Blum with an even more vicious assault on the minister of the interior, Roger Salengro. His refusal to preserve order made Salengro a constant target of abuse from the Right. Henri Becquart, a recently elected deputy from the Nord, sought parliamentary prominence by discrediting the Socialist minister. In November, 1936, resurrecting an old scandal concerning Salengro's war record, he accused him of having deserted to the Germans in 1915 and of having betrayed his comrades in the trenches. Salengro had, in fact, been captured by the Germans while on a burial detail but, in the face of his unexplained absence, had been sentenced to death in absentia by a military tribunal. The sentence had been annulled when Salengro escaped from the Germans and returned to the French front. Becquart, however, told the Chamber that inexplicable discrepancies existed in Salengro's subsequent story and that no record remained of his having justified his capture before a court-martial. Becquart's charges had often been made over the years, initially by Salengro's Communist opponents in Lille, more recently by the extreme right-wing newspaper *Gringoire*. Becquart did not

37. The Marin Papers (carton 74) contain a letter from a Jewish immigrant requesting membership in the party as late as 1938. No less a figure than Xavier Vallat admitted that there were Jews in the Federation (*L'Oise Nationale*, February, 1936). *Le Réveil du Beaujolais*, August 10, 1938; *L'Union Républicaine du Rhône*, June 14, 1936.

38. Utterly frustrated by the constant badgering from the benches of the Right, Blum had once yelled out his hatred for his adversaries. The name *Je Vous Haïs* stuck. In fact, even an inveterate anti-Semite like Xavier Vallat was not preoccupied by the Jewish problem. Vallat never hid his dislike and distrust of Jews, but his weekly column in the *Gazette d'Annonay* made few anti-Semitic references and was almost never devoted exclusively to anti-Semitic propaganda.

have a very substantial case against Salengro, but by making his charges in the Chamber he helped expand it into a major political scandal. The resultant campaign of vilification drove the harried Salengro to commit suicide. Although some members of the Federation (Louis Marin in particular) were embarrassed by his sordid little enterprise, Becquart's hate campaign received the support of the quasi totality of the party's deputies. They were among the hard core of sixty-three deputies who condoned Becquart's attack on what proved to be an innocent man. The "Sixty-three" became a symbol of an irreducible core of unrepentant reactionaries.[39]

When Léon Blum's Popular Front government was forced first to "pause," and then to resign in favor of a more moderate one under the Radical Camille Chautemps, the Federation dropped some of its hysterical rhetoric. But concern for the security of the existing order persisted, as did anxiety about the Communists and the working class. In February, 1937, Gustave Gautherot conceded in the Senate that in many areas "French good sense" had triumphed over revolutionary disorder, but he assured his listeners that he did not share "the present euphoria" about the future of France. As long as the Communists remained a powerful force, enjoying the protection of the government, France could not discount the possibility of revolution.[40] Louis Marin now argued that the failure of the Popular Front had been predictable, since relations between the composite parties had been strained to the breaking point. But he insisted that there was "still plenty of gold coming from Moscow . . . and vast associations that are more or less Bolshevik" to threaten the domestic peace of France. Despite repeated checks, the Communists and their allies still sought to drive the nation to ruin. Marin refused to enter Léon Blum's proposed national coalition with the Communists in March, 1938, on the grounds

39. *Journal Officiel*, November 13, 1936, pp. 2997–3004; *Vendémiaire*, November 18, 1936; *Aux Ecoutes*, November 21, 1936; *Le Populaire*, throughout the spring of 1937. A total of 103 deputies had initially voted in support of Becquart; of them, 40—including Bousquet, Oberkirch, Lucas, and Dubois-Fresney of the Federation—subsequently changed their votes to abstention.

40. *Journal Officiel, Sénat*, February 2, 1937, p. 7378.

that a government including the Communists could not work for the national interest. Nor did the Federation vote for Blum's successor, Edouard Daladier, despite the presence in his government of such conservative figures as Paul Reynaud, Georges Mandel, and Auguste Champetier de Ribes. Although it recognized that successive governments of the Popular Front were growing weaker, the Federation noted that disorder continued, such as "revolutionary strikes" in the Parisian metallurgical industries. The only government that the Federation could trust was one which "affirms itself and returns to a state of order."[41]

Not until the general strike of transport workers was crushed on November 30, 1938, did the Federation begin to feel that order might be restored to France. The strike, called by the Confédération Générale du Travail to protest modifications of the forty-hour laws as well as the recent Munich settlement, failed completely. Its collapse was due to a lack of enthusiasm among the workers and to the firm action of the Daladier administration, which requisitioned the transport facilities and threatened the strikers with severe sanctions. The failure of the strike marked the definitive end of the Popular Front and destroyed the power and influence of the Confédération, whose numbers dropped sharply in the succeeding months. It also led to a rupture within the Socialist party and to a corresponding decline in its élan.

The Republican Federation was immensely relieved at what Marin termed "the victory of November 30." At last a government had shown the courage to repress the forces of disorder, and France could begin to repair the damage done by the Popular Front experience. Victor Perret rejoiced at the prospect of the nation's being able to look forward to the day when social peace would not be disturbed by "foreign leaders . . . and troublemakers, paid to bring about class war." On December 10, 1938, for the first time in three years, the Republican Federation voted confidence in the government. Explaining the vote of the Federation, Camille Blaisot recalled the railway

41. *La Nation*, April 6, May 7, 1938.

workers' strike of October, 1910, when Aristide Briand had mobilized the *cheminots* to force them back to work. Although then in the opposition, "the elders of the Republican Federation" had voted confidence in the Briand government and its campaign against the extreme Left. Twenty-eight years later, the Federation was once again prepared to forget party labels and vote for the defenders of public order. Until the coming of the Vichy regime eighteen months later, the Federation remained alert to the Communist menace and to the latent disruptive forces in French society. But after November 30, or as Jean Fernand-Laurent put it, after the triumph of "national good sense," the era of systematic opposition based on a profound fear for the social order was over.[42]

The Popular Front fell apart because of insurmountable economic difficulties, the entrenched resistance of France's social and economic elite, mounting international problems, and unresolvable differences within the left-wing coalition. The Popular Front fell victim to the same two-year rule that nullified the Left's electoral victories in 1924 and 1932 within two years. The contribution of the Republican Federation to the collapse of the Popular Front was minimal.

The experience of the Popular Front, however, wrought important changes in the Republican Federation. It forced the party to reassess important aspects of its program, and it brought into sharp relief some disturbing latent qualities of French conservatism. Their exaggerated fear of the Left drove the traditional conservatives of the Republican Federation into an alliance with elements on the Right that bore disquieting similarities to foreign fascist movements. Anxiety over the future of France and French society also forced the Federation to reconsider its deeply rooted anti-German nationalism. As a result of the Popular Front, the Republican Federation evolved in a direction that would have horrified the founders of the party.

42. *Ibid.*, December 10, 31, 1938; *Journal Officiel*, December 8, 1938, p. 1652, December 9, 1938, pp. 1729–30.

IV. *The Leagues*

The crises of the 1930s stimulated a revival of the anti-republican and antiparliamentary political current that ran through the Third Republic. This current, varying in intensity with the social and political climate, had previously climaxed during the Dreyfus affair and the experience of the Cartel des Gauches. Faced with repeated parliamentary scandals, governmental instability, a severe economic crisis, and the growing strength of the Left, a segment of the French middle class once again turned toward the antiparliamentary Right. To an increasing number of middle-class Frenchmen the parliamentary regime appeared to be both outmoded and unstable; only the dynamic and authoritarian alternatives proposed by the right-wing leagues seemed capable of preserving the social order and restoring national dignity. Not only did this so-called "new" Right distrust parliamentary institutions, but it also engaged in mass politics and sought to attract a large popular following. Unlike the traditional conservatives, the formations of this "new" Right adopted some of the trappings of mass political movements. Although the "new" Right preserved most of the values and goals of traditional French conservatism, its style was suggestive of foreign, and particularly Italian, fascist movements. It was also sufficiently appealing to attract substantial numbers of adherents during the crisis of the middle 1930s.

The revival of authoritarian and antiparliamentary movements posed a fundamental dilemma for a representative of the "old" Right, such as the Republican Federation. From its foundation the Federation had expressed distrust for Bonapartism. The party reflected the sentiments of its political ancestors, the rallied Orleanists of the early Third Republic, who preferred a parliamentary republic in which they would always have substantial representation to a plebiscitarian dictatorship, which would effectively exclude them from decision making. As long as the Third Republic proved itself to be a reliable instrument for preserving the social order, political adventurism of the Right seemed almost as fraught with danger as adventurism of the Left. An elite party, the Federation was inherently suspicious of the active participation of the masses in politics and only slightly less distrustful of mass parties of the Right than of the Left.

But the social and political crises of the 1930s raised disturbing questions about the viability of the Third Republic and especially about *la république conservatrice*, which had once been so appealing. It also gave the Federation reason to reflect on the weaknesses of elitist conservative political parties. Without any mass base, incapable of mobilizing its constituency except during elections (and then only moderately), a party like the Federation felt itself to be highly vulnerable during periods of political upheaval. It could not match the electoral performance of the Left, nor did it enjoy the large number of shock troops that the Left had at its disposal. In the event that disorder spread into the street, unchecked by a leftist government, the Federation was in no position to rally conservative forces to preserve the social status quo or to head off a potential revolutionary thrust. The elite of *notables*, upon whom the Federation relied, were of little value against a possible mass uprising.

Under these circumstances the existence of right-wing leagues, whose goals (rhetoric notwithstanding) were similar to those of the Federation and whose membership was large and imposing, could be a source of some comfort to the Federation. Working in cooperation with conservative parties, the leagues could furnish the *militants* that the Federation did not have. Furthermore, should it prove necessary, the leagues could provide counterrevolutionary shock troops to parry the disruptive forces of the Left. But the partnership was likely to be at best an uneasy one. The leagues arose, in some measure, as a reaction to the sterile conservatism of the *modérés* and were consequently unenthusiastic about the secondary and subservient role assigned them by the Federation. They tended, therefore, to strike out on their own. What ideally ought to have strengthened French conservatives frequently seemed to provoke only division on the Right.

The early Republican Federation had made much of its republican orthodoxy and the republican pedigree of its founders. Under Louis Marin's leadership the Federation drifted to the Right; but Marin's republicanism was unimpeachable, and his devotion to the parliamentary process was nearly as well known as his aversion to Germany. Léon Blum once remarked that Marin's attachment to parliamentary democracy exceeded even his. Charles Maurras noted wistfully that there was no doubt about the "loyalty, the sincerity and the depth of his republican convictions," and representatives of the extreme Right occasionally found his "parliamentary fetishism" exasperating. In the 1930s the official position of the Republican Federation remained unequivocal. The party declared in 1933: "The Republican Federation refuses to lay the responsibility for the trials and disappointments of the times on democratic institutions. These are the fault neither of the democratic principle in general nor of the parliamentary republic in particular, but of the bad use to which the French electoral majority have put the one and the other."[1] Yet the Federation's official republicanism did not segregate the party from those whose allegiance to the republic was a good deal less certain. Its formal pronouncements notwithstanding, in the 1930s the Federation's rhetoric and its personnel often resembled that of the antiparliamentary Right.

The Federation demanded a number of modifications in the representative system and in the operation of parliament—reforms that were clearly intended to remove some of the perceived abuses of the parliamentary system. The party called for

1. *Journal Officiel*, February 15, 1934, p. 456; *L'Action Française*, May 30, 1932; *Je Suis Partout*, November 16, 1935; *La Nation*, June 3, 1933.

the introduction of women's suffrage, proportional representation, the obligatory vote, and a weighted vote for the heads of
families. Behind the lofty justifications for such measures lay the
assumption that their implementation would significantly increase conservative representation in parliament.[2] In line with
its deflationary economic policies, the Federation advocated reducing by half the number of deputies and senators and depriving deputies of the right to introduce money bills. Finally, the
party favored granting the premier the right to dissolve parliament, thus ensuring that France would be governed by firm and
resolute majorities and not by a series of unnatural and unpro-
ductive coalitions. None of these reforms were inherently un-
democratic or antiparliamentary; indeed most of them pushed
France in a more democratic direction. But as long as critical
segments of the political elite opposed these reforms (often for
rather shabby motives) and as long as the operation of the parliamentary republic remained imperfect, certain members of the
Federation did not hesitate to denounce *la république des
camarades* in terms that were often strikingly similar to the
rhetoric of those who were less committed to parliamentary
democracy.

In 1935, for example, Victor Perret wrote: "the great majority
of all Frenchmen today condemn parliamentarianism." Responsible patriots, he indicated, would make "the elimination of parliamentarianism" their first goal. It was evident from the context
of his remarks that by parliamentarianism Perret meant the various abuses in the existing parliamentary system: the single-
member constituency, the excessive number of deputies, and
the right of deputies to initiate financial legislation. Yet the
article was immediately reprinted by the local branch of the
Jeunesses Patriotes.[3] Whatever meaning Perret had intended to
convey by his critique of parliamentarianism, it was highly appreciated by the staunchly antiparliamentary Jeunesses Patri-

2. This assumption also lay behind the stubborn resistance of the Radicals to such
proposals as women's suffrage.
3. *L'Union Républicaine du Rhône*, September 15, 1935; *L'Alerte*, October, 1935.

otes of the Rhône. This practical blurring of the Federation's unqualified republicanism blunted the distinction between the party and certain of the antiparliamentary leagues. The Federation could still approach the leagues in its denunciation of the inefficiency and corruption of the existing unreformed parliament. Since certain of the leagues were prepared to qualify themselves as reformist republicans, the formal ideological distance between them and the Federation was slight.

The oldest and best known of the antiparliamentary movements in France was the Action Française. Although declining as a political force in the 1930s, the Action Française still exerted an influence, particularly on young middle-class intellectuals. Because the Action Française was openly monarchist, the Federation could have little contact with it, and *La Nation* rarely mentioned the French royalists. Nonetheless, some of the conservatives who joined the Federation in the 1930s, including Xavier Vallat, Jacques Debû-Bridel, Victor Rochereau (deputy from the Vendée), and François Valentin (deputy from the Meurthe-et-Moselle), began their political careers in association with the Action Française. In 1936 a number of deputies from the monarchist stronghold of the Loire-Inférieure, whose sympathies for the Action Française were well known, affiliated with the Federation.[4]

In the early 1930s, the Action Française took an active interest in the Republican Federation and openly intervened in its internal problems. It warmly praised Marin's firm nationalism and castigated his opposition within the party. Although the electoral role of the Action Française was minimal in the 1930s, it occasionally supported sympathetic candidates of the Federation, particularly if they ran against the "Red-Christians" of the Parti Démocrate Populaire. Such help was not always appreciated or acknowledged. Augustin Michel, who in 1932 with the active support of the Action Française regained his seat from a

---

4. These included Henri de la Ferronnays, Jacques de Juingé, and Jean Le Cour Grandmaison. Eugen Weber, *Action Française* (Stanford, 1962), 145.

Popular Democrat, spent the first few weeks after his election denying that he had solicited or desired such support. As Maurras admitted, his own high praise for Louis Marin had compromised Marin in 1932 and reduced his majority by several thousand votes.[5] After 1933 the Action Française's interest in the Federation waned, and the two groups rarely mentioned one another officially during the rest of the decade.

At the local level during the 1920s and 1930s, branches of the Federation often carried on a reasonably amicable dialogue with their counterparts in the Action Française. The Federation of the Morbihan, while stressing its republicanism, admitted that on all major issues—questions of religious, social, and foreign policy—the Federation and the monarchists had "a common soul." In 1934 in the Nord, a traditional stronghold of the Action Française, one local Royalist journal publicly praised Eugène Warein (the president of the Federation's branch in Hazebrouck) for his courageous defense of the demonstrators of February 6. Could this not, the journal wondered, signify the beginning of a policy of "no enemies to the right." Warein replied that he and his group had never been afraid to look to their right and had "never ceased to demand the support of all those who were on the Right and who must immunize themselves against the *gauchite.*" In the Rhône in the early 1930s, the local royalist newspaper, *La République Lyonnaise*, published long letters by Alexandre Bosse-Platière, Pierre Burgeot, and Victor Perret as part of a debate on the respective merits of the monarchy and the republic. Throughout this debate the royalists treated the pro-Marin leaders of the Federation of the Rhône as kindred spirits and periodically addressed good-natured open letters to them trying to convince them of the futility of supporting the democratic regime. For the disciples of Charles Maurras, the Marin wing of the Federation consisted of essentially right-thinking Frenchmen, who were still wasting their time with the electoral process. It was precisely because the Action

5. *Ibid.*, 303, 371; *Le Charivari*, May 24, 1932; *L'Action Française*, May 30, 1932.

Française did not "consider [the Federation] to be an adversary" that it felt obliged to point out "its weaknesses and timidities."[6] But the monarchy was a lost cause by the 1930s, and the Action Française was losing its popular support. The Jeunesses Patriotes and the Croix de Feu, on the other hand, were far larger and more popular political movements. They were also formally republican.[7] Consequently, they were of more immediate interest to the Federation.

The Jeunesses Patriotes was founded on December 18, 1924, by Pierre Taittinger, deputy from Paris. Initially, the Jeunesses Patriotes began as a youth section of the Ligue des Patriotes, founded by Paul Déroulède during the Dreyfus affair. The Ligue des Patriotes had virtually disappeared after World War I but was revived after the victory of the Cartel des Gauches in 1924 by Alexandre Millerand and General de Castelnau. Taittinger intended that the Jeunesses Patriotes would have the same relationship with the Ligue des Patriotes as the Camelots du Roi had with the Action Française, although he expected the Jeunesses Patriotes to be a larger and more popular force.[8] Within a few months the Jeunesses Patriotes proved to be far more active than the parent body and formally separated from the moribund Ligue.

The Jeunesses Patriotes represented a direct continuation of the Bonapartist tradition in French politics. The league was founded and it flourished during a period of demonstrated parliamentary inability to deal with the pressing issues facing France. As an alternative, the Jeunesses Patriotes proposed an authoritarian leadership in the form of a powerful chief-of-state elected by the various *notables* and *corps* of French society. The power of parliament would be correspondingly reduced,

6. *La Liberté du Morbihan*, May 1, 1923; *L'Entente Républicaine Démocratique de Hazebrouck*, April, 1934; *La République Lyonnaise*, November 30, 1929, April 23, June 18, July 2, 1932, April 29, 1933.

7. The nominal republicanism of most of the leagues, except the Action Française, led one historian of the leagues, H. Maizy, to entitle his work, *Les groupes anti-parlementaires républicains de droite en France de 1933 à 1939* (Paris, 1951).

8. Archives de la Préfecture de Police (hereafter cited as APP), 79.501–508A, C328, May, 1925.

ministers would no longer be chosen from its midst, deputies would lose all initiative on financial matters, and parliament would be limited to controlling public expenses and voting laws proposed by the chief-of-state and his ministers. The program of the Jeunesses Patriotes called for the end of the *parlement roi* and the restoration of discipline and authority to French government. Spiritually, the Jeunesses Patriotes harked back to the plebiscitarian dictatorship of the second Empire, but in the 1930s certain elements in the Jeunesses Patriotes also seemed akin to more contemporary dictatorships. The blue windbreakers and basque berets worn by the Jeunesses Patriotes reminded contemporary observers of the Italian Blackshirts. In the Rhône, *Alerte* (the local journal of the Jeunesses Patriotes) lauded the youth who had purged Germany, Spain, and Italy of Marxism and singled out for praise the Squadristi, the cadets of the Alcazar, and such German patriots as Horst Wessel. Reflecting upon one of the Jeunesses Patriotes' favorite proposals, the replacement of parliament by a Committee of Public Safety, the leaders of the Jeunesses Patriotes of the Rhône noted: "This may be fascism. But in any case it is a very republican fascism." In 1935 *Alerte* insisted that France needed "a dictator plebiscited by the nation" and insisted that only one man could fill the role: Marshal Pétain.[9]

But the intensity of the antiparliamentarianism of the Jeunesses Patriotes was always tempered by the fact that a substantial number of them were deputies and its leader, Pierre Taittinger, a notoriously ambitious one. In 1935 it was estimated that at least seventy-six deputies belonged to the Jeunesses Patriotes.[10] Throughout its history the Jeunesses Patriotes felt the strain of being a nominally antiparliamentary movement, in principle hostile to *la république des camarades*, a good part of whose leadership nonetheless consisted of deputies who were

9. *L'Alerte*, May, June, 1935, November, 1936.
10. *Le Temps*, February 10, 1935. E. Beau de Loménie gave the figure of seventy-seven deputies for the 1928–1932 legislature. Emmanuel Beau de Loménie, "Verrons nous se faire un regroupement national," *La Revue Hebdomadaire*, November 30, 1935, p. 607.

thoroughly at home in the Palais Bourbon. From the beginning, elements within the Jeunesses Patriotes challenged Taittinger's leadership and the predominance of parliamentarians in the league. As early as December, 1925, a subgroup of the Jeunesses Patriotes, the Légion, attempted to remove Taittinger from the presidency and cleanse the directing bodies of the league of deputies. Taittinger succeeded in expelling the dissidents, who shortly afterward joined Georges Valois' far less ambiguous Faisceau. Discontent continued, however, especially among the youthful elements within the league, the student Phalangeards. In 1929 the leader of the Phalange, Pighetti de Rivasso, addressed the congress of the Phalangeards and complained of the gap that separated Taittinger's words from his actions. The Jeunesses Patriotes, he insisted, was not meant to be an *officine électorale*, as so many of its present leaders seemed to believe. He demanded that Taittinger put his leadership of the Jeunesses Patriotes ahead of his other interests, notably being deputy from Paris, member of the Republican Federation, and especially president of the Commission des Colonies. Taittinger fired him on the spot, and Pighetti replied by accusing him of converting the Jeunesses Patriotes into the Jeunesses Opportunistes et Parlementaires. Taittinger's faithful support of Briand's foreign policy throughout 1929 and 1930 intensified the suspicion that he was more interested in obtaining the portfolio of Minister of Colonies than in cleansing the parliamentary regime. His apparent sacrifice of principle on the question of the interallied debts and the Young Plan earned him the enmity of the Action Française and provoked a number of resignations from the Jeunesses Patriotes.[11]

Throughout the early 1930s there were continuing reports of a malaise within the Jeunesses Patriotes resulting from the league's equivocal attitude. One vice-president of the Jeunesses

11. APP, 79.501–508B, D328, November 15, 1925; in the same file see the report from the Ministry of the Interior, January 21, 1926; APP, 79.501–508, F–2, March 2, 1929; Jean Philippet, *Les Jeunesses Patriotes et Pierre Taittinger, 1924–1940* (Paris, 1967), 67–79.

Patriotes, Henri Provost de la Fardinière—a man of deep Bonapartist and plebiscitarian roots—launched a long, although ultimately unsuccessful, campaign to force Taittinger to adopt a genuinely antiparliamentary stance. The Parti de l'Appel au Peuple, the tiny Bonapartist party, accused the Jeunesses Patriotes of having abandoned their founding principle and of having become "the more or less conscious defenders of the parliamentary system." The leadership did nothing to dissipate the league's political ambiguity. Its weekly newspaper, Le National, frequently alluded to the Révolution Nationale and violently attacked la république des camarades, but it also assured its readers that members of the league were republican reformists. Pierre Taittinger told a parliamentary commission that, although many of his followers came from diverse political backgrounds, the league accepted the existing form of government and was 99% republican.[12]

Despite periodic disparaging references to the modérés, the Jeunesses Patriotes enjoyed close personal relations with the Republican Federation. Many of the directing personnel of the league belonged to the older party. Taittinger, Edouard Soulier, and Jean Ybarnegaray, all vice-presidents of the Federation, were three of the leading figures in the Jeunesses Patriotes.[13]

12. APP, 79.501–508A, D328, April 18, August 5, 1933, and 79.501–508D, D328, January 13, 1933, January 21, 1935; Brumaire, February, 1933; Le National, February 24, 1934; Chambre des Députés, Rapport fait au nom de la commission d'enquête chargée de rechercher les causes et les origines des événements du 6 février 1934, II, 1711.

13. Taittinger and Soulier quietly resigned as vice-presidents of the Republican Federation in the early 1930s, although they resigned over issues that were unrelated to their membership in the Jeunesses Patriotes. Both had been at odds with Marin and the refractory wing of the party about foreign policy and about the management of the party. Taittinger precipitously resigned as vice-president because he thought that the Federation had accepted the open support of the Action Française at a rally that the party sponsored in the Vélodrome d'Hiver in May, 1931, to protest the proposed Austro-German customs union. The Action Française had concentrated its venom on Taittinger for some time because of his Briandism and his opportunism. Although Taittinger proved to be mistaken on this point, he did not withdraw his resignation. L'Echo de Paris, May 3, 1931; La Nation, May 30, 1931. Soulier resigned as vice-president after the expulsion of the Pernot group. Both men nevertheless remained active members of the party. Jean Ybarnegaray ceased to play an active role in both the Federation and

In 1934, of the six vice-presidents of the Jeunesses Patriotes, three—Ybarnegaray, Michel Parès, and Fortuné d'Andigné— were deputies of the Federation; and a fourth, Charles des Isnards, was soon to be one. The executive committee of the Jeunesses Patriotes included René Russier, assistant secretary-general of the Federation; Georges Bonnefous, a vice-president; and three deputies of the Federation, Edouard Moncelle, Charles Coutel, and Augustin Michel. A large number (probably a majority) of the senators and deputies of the Jeunesses Patriotes also belonged to the Republican Federation. Many of the municipal councilors of Paris also belonged to the two organizations.[14] At the local level the same individuals often headed the branches of both the party and the league. André Mutter, secretary-general of the Republican Federation of the Aube, was also president of the regional branch of the Jeunesses Patriotes. Georges Bricard was simultaneously president of the Federation and the Jeunesses Patriotes of the Maine-et-Loire. Elsewhere the two groups often cooperated closely. In the Rhône, for example, the Jeunesses Patriotes often provided the *service d'ordre* for meetings of the Federation and referred to

---

the Jeunesses Patriotes sometime after 1934. A prolonged illness kept him from Paris for nearly a year, and his return was the occasion for his famous offer of December 5, 1935, to disarm the leagues. This led to an abrupt break with the Jeunesses Patriotes, of which he was still technically a director. His formal break with the Federation came later when he entered the Parti Social. Français. *Le National*, December 14, 1935.

14. The press and police files on the Jeunesses Patriotes reveal at least thirty-five deputies or former deputies of the Federation as members of the league during the early 1930s. They included Fortuné d'Andigné, Bertrand d'Aramon, Etienne d'Audiffret-Pasquier, Camille Blaisot, Edmond Bloud, Georges Bonnefous, Désiré Bouteille, Alexis Calliès, Paul Chassaigne-Goyon, Charle Coutel, Henry Cravoisier, Louis Delsol, Joseph Denais, Louis Dumat, Alexandre Duval, Louis Duval-Arnould, Emile Faure, Désiré Ferry, Emmanuel Evain, Henri Fournier-Sarlovèze, Henri Groussau, Maurice Le Corbeiller, Charles de Lasteyrie, Augustin Michel, Edouard Moncelle, Michel Parès, Charles Pechin, Georges Pernot, Auguste Sabatier, Robert Serot, Edouard Soulier, Lionel de Tastes, Xavier Vallat, Edouard de Warren, François de Wendel, Jean Ybarnegaray. The municipal councilors of Paris who belonged to both groups included Jean Ferrandi, Félix Lobligeois, Charles des Isnards, and Edouard Frédéric-Dupont. Frédéric-Dupont and des Isnards became deputies of the Federation in 1936. Frédéric-Dupont was a particularly dedicated member of the Jeunesses Patriotes, having been wounded in both of its most famous skirmishes: Rue Damrémont in 1926 and the Pont Royal on February 6, 1934.

the older party as "the big sister of the Jeunesses Patriotes."
In his report on party policy, given at the 1929 congress of the
Federation, Edouard Soulier expressed the Federation's appre-
ciation of the work of "the vigilant defenders of order and public
liberty" and acknowledged that the principles of the Federation
"were identical with those of the Jeunesses Patriotes."[15]

The Federation had good reason to desire an intimate relationship with the Jeunesses Patriotes. The league could attract
a far greater following than the Federation ever could and was an
ideal instrument for defending public order and providing conservatives with electoral support. The exact size of the Jeunesses
Patriotes is uncertain, but Taittinger claimed 240,000 members
in 1934 and some 325,000 in 1935. Inherently more plausible,
however, are the estimates of the Prefecture of Police, which
placed the membership of the Jeunesses Patriotes at 80,000 at
the end of 1935.[16] Nonetheless, in comparison with the Federation the Jeunesses Patriotes had a mass membership and seemed
to be an ideal partner for the elite party.

The partnership, however, was predicated upon the league's
docile acceptance of the Federation's political leadership. But in
the 1930s several factors militated against such an acceptance.
One was Taittinger's political ambition. In October, 1930, Taittinger announced the creation of a new political party, the
Parti Républicain National et Social (PRNS). The PRNS was
Taittinger's response to the incoherence and organizational
weakness of the modérés. At the present time, he affirmed, "the
remnants of parties, groups, associations and leagues wrangle
over members and votes. . . . These organizations which were
conceived for other times have been able neither to renovate
themselves nor to adapt completely to the exigencies of modern

15. L'Union Républicaine de l'Aube, January, 1930; Le Journal de Rouen, May 25,
1931; L'Alerte, June 1, 1930; La Nation, June 22, 1929.
16. Chambre des Députés, Rapport . . . événements du 6 février 1934, II, 1686;
Le Temps, February 19, 1935; APP, 79.501–508D D328, November 12, 1935, where
Taittinger reportedly gave an estimate of 327,000 members. APP, 79.501–508A, D328,
November 4, 1936. The report also estimated that membership in the league had declined to 70,000 members by the middle of 1936.

life." The PRNS was being formed because the traditional conservative parties had proven "incapable of effective organization." Taittinger emphasized, however, that he did not intend the PRNS as a rival of the traditional parties but as a means for tapping a segment of the electorate that had been unwilling to respond to the traditional conservatives. Drawing a parallel with the army, he observed: "Just as the scout does not want to be an infantryman and the cavalryman does not want to serve in the artillery, the citizen who does not want to serve in the Federation joins the Parti Républicain National et Social." Leaders of the PRNS reiterated that their political activity would be concentrated in the forty-three departments which, they claimed, lacked any effective conservative organization. Far from seeking to divide the ranks of the *modérés*, the new party intended to bring conservative forces together in preparation for the 1932 election.[17]

These arguments did not impress the Federation. It appreciated the role of the Jeunesses Patriotes but regarded the Parti Républicain National et Social as an unnecessary nuisance. The spectacle of a vice-president of the Republican Federation founding a new political party in the name of unity prompted some pointed rejoinders. The Republican Federation of the Seine noted that despite Taittinger's promise not to recruit from within the Federation, many members of the executive committee of the Federation received application forms from the PRNS. Nor was the PRNS well received within the Jeunesses Patriotes. The creation of political parties struck many as being incompatible with the avowed aims of the league, and some thought they scented in the PRNS another vehicle for Taittinger's well-known ministerial ambitions.[18]

17. Cited in *L'Action Sociale et Nationale*, November 15, 1930; *Le Sud-Est Républicain*, July 8, 1933 (probably a reprint from *Le National*, a number of issues of which are missing from the collection in the Bibliothèque Nationale); APP, 79.501–1210–3, D3299, November 18, 1930, March 22, 1932, and 79.501–1210–3, D329, May 20, 1931.

18. Louis Marin protested the formation of the new party at the Federation's 1931 congress; *La Nation*, May 30, 1931. *L'Action Sociale et Nationale*, November 15, 1930; minutes of the Republican Federation of the Seine, November 7, 1930, in Marin Papers, carton 82; APP, 79. 501–1210–3, D329, November 18, 1930.

As it happened, the Parti Républicain National et Social was not a notably successful venture. Although a number of deputies of the Federation showed some interest, the new party was generally received with indifference. A series of public meetings failed to attract much attention, and within a year it was obvious that the PRNS could attract neither popular support nor financial backing.[19] Following the 1932 election the PRNS ceased all activities, thus eliminating a potential source of conflict between the Federation and its sister league.

A growing restlessness within the league, particularly among the young, caused more serious trouble in its relations with the Republican Federation. As the political and social crisis deepened and as the leagues increasingly flexed their political muscles, many began to chafe at the docile role they played with respect to conservative parliamentarians. The provincial branches of the Jeunesses Patriotes, somewhat removed from the Bonapartist passions of Paris, usually managed to reconcile membership in the league with support of parliamentary conservatives. But even here some of them began to complain of being treated by the *modérés* as if they were a mere "civic guard." The president of the Jeunesses Patriotes of the Meurthe-et-Moselle suspected that the conservative deputies had been "completely contaminated by politics" and asked of them: "Will you have the courage to break with your present egotism and that of your outmoded and sterile parties?" The tone of *Le National* also changed. Whereas in the early 1930s *Le National* treated the Federation with deference and reported its congresses sympathetically, by 1935 it could say little about the Federation except that its congresses were exceedingly dull. The dissidents in the league never gained control, however, and in the climate of the mid-1930s the Jeunesses Patriotes began to seem too genteel

19. The interested deputies included Etienne d'Audiffret-Pasquier, Désiré Bouteille, Henry Cravoisier, Joseph Denais, Alexandre Duval, Emmanuel Evain, Henri Fournier-Sarlovèze. Edmond Bloud, Charles de Lasteyrie, and Maurice Le Corbeiller, all of whom remained in the Federation. APP, 79.501–508A, D328, an undated report made in 1932, and 79.501–1210–3, D329, November 18, 1930, May 13, September 15, 1931.

for the more spirited elements on the Right. By 1935 many Parisian Phalangeards, disgusted with Taittinger's parliamentarianism, began a steady migration to Colonel de la Rocque's recently founded Croix de Feu.[20]

The Croix de Feu was by far the largest and most dynamic of the leagues of the 1930s. Founded in 1928 by Maurice Hanot as an organization of veterans, the Croix de Feu was initially nonpolitical. Colonel de la Rocque, recently retired from the army, entered the Croix de Feu in December, 1930, and became vice-president of what was still little more than a modest veterans' organization. De la Roque soon emerged as the dominant figure in the Croix de Feu, giving the league an overtly political orientation. With the election of 1932 the Croix de Feu began to take an active interest in politics and politicians. Unlike the Jeunesses Patriotes, however, de la Rocque and the Croix de Feu made a deliberate effort to avoid open contact with traditional political parties. In 1931, for example, the Federation sponsored a rally against the proposed Austro-German customs union and invited the Croix de Feu to participate. The executive committee of the Croix de Feu replied that "the Croix de Feu . . . make it a rule to act completely independently of political parties. It cannot appear officially at a rally held exclusively under the auspices of such a party."[21] Subsequently, however, de la Rocque's critics would charge that he maintained intimate but clandestine contacts with the French political elite.

The exact political stance of the Croix de Feu was vague. In particular the league could not or would not state precisely

20. *Le Chardon*, March, 1933; *Le National*, February 14, 1932, April 20, 1935; APP, 79.501–508F–2, D329, December 18, 1934, January 7, 25, October 30, November 12, 1935, March 3, 1936.

21. On the early history of the Croix de Feu, see Paul Chopine, *Six ans chez les Croix de Feu* (Paris, 1935); Philippe Rudaux, *Les Croix de Feu et le PSF* (Paris, 1967); Edith and Gilles de la Rocque, *La Rocque tel qu'il était* (Paris, 1962); René Rémond, "Les anciens combattants et la politique," *Revue française de science politique*, V (1955), 267–90; Philippe Machefer, "Les Croix de Feu: 1927–1936," *L'Information Historique*, January–February, 1972, pp. 28–34; Robert Soucy, "France: Veterans Politics Between the Wars," in Stephen R. Ward (ed.), *The War Generation: Veterans of the First World War* (Port Washington, Wisconsin, 1975), 59–103. *L'Echo de Paris*, April 14, 1931.

where it stood with respect to parliamentary democracy. The Croix de Feu's profound discontent with the existing political system was matched by its highly ambiguous remedies. The president of the Croix de Feu in Marseilles was typical of the league's leaders when he remarked in 1935: "As long as there is a parliament like the one we have now, there is nothing to be hoped for. It is up to the Croix de Feu to make the necessary revolution by following strictly the orders of our leaders."[22] Such a comment could be interpreted in several ways. It might have represented no more than a call for a more effective group of deputies in the next legislature, or it might have been a covert appeal for the violent replacement of the existing political system by a more authoritarian one.

De la Rocque was no more informative, and his political pronouncements usually consisted of vapid and essentially meaningless generalizations. He readily denounced the old conservative leaders who, "for the sake of electoral and political expediency, betrayed the men who had confidence in them," and he scorned the *modérés* and the *bien pensants* who were "incapable of serving without looking for votes or a constituency." When asked in 1935 by Georges Suarez if the Croix de Feu had "a definite political attitude," de la Rocque replied: "If, by definite political attitude, you mean adhering to any man or group, whether political or para-political, the Croix de Feu gives proof, in all circumstances, of obstinate eclecticism." Typical of de la Rocque's rhetoric was his comment about the antiparliamentary quality of the Croix de Feu: "We are not anti-parliamentary in the sense that we are in any way opposed to genuine, popular representation. On the contrary. We are enemies of the present parliamentary chaos and all its causes and we demand a careful, courageous, renovating and durable reform of the constitution as well as of our social and political condition of life."[23]

22. APP, 79.501–1108–1–B, report of a meeting organized by the Croix de Feu in the Salle Wagram, January 28, 1935.
23. Cited in Georges Suarez, "Les Croix de Feu," *Le Document*, June, 1935, pp. 6, 7, 11; *Le Flambeau*, January 4, 1936.

This imprecision, far greater than in the Jeunesses Patriotes, probably reflected a confusion in de la Rocque's mind as to exactly what he wished to do. It also served to mask some of the more disturbing aspects of the Croix de Feu. The overtly paramilitary quality of the league, its penchant for cryptic orders to its *dispos*, veiled allusions to H-hours, speeding convoys of automobiles and motorcycles, massive and disciplined parades were softened somewhat by the fuzzy and rather innocuous political statements of its leaders.

The haziness of the Croix de Feu's political position facilitated the adherence of a number of *modéré* politicians. Although there were fewer parliamentarians in evidence in the Croix de Feu than in the Jeunesses Patriotes, a number of deputies of the Republican Federation belonged simultaneously to the Croix de Feu. Xavier Vallat, François de Wendel, Louis Duval-Arnould, Jacques Poitou-Duplessy, and Jean Ybarnegaray—all at one time or other vice-presidents of the Federation—also adhered to the Croix de Feu.[24] Membership in an organization that was supposedly both apolitical and antiparliamentary posed no fundamental problem for the Federation's deputies. As conservative and nationalistic politicians, many members of the party found membership in an association like the Croix de Feu to be a political asset and, without worrying about the exact nuances of its program, were prepared to use the good auspices of the league to further their electoral fortunes. Colonel de la Rocque ironically described the kind of relationship that often existed between the antiparliamentary league and aspiring politicians.

Among the new "friends" who, during the last half year, have requested an audience with me for an "important conversation," there have been several whose visits, give or take a few details, could be summarized by the following monologue: First act; my guest is congratulatory, rapturous and encouraging. Second act; my guest de-

24. It is difficult to say exactly how many deputies of the Federation belonged to the Croix de Feu, but the instances of divided loyalties that arose when the Croix de Feu became a rival political party suggest that a substantial number belonged to the league.

nounces parliamentarianism, details its flaws, vilifies the deputies. Third act; my guest asks me what the Croix de Feu might do in the up-coming elections. He develops one or two hypotheses and furnishes me with the details of constituencies he knows well. Fourth act; struck by a sudden inspiration . . . my guest suggests at random a list of Croix de Feu or Volontaires Nationaux who might be candidates. Casually, and merely as an example, he mentions that he himself has some well-placed friends who have (fancy that!) offered him a constituency. At that the rascal leaves, doubtlessly believing that he has laid some foundations.[25]

The Croix de Feu had an obvious appeal for a party like the Republican Federation because by the mid-1930s it had become a genuine mass movement. In July, 1935, Colonel de la Rocque estimated that the Croix de Feu, including auxiliaries like the Volontaires Nationaux, was growing at a rate of 15,000 members a month. He placed the total membership of the league at between 300,000 and 500,000. De la Rocque undoubtedly exaggerated, but a police report in the same month estimated the total membership in the Croix de Feu to be approximately 240,000. The most recent scholarly estimate of the size of the Croix de Feu suggests that the league had a maximum of 450,000 members on the eve of the 1936 election.[26] Such figures could be envied by any French political party of either the Right or the Left and made the Croix de Feu a potentially valuable ally of elite parties like the Federation. With large numbers of *militants* but no political elite and only a vague political philosophy, the league could serve as a useful instrument for the *modérés*.

The violence of the night of February 6, 1934, placed the leagues at the center of French politics. The spectacle of the various right-wing leagues converging on the Palais Bourbon to protest parliamentary corruption profoundly frightened many Frenchmen, who saw in the episode an abortive fascist coup. Subsequently, historians have argued that there was no coordi-

25. Suarez, "Les Croix de Feu," 17–18.
26. *Ibid.*, 4; APP, 79.501–1108–1–B, July 10, 1935; Philippe Machefer, "Le Parti Social Français en 1936–1937," *L'Information Historique*, April–May, 1972, p. 74.

nated plan to overthrow the Republic, that the leagues were simply protesting against undeniable parliamentary corruption, and that at a maximum the most violent elements simply wanted a chance to *fesser les députés*.[27] The incoherence of the principal leagues on February 6 would seem to support this interpretation. But to many contemporaries, February 6 simultaneously conjured up memories of Boulangist agitation against the Republic and contemporary fascist seizures of power in Italy and Germany. February 6 prompted the reconciliation of the disparate elements on the Left and Center-Left and the formation of the Popular Front to save the Republic. The Right, on the other hand, and particularly the Republican Federation, treated the night of violence as a wave of genuine popular protest against the corruption and inefficiency of the government. Far from viewing February 6 as an act of illegal violence, the Federation maintained that it represented a legitimate act of protest, which had resulted in the partial cleansing of French politics.

Although the Federation did not officially participate in the demonstrations of February 6, a number of party members played an active role. Charles des Isnards, Pierre Taittinger, Edouard Frédéric-Dupont, Jean Ferrandi, and Dr. Félix Lobligeois, representatives of the Federation in the Municipal Council of Paris, were among the leaders of the column that advanced on the Chamber of Deputies from the Hotel de Ville. Des Isnards, a future deputy of the Federation, who has been described as "the brains behind February 6," played a particularly provocative role in the events of that night. When subsequently questioned about the propriety of a man of order attempting to change the government by violent demonstrations, des Isnards replied: "there are moments when insurrection is the most sa-

27. For the subsequent debate on the significance of February 6 see: Marcel Le Clère, *Le 6 février* (Paris, 1967): Maurice Chavardès, *Le Six février 1934* (Paris, 1966); Maurice Chavardès, *Une Campagne de presse: La droite française et le 6 février 1934* (Paris, 1970); Max Beloff, "The Sixth of February," in James Joll (ed.), *The Decline of the Third Republic* (London, 1959); René Rémond, "Explications du six février," *Politique*, n.s., I (1959), 218–30.

cred of duties." At the head of a column composed principally of several thousand Jeunesses Patriotes, des Isnards and his fellow councilors attempted to force a police barricade at the Pont Royal. In the resulting fracas, Lobligeois, Ferrandi, and Frédéric-Dupont were seriously injured. Des Isnards and three other councilors managed to break through the line and succeeded in entering the Chamber, thanks to Edouard Soulier, who let them in a back entrance. After demanding Daladier's resignation, they were unceremoniously shown the door. Although the municipal councilors acted in their capacity as members of the Jeunesses Patriotes, their attitude indicated that violent street demonstrations were not altogether foreign to the mentality of some in the Federation.[28]

Almost without exception the leaders of the Federation praised, sometimes in extravagant terms, the men of February 6. The violence of that night did not cause them to reconsider their attitude toward the leagues. Far from disavowing the leagues, the Federation viewed them as gallant and martyred bands of patriots. Philippe Henriot, who made his parliamentary reputation by his stinging attacks on the government's handling of the Stavisky affair, became the official apologist for the leagues. In his book, Le 6 février, the young vice-president of the Federation ridiculed the suggestion that there had been a plot to overthrow the Republic. The leagues, according to him, had shown a surprising degree of moderation, and he marveled at "their docility, their discipline and their wisdom." He admitted that there had been "disorderly elements" in the crowd, and he deplored "isolated incidents" of violence. But the rioters of February 6 had not threatened the Republic; they had been merely "warning the state and reminding it of its duty."[29]

Henriot's position was not exceptional. Camille Blaisot, also a vice-president of the party, justified February 6 even more extravagantly. He described the night as: "The uprising of the

28. Le Clère, Le 6 février, 161; Chambre des Députés, Rapport . . . événements du 6 février 1934, II, 1503.

29. Philippe Henriot, Le 6 février (Paris, 1934), 107, 173, 226.

healthy, hardworking and vibrant population of the capital against the weakness of a decadent parliamentary regime . . . [composed of] a majority of deputies and senators who are blinded by the most cowardly obedience to the orders of the Lodges." February 6, he contended, would be remembered "as a day having as much importance as September 4, 1870 which substituted the Third Republic for the defeated Empire."[30] It is significant that Blaisot equated February 6 with September 4. Although September 4 had a healthily republican ring about it, that date had been (as Blaisot must have realized) the occasion for the violent overthrow of one political regime and its replacement by another. For Camille Blaisot February 6 was more than a street riot that had gone out of control; it was a revolutionary *journée* that had swept away yet another corrupt regime. The replacement of the 1932 majority by the more conservative coalition headed by Gaston Doumergue did not, of course, amount to a change of regime, but Blaisot did not appear disturbed at the prospect of individual governments falling as a result of agitation in the street. Philippe Henriot was one of the youngest and least orthodox members of the Republican Federation. Camille Blaisot was one of the oldest and most traditional. Yet both agreed that the demonstrators of February 6 had performed a service for France and were worthy of praise.

Their feelings were shared by virtually all elements within the Republican Federation. A typical reaction was that of the vice-president of the Federation's committee in Hazebrouck: "A few martyrs, who can never be sufficiently praised or honored, have paid with their lives . . . but as was the case nearly two thousand years ago, we can say *Sanguis martyrum, semen Christianorum*. The blood poured out on February 6, 1934 will be the seed of a great national awakening." Other local branches echoed these sentiments, denouncing the government's "criminal *coup de folie*" and lauding the "generous hearts" which "cried out in disgust." Louis Marin, who became Minister of State in Doumergue's new government, distrusted the street as

30. *La Nation*, April 21, 1934.

a substitute for political and parliamentary action. But even he could find no words of blame for the leagues. "The blood of good Frenchmen," he wrote, "flowed as the result of the frightful and idiotic errors of incompetent governments."[31]

The events of February 6 did not cause the Federation to reexamine its relationship with the leagues, but subsequent events did. From the conservative point of view the salutary effects of February 6 were of short duration. Doumergue's government of national salvation lasted only six months and accomplished virtually nothing. More seriously, February 6 provoked a counterattack from the Left in the form of the Popular Front, which threatened to be far more dangerous than a corrupt Chautemps ministry. The defeat of Doumergue's government in November, 1934, seen by many conservatives as "the revenge of February 6," demonstrated that governments placed in power by street demonstrations could as easily be removed by devious maneuvers in the corridors of the Palais Bourbon. On this occasion Camille Blaisot concluded: "We must no longer rely only on the street to straighten things out; in a parliamentary regime, even a faded, outmoded, discredited one . . . we must not attempt adventure."[32] Blaisot's earlier enthusiasm for the demonstrators of February 6 was now tempered by an increasing realization of the limitations of extraparliamentary action.

At the same time the leagues experienced an unprecedented growth, attributable largely to the deepening social and political crisis and the growing fear of communism. As the leagues grew, they began to assert with increasing stridency that they alone, and not the traditional politicians of the Right and the Left, could resolve the social, economic, and political problems of France. Even the Jeunesses Patriotes, despite its close connection with traditional conservative politicians, became increasingly abusive of the *modérés*.

31. *L'Entente Républicaine Démocratique de Hazebrouck*, March, 1934; Victor Perret, *L'Union Républicaine du Rhône*, February 18, 1934; *L'Union Républicaine de l'Aube*, January–February, 1934; German Favre (president of the Federation of the Loire), *L'Union Républicaine du Rhône*, February 18, 1934, January 13, 1935; *Voir Clair en Politique*, March 6, 1934.

32. *La Nation*, November 11, 1934.

The Federation was of two minds about the league. Acutely aware of the need to attract the support of the more dynamic elements on the Right, the Federation realized that whereas it could not (and probably did not want to) mobilize the masses, the leagues were an ideal instrument for galvanizing popular support in defense of the existing social order. In the face of the newly formed Popular Front and the growing importance of the Communists, the leagues could be, as Philippe Henriot noted, "a useful barrier of resolute men against the threatening violence of the revolutionary forces."[33] Jacques Poitou-Duplessy, deputy from the Charente, wrote: "The admirable and generous movement of the leagues . . . has fortified many sagging spirits and given birth to fervent hopes. These formations presently contain good and ardent patriots who are resolved, even at the cost of losing their lives, to oppose the mad and bloody rise of the extremists of the Left. One cannot praise too highly their devotion, their self-denial, their civic spirit and their desire to serve. We must encourage them in their role as "defenders of order."[34] At the same time the Federation knew that the leagues had more in mind than simply preserving order. They wanted more fundamental changes. Although their programs were usually nebulous, some elements within the leagues contemplated a violent seizure of power. A number of members of the Federation were alert to the possibility that such ambitions could prove to be counterproductive.

Jacques Poitou-Duplessy, who was a member of the Croix de Feu as well as vice-president of the Federation, analyzed the possibilities of securing a change of regime by violent means.

It would, in our opinion, be singularly dangerous to follow certain elements in the leagues, who, doubtful of the possibility of renewing the nation by legal means, do not hesitate to consider the forceful conquest of power. For several reasons we are clearly opposed to that point of view. The first reason is that, while recognizing the

33. Quoted in Emmanuel Beau de Loménie, "Verrons nous," October 19, 1935, p. 325.

34. La Nation, August 10, 1935.

vices of the present parliamentary regime, we are convinced of the possibility of improving it by a fundamental reform of the state. This can be realized once we have reformed the electoral system. The second is that, while wishing to safeguard our country from the horror of foreign war, we must all strive to protect our beloved France from the greater threat of a fratricidal struggle. We must seek to avoid the worst internal ruptures and the dark, mysterious unknown which is civil war.

A civil war would inevitably produce foreign complications and could lead to a foreign war. More important, an internal struggle would not result in the desired cleansing of French politics. Quite the contrary:

In reality, as soon as the internal conflict became serious, the army and the police would intervene fatally and tip the balance in favor of those whom they serve. In short, the last word would remain with those who control the "levers of command," that is to say, with the government in power.

He concluded:

The nationalistic leagues are marvellous instruments of resistance against the revolutionary thrust but it would be unwise to rely completely on this sympathetic movement. . . . Nothing should excuse us from the urgent and essential task which we must carry out on the electoral level by reinforcing the organized nationalist parties.[35]

Poitou-Duplessy's assessment of the possibility of a right-wing coup is significant because the crux of his objection to a counter-revolutionary seizure of power was his conviction that it would not succeed. Neither the police nor the army appeared likely to support an "adventure" by the Right. The state was, in his view, more vulnerable from the Left than from the Right, rendering an attempt by conservative forces to seize power far too risky.

Charles-Maurice Bellet, president of the Republican Federation of the Seine, shared Poitou-Duplessy's reservations. Near the end of 1934, in the midst of a prolonged discussion within

35. *Ibid.*

the Federation of the Seine about the need to enlist the support of the more youthful elements, Bellet observed:

> Our role is above all to counsel caution and not to be drawn into a course of violent action which might well appeal to youth who have not yet acquired the experience of their elders and who are unaware of the serious repercussion which such a policy could have for the country. We must advise and moderate the youthful elements, not excite them. It must not be a question of smashing everything without knowing what might happen afterwards. Everyone knows that at the present time many citizens desire a dictatorship but it is to be feared that if such a dictatorship could be established it would be a dictatorship of the Left.[36]

Bellet feared that if the more adventuresome elements on the French Right got out of control, far from serving as a useful guarantee against revolution, they might so weaken the existing political order as to establish the conditions for, at a minimum, a substantial leftward shift in the political balance and, at a maximum, a revolution. French conservatives would have to use legal and parliamentary means to gain power, and to do so meant strengthening existing parties like the Federation.

Spokesmen for the Federation also argued that the necessary leadership in the struggle against the Popular Front must come from the conservative parties. The leagues could not provide this leadership because, as Jacques Debû-Bridel argued, they lacked the political acumen to act effectively outside the tutelage of the more mature conservatives. The leagues, he reasoned, could not be called fascist precisely because, unlike the Nazis or the Fascists, they were not guided by a political party or a parliamentary formation. Whereas foreign fascist movements put forth their own candidates, had representatives in parliament, controlled city councils, and generally engaged in serious political activity, the Croix de Feu and the Jeunesses Patriotes officially did none of these things. Thus, their rhetoric and their

36. Minutes of the Republican Federation of the Seine, December 20, 1934, in Marin Papers, carton 82.

parades notwithstanding, the leagues were basically weak, lacking "a politically organized, politically enlightened, politically directed and electorally involved party." Without this kind of leadership the leagues were unable to play a commanding role in politics. The Jeunesses Patriotes, for example, had courageously risked their lives on February 6 to rid France of a corrupt government but had been unable to exercise much influence on succeeding governments. The Croix de Feu had created a magnificent organization and yet had contributed nothing to the 1935 municipal elections. Debû-Bridel concluded that because of the "gap which separates our leagues from political action and from the electorate" they could achieve little on their own and would have to rely on the guidance of the established conservative parties.[37]

The leadership of the Republican Federation conceived of the relationship between the leagues and the conservative parties as a symbiotic one. The role of the leagues was to mobilize support for the conservative cause, to defend the nation against the forces of revolution, and occasionally to chase a corrupt government from office. The more complex and demanding work of political leadership would remain the domain of the traditional conservative parties. Philippe Henriot revealed the kind of cooperation that he thought would be ideal:

> The collaboration [between the parties and the leagues] should be a simple matter, provided that each sticks to its own terrain. Unlike political parties, the leagues do not group their adherents around a political doctrine. They enroll men of good will in order to demand or prevent, by their cohesion, by their discipline or by their force, a specific state of affairs. Furthermore, they can assemble such large numbers only because it is precisely a question of a limited and temporary goal. Consequently, while the parties should provide the core of the troops [*troupes de fond*], the leagues constitute the shock troops.[38]

37. *L'Union Républicaine du Rhône*, October 13, 27, 1935.
38. Beau de Loménie, "Verrons nous," October 19, 1935, p. 325.

The leagues and the conservative parties could work in perfect harmony if each would accept what Jean Baudouin called its "parallel, but different and autonomous" tasks.[39]

The leagues, however, were not prepared to play the subordinate role that the Federation had cast for them. As they grew in size, they demanded a more important role than that of serving as a praetorian guard for the *modérés*. The Croix de Feu scorned the sterile conservatism of the *modérés* and energetically vilified the "professional patriots" whose principal ambition was "to get their hands on a portfolio." *Le Flambeau*, the house organ of the Croix de Feu, advised the *modérés* to admit their past failures and "follow silently and modestly in the ranks in the hopes of being forgotten."[40] Significantly, it was at this time that the Croix de Feu adopted the slogan: "One does not annex the Croix de Feu, one follows it." The Jeunesses Patriotes, although less harsh with the *modérés*, also insisted that it did not wish to be "in tow of" anyone.

The evident unwillingness of the leagues to act as docile auxiliaries disquieted the Federation. Jean Corbière, a staff writer for *La Nation*, complained of the leagues' "systematic denigration" of the work of the conservatives and reminded the younger formations that the birth of parties like the Federation at the beginning of the century had been due to the political failure of the leagues of that period. Furthermore, he found it paradoxical that the extraparliamentary forces of the Left actively defended the left-wing parties, while those of the Right seemed to have "as their first object, the demolition of the 'old parties.'" Philippe Henriot argued that if the leagues refused to cooperate with the conservative parties and attempted to play an independent role they were doomed to sterility and would achieve little except to sow confusion among the *modérés*.[41]

Local organizers often feared that if the leagues persisted in acting as rivals, instead of bringing much-needed ancillary

39. *La Nation*, July 6, 1935.
40. *Le Flambeau*, April 6, 1935.
41. *La Nation*, July 6, 1935; Beau de Loménie, "Verrons nous," October 19, 1935, p. 325.

troops to the conservative cause, they would simply seduce both members and funds away from parties like the Federation. At the beginning of 1935, Jean Baudouin cheerfully lauded the Croix de Feu in the Seine-Inférieure, assuring members of the Federation that the league was not in competition with the party and could make only "fruitful contributions" to its political and electoral action. But seven months later he complained of the impatience of certain of the party's *militants*, who appeared to prefer the aggressive luster of the Croix de Feu to the "circum-spection and abnegation" of the leaders of the Federation. Such impatience weakened the Federation instead of stimulating it to productive political activity. Gabriel Boissou, administrative secretary-general of the Federation of the Rhône, pleaded: "Whatever your personal preference, whatever your taste for this or that nationalistic league, you must not abandon your political party. You must not withdraw your moral and financial support from the group which is the only official defender of your interests . . . the Republican Federation of France."[42] In-sofar as the leagues refused to subordinate themselves to the *modérés* and threatened to replace the established parties, they became a source of concern for the Federation.

Yet as long as the Croix de Feu and the Jeunesses Patriotes retained the status of leagues, the tension between them and the Federation remained muted. The blustering rhetoric of *Le Flambeau* might have been irritating, but it was to be expected and could be ignored. The prospect of losing members to the more exciting leagues was disturbing for local organizers, but the Federation was not a mass party and its strength did not lie in the number of its *militants*. The leagues were troublesome and occasionally unpredictable partners, whose public attitude toward the *modérés* was at best abrasive. Nevertheless, they still represented valuable allies. Even the Croix de Feu was far more tractable in practice than its public rhetoric might have sug-gested. For example, during the 1936 elections the Croix de Feu

42. *Voir Clair en Politique*, January 1, 1935; *La Nation*, July 6, 1935; *L'Union Républicaine du Rhône*, July 6, 1936.

(although not presenting candidates of its own) insisted that it would play an independent role and broadly hinted that, instead of supporting the worn-out incumbents in the conservative camp, it would encourage new men. The Croix de Feu even refused to participate in the Comité d'arbitrage des partis nationaux in the Parisian region because that committee had decided to support all conservative incumbents. De la Rocque characteristically failed to specify exactly who the Croix de Feu would support, but he solemnly affirmed that it would oppose the *"fatigués"* and the *"dauphins,"* or hereditary seat-holders— in other words, a large number of the incumbent *modérés*. Yet despite these brave boasts, the Croix de Feu almost certainly supported many *modérés*. There is evidence to suggest that the league supported a number of candidates of the Federation, many of whom belonged to the Croix de Feu and most of whom were incumbents. The Croix de Feu, in any case, never opposed any of the Federation's candidates.[43]

Until the summer of 1936 the Federation could be satisfied, on the whole, with its relations with the leagues. Although they sometimes did so reluctantly, the leagues usually furnished what the Federation sought: a reliable and effective electoral ally and a comfortably large number of right-wing shock troops capable of parrying a potentially revolutionary thrust. But, when the leagues were forced to reconstitute themselves as political parties, the former partners became potential rivals.

43. *Choc*, March 5, 1936; François de la Rocque, *Autour des élections: Principes d'arbitrage du mouvement Croix de Feu* (Paris, 1936). Maizy, *Les groupes anti-parlementaires*, pp. 139–167, has an extended discussion of the Croix de Feu and the 1936 elections. He estimates that at least fifty-five of the deputies elected in 1936 had the support of the Croix de Feu; of these, thirty-one were members or former members of the Republican Federation. Maizy's estimate is, however, little better than a guess, since he does not prove that any of the fifty-five deputies actually received electoral support from the Croix de Feu. He arrives at his figure of fifty-five by adding the names of the forty-seven deputies who belonged to the Comité parlementaire de défense des libertés et de sympathie pour le Parti Social Français to those of the eight who sat with the Parti Social Français. As he admits, his figures do not include Camille Blaisot, who belonged to neither group but who almost certainly had the support of the Croix de Feu, nor Xavier Vallat, an active member of the Croix de Feu at the time of the elections who subsequently broke with de la Rocque and did not sit with the group of sympathetic deputies.

V.   *The New Parties*

The possibility of becoming political parties in their own right, instead of mere auxiliaries to existing parties, often tempted the leagues and correspondingly dismayed the conservatives. Even in the 1920s the Federation periodically complained about the tendency of otherwise sympathetic leagues to encroach on the territory of political parties.[1] Personal ambitions often dictated these metamorphoses, as in the case of Taittinger's experiment with the Parti Républicain National et Social in 1930. But in 1936 it was the antifascism of the victorious Left that prompted the transformation of the leagues. Since the principal bond holding the Popular Front together was its opposition to the menace from the extreme Right, one of its major demands was the dissolution of the leagues. Once these demands were implemented, the leagues were forced to seek the protective cloak of political party status.

The Federation bitterly resisted the proposed dissolution of the leagues. Despite occasional misgivings about the leagues, the Federation denied that they were responsible for the climate of violence in France and charged that the government's measures against the leagues were part of a revolutionary project of the Communists. When the government dissolved the Ligue d'Action Française because of its attack on Léon Blum in Febru-

1. For example, see the protests of Georges Cousin, vice-president of the Federation of the Seine and later one of the party's deputies, against the Ligue Républicaine Nationale. He expressed some anxiety that the league seemed in danger of becoming a rival party, rather than retaining the function initially assigned to it—that of being a *grand État-Major* standing above the major conservative parties. Minutes of the Republican Federation of the Seine, May 23, July 20, 1927, November 9, 1938, in Marin Papers, carton 82.

ary, 1936, leaders of the Federation protested sharply. Edouard Soulier deplored the aggression against Blum, but contended that the leaders of the Right were constantly subjected to similar assaults by the Communists. Louis Marin decried the "draconian and revolting measures" taken against the Action Française and suggested that the "infinitely more guilty" forces of the Left were tacitly encouraged by the government. The Federation was predictably outraged when in June, 1936, after a period of sustained violence by the Confédération Général du Travail, the government dissolved the leagues instead. Marin described the dissolution as "an act of fanatic arbitrariness," and Xavier Vallat accused the government of suppressing the leagues in order to begin more easily the planned *vacances de la légalité.*" By dissolving the leagues the Popular Front had struck at one of the last barriers against revolution.[2]

The Jeunesses Patriotes, anticipating the dissolution, became a political party as early as November, 1935. At the same time that the Chamber was about to debate an early proposal to dissolve the leagues, Pierre Taittinger moved to found the Parti National Populaire, which would be immune from possible antileague legislation. At its inception, Taittinger made extensive claims for the Parti National Populaire (PNP), some of which (had they been well founded) might have disturbed the Republican Federation. He predicted two million members within six months and announced that in the forthcoming elections the new party would present candidates everywhere possible. The PNP would engage in the electoral struggle "outside of the old parties that were worn out and worn down by thirty years of endless struggle." The new party even promised to form a separate group in the Chamber. His ambitions exceeded the capacities of the PNP, however, and within a few months Taittinger admitted that his new party would support candidates of neighboring parties. "In one constituency," he noted, "we will support a member of the Republican Federation because he repre-

2. *Journal Officiel*, February 13, 1936, p. 381, June 30, 1936, p. 1636; *La Nation*, February 22, June 30, 1936.

sents our nationalistic ideas, in another we will support the Croix de Feu." In the 1936 election the Parti National Populaire supported at least thirty-three members or former members of the Federation and in no case opposed an incumbent deputy of the party.[3]

So many directors of the new party were also members of the Federation that the two movements could hardly have been rivals. Five of the Federation's deputies sat on the executive committee of the PNP. After the elections, the PNP made no attempt to establish a separate group of deputies. Although it claimed to have elected twelve deputies, eight of them belonged to the Republican Federation, and a ninth associated himself with the Federation's parliamentary group. In spite of Taittinger's claims, the PNP acted as little more than an electoral instrument for *modérés*, most of whom sat with the Federation.[4]

The Popular Front was unimpressed by the republican credentials of the Parti National Populaire and dissolved it along with the rest of the leagues in June, 1936. In response Taittinger revived the Parti Républicain National et Social, which had never formally ceased to exist and which, by virtue of five years of token existence, was deemed by the government to be sufficiently respectable. The PRNS was also intimately linked with the Federation, and its executive committee consisted largely of members of the older party. Taittinger was president; Soulier, honorary-president; Henriot and des Isnards, vice-presidents; and Denais, Vallat, and Parès, members of the executive committee. The new party had no parliamentary formation, ran no candidates under its own flag, and in no way challenged the Republican Federation. It preserved some of its former antiparliamentary rhetoric, persisted in the use of violent

3. *Le National*, November 16, 23, 1935, January 11, April 4, 25, 1936; Jean Philippet, *Les Jeunesses Patriotes et Pierre Taittinger, 1924–1940* (Paris, 1967), 240.

4. Parès, Evain, des Isnards, Le Corbeiller, and Denais were Federation deputies who sat on the executive committee of the Parti National Populaire. Denais, Frédéric-Dupont, Fernand-Laurent, des Isnards, Soulier, Cousin, Henriot, and Taittinger—elected as deputies of the Parti National Populaire—belonged to the Republican Federation. René Dommange was an *apparenté*. The other three, Kerillis, Scapini, and Pinelli, sat as independents.

language, and retained a pronounced undercurrent of anti-Semitism. But unlike its sister Parti Social Français, the Parti Républicain National et Social avoided abusing the old parties and limited its attacks to the Popular Front. Like its predecessor the PNP, the PRNS acted very much like a propaganda auxiliary for the Republican Federation. That the PRNS took on such a benign appearance increasingly disaffected certain of the more militant elements within the party. The youthful Phalangeards in particular disliked Taittinger's growing tendency to counsel patience and discipline rather than to act. In Paris and in some departments, large numbers of former Jeunesses Patriotes reportedly abandoned the docile PRNS for the more active Parti Populaire Française. At the 1938 congress of the PRNS some party members complained that a political party, working with other political parties, could hardly sustain the dynamism of a league. When it was moved that the party, "heir to the spirit of Déroulède and Barrès," acknowledge the failure of the parliamentary regime and plan common action with the other opposition parties, the more militant *congressistes* denounced the proposal as a classical *nègre-blanc* motion, which deliberately left the purposes and mission of the PRNS unclear. Some of the rank and file, well aware of the party's numerous organic links with the Republican Federation, despaired of an independent role for the PRNS and actually proposed a union with the older party.[5]

The Croix de Feu, which had always maintained a greater distance from the conservative political parties than had the Jeunesses Patriotes, followed a far different course after dissolution. Contrary to the advice of several associates, Colonel de la Rocque responded to the government's dissolution of the Croix de Feu by founding the Parti Social Français. He intended the new party to be more than a facade. At the first meeting of the Parti Social Français (PSF) on July 12, 1936, de la Rocque an-

5. APP, 501–1210–3, D329, May 28, 30, June 21, 1938, and 79.501–1210–3, D329, August 1, September 30, October 10, 1936, January 2, May 21, 1937, November 20, 1938; *Le National*, November 26, 1938.

nounced that the new party would resemble the French Socialist party, rather than "a party like that of M. Marin." He did not wish to create "a party of conservatives or of *modérés* who think only of making speeches and who take no action." His party would, on the contrary, be coherently organized at the national, the departmental, and the communal levels. In order to have some parliamentary representation, de la Rocque attempted to reunite the thirty-eight deputies who had belonged to the disbanded Croix de Feu and form a separate parliamentary group of the PSF.[6] Since a large number of these deputies also belonged to the Republican Federation, the formation of the new group inevitably provoked a conflict of loyalties. Xavier Vallat and a majority of the deputies concerned opposed the creation of yet another parliamentary group. Although de la Rocque and his lieutenant Ybarnegaray persisted, the group of the PSF attracted only five (later eight) deputies.[7]

Jean Ybarnegaray, the president of the new group, was incensed at the betrayal of the former members of the Croix de Feu and publicly attacked them as "decadent *salonards.*" Vallat explained his refusal to join the PSF in a lengthy article in the right-wing weekly, *Choc.*

I was, I am and I will remain Croix de Feu member number 2,850. At the same time, I, like almost all of the deputies who belonged to the Croix de Feu, did not believe that I should join the Parti Social Français. My reasons? The first is that I don't see the need to form yet another party when everyone is complaining about the disper-

6. APP, 79.501–2726–2, C327, July 12, 1936; *Le Petit Parisien*, July 13, 1936. Xavier Vallat, *Choc*, August 13, 1936; Xavier Vallat, *Le Nez de Cléopâtre* (Paris, 1957), 132, gives the figure of forty-seven deputies belonging to the Croix de Feu. In neither case did he give any names, although many of the deputies concerned later belonged to the intergroup that was sympathetic to the PSF.

7. These were Jean Ybarnegaray (Basses-Pyrénées), François de Polignac (Maine-et-Loire), Paul Creyssel (Loire), Eugène Pébellier (Haute-Loire), Stanislas Devaud (Constantine), Fernand Robbe (Seine-et-Oise), Emile Peter (Moselle), and François Fourcault de Pavant (Seine-et-Oise). Ybarnegaray and Polignac were former members of the Federation (although de Polignac had seceded with Pernot in 1932). Creyssel and Robbe were former Radicals who had gradually shifted to the Right. Pébellier, Devaud, and Fourcault de Pavant sat with the successor to the *groupe Pernot* before the formation of the PSF. Peter sat with a group of independents from Alsace and Lorraine.

sion of the nationalists into so many diverse groups. The second is that I have found nothing original in the program of the new party. Every aspect of its program can be found in the program of the Republican Federation to which I belong. Political party for political party, why should I leave a group which is the only party of the Right to have registered an electoral victory.[8]

Vallat defended his personal loyalty to Louis Marin and concluded: "The events of the last few weeks have led me to prefer the bow tie of Louis Marin to the commander's baton of Colonel de la Rocque." Vallat was one member of the Republican Federation who, both by background and by temperament, might have found the new party most appealing. His loyalty to the Federation had little to do with repugnance for the authoritarian and paramilitary character of the PSF. Vallat had appreciated the role of the Croix de Feu but failed to see why France needed another conservative party, particularly one that took its role seriously.

The Federation reacted coolly toward the new party. Marin complained that he had seen the formation of many new parties during his political career, and none of them had contributed significantly to the conservative cause. Party leaders agreed that it was sometimes necessary to form pseudoparties to avoid the arbitrary decrees of the sectarian government, but they felt that these parties ought not to attempt to become real political parties that rivaled existing ones. At the Federation's National Council meeting on November 4, 1936, the PSF and its challenge to the Federation were the principal questions on the agenda. Many delegates expressed concern about the growing and often unfriendly rivalry of the PSF. But both Marin and Vallat pointed to the large membership of the PSF and insisted that since dissolution and a new election seemed a distinct pos-

---

8. *Le Flambeau*, July 18, 1936. It was rumored at the time that Vallat had refused to join the PSF because he had not been picked as president of the parliamentary group; the PSF repeated the charge as late as 1938 (*Je Suis Partout*, August 5, 1938). Vallat scoffed at the suggestion that after fourteen years in parliament he could be seduced by the presidency of a group with only eight members (*La Gazette d'Annonay*, August 21, 1937). *Choc*, August 13, 1936.

sibility, it was important that the Federation not sever relations with a neighbor whose services could be invaluable to the older party.[9]

Louis Marin nonetheless expressed serious misgivings about the PSF, and his reasons are significant. He complained that the new party had no program except one stolen from the Federation and embellished slightly with some demagogic social claims. He also charged that the PSF had betrayed the spirit of the Croix de Feu. Those who had supported the Croix de Feu "had believed . . . that the Croix de Feu was preparing, not to be a party, but for the day when there would be disorders in the street." Many of the Croix de Feu, Marin suggested, were surprised and disappointed that de la Rocque did not consider the occupation of the factories to be an appropriate time to intervene in force with his shock troops. They hoped for a more vigorous response from the Croix de Feu in the future and certainly did not expect to become part of another political party. As far as the Republican Federation was concerned, Marin reported: "I know some very ardent people who, from the political point of view remain faithful to us and who tell us: 'We don't expect the Federation to supply shock troops that could, if necessary, march.'" Marin was in effect saying that the Federation was in the business of providing political and parliamentary leadership and not street battalions. Shock troops that could march when there were disorders in the street were the responsibility of the Croix de Feu. Louis Marin found the idea of having readily available shock troops appealing and wished only that Colonel de la Rocque and his followers would get on with that particular task and not attempt to duplicate the activities of the Republican Federation. The older party wanted to preserve the division of labor that had existed before the dissolution of the leagues and feared that the creation of the PSF would disrupt that partnership.

9. *Voir Clair en Politique*, August 1, October 1, 1936; *Réunion du conseil national de la Fédération Républicaine*, November 4, 1936, in Marin Papers, carton 82 (virtually the only example of such a transcript that seems to have survived).

Throughout 1936 relations between the Federation and the PSF remained chilly. Some deputies attempted to form a parliamentary intergroup to facilitate informal contact between the deputies of the PSF and other conservative deputies. Forty-seven deputies, including twenty-two from the Federation, joined the Comité parlementaire de défense des libertés et de sympathie pour le PSF.[10] But the Comité only met once. A few members of the Federation were received warmly at local rallies of the PSF, but usually the PSF chose to keep its distance from the Federation. In January, 1937, when Paul Creyssel, the former independent Radical and now a PSF deputy from the Loire, addressed the annual congress of the Federation of the Rhône with a number of conciliatory remarks, the Federation anticipated an era of "loyal collaboration" between the two parties. The leadership of the PSF suspected correctly, however, that "loyal collaboration" meant that it should renounce its independent political ambitions. Hence, headquarters of the PSF hastened to clarify Creyssel's remarks, assuring the membership that the party was not in "tow of" the Federation and had not modified its "total disgust for the old groupings of politicians." The PSF denied any desire for an alliance with anyone and soon issued regulations prohibiting its members from addressing the meetings of other parties.[11]

The PSF represented a serious challenge to the Republican Federation. By 1937 it was a vigorous and rapidly growing party, claiming two million members. While this figure is certainly an exaggeration, it has been suggested that a membership of between 600,000 and 700,000 would not be unreasonable.[12] If

10. Deputies of the Federation included d'Aillières, d'Aramon, Becquart, Burgeot, Crouan, Cousin, Daher, Frédéric-Dupont, Duval, de Frammond, Guerin, des Isnards, de la Ferronnays, Lardier, Martin, Michel, Poitou-Duplessy, Roulleaux-Dugage, de Saint-Just, Soulier, and Temple. Nine other former members of the Federation included: d'Audiffret-Pasquier, de Kerillis, Peissel, Plichon, Sallès, Taudière, de Tinguy du Pouët, and Weidemann-Goiron. Le Flambeau, December 19, 1936.

11. Philippe Machefer, "Le Parti Social Français en 1936–1937," L'Information Historique, April–May, 1972, p. 74; Le Flambeau, November 21, 1936; L'Heure Française, March 3, 20, April 4, 1937; L'Union Républicaine du Rhône, January 17, 1937; La Nation, February 6, 1937; Volontaire 36, January 15, 1937.

12. Philippe Machefer, "L'Union des droites: Le PSF et le Front de la Liberté, 1936–1937," Revue d'histoire moderne et contemporaine, XVII (1970), 118.

true, the PSF was the largest political party in France and would have outstripped the Republican Federation many times over. The extensive party press of the PSF is indicative of its mass base. By 1937 the party had at least twenty-five regional weekly press organs.[13] Furthermore, in 1937 the party gained control of the Parisian daily, *Le Petit Journal*.

The PSF also created a mass party organization. The newly founded party began with a burst of activity and created a large number of departmental sections almost overnight. By the middle of August, 1936, the party had opened 670 regional offices. Within a few months it had a far more extensive departmental organization than the Federation had ever achieved. In Calvados, for example, where the Federation had many voters but virtually no permanent organization, the PSF claimed fifty-five sections by November, 1936.[14] No doubt much of this organization would not have survived the early enthusiasm of the movement, but in 1937 it made the PSF appear as an extremely energetic rival of the Federation.[15] Organizers of the PSF were quick to point out their party's superiority in this respect. In an exchange of letters with Jacques Poitou-Duplessy, the president of the party in the Charente observed that he had been unable, except in Poitou-Duplessy's constituency, to discover any evidence of a permanent organization of the Republican Federation.[16] The conviction that parties like the Federation did not have much significance outside of Paris and had made relatively little impact on the provincial middle classes made the leaders of the young party all the more aggressive.

It was precisely the aggressive and popular image of the PSF

13. Only about half that number are actually preserved in the Bibliothèque Nationale. The above figure includes journals cited in the various lists of party publications that occasionally appeared in its newspapers. Only those journals that gave evidence of actually having appeared are included.

14. Machefer, "Le Parti Social Français," 74; *Le Flambeau*, November 21, 1936.

15. In 1939, for example, the president of a branch of the PSF in Autun in the Saône-et-Loire, complained of "a relaxation and slowing down of our efforts, marked absences at our meetings and an obvious unwillingness to loosen the purse strings when visited by our delegates." He ascribed this condition to the fact that the revolutionary danger seemed to be past and the fact that the PSF no longer appeared to be doing very much. *Le PSF Autunois*, March, 1939.

16. *Le Réveil Charentais*, June 6, 1937.

that accounted for its rapid growth in 1936 and 1937. It was new, different, and actively involved with those elements of the French population who were frightened by the experience of the mid-1930s and sought a change. Colonel de la Rocque attributed the party's phenomenal growth to its social program, which he believed transcended the sterile conservatism of the *modérés* and appealed to Frenchmen of all classes and ideological persuasions. The PSF prided itself on having drawn adherents from all sides of the political spectrum and on being unlike the reactionary conservative parties. Yet, as the Republican Federation frequently noted, the social program of the PSF did not differ significantly from that of the *modérés*.[17] The regional journals of the PSF read very much like those of the *modérés* with the same articles decrying the decline of natality, the rural depopulation, and the proliferation of costly and irresponsible civil servants. The social program of the PSF resembled that of the Federation in its loud claims to social awareness and its unmistakable and only thinly disguised social conservatism. The PSF did make a more overt appeal to the working classes than did the Federation; but even in publications that were explicitly directed toward the factory worker, the PSF managed to sound as paternalistic and as implausible as the more traditional conservatives. The party's short-lived *Ouvrier Libre*, for example, could openly advertise its upcoming Congrès des Patrons, while at the same time loudly proclaiming the party's "total independence with respect to the capitalist forces."[18]

A far more likely area of recruitment for the PSF was from the ranks of the *modérés*. Although its message was approximately the same as that of the Federation, its style was more exciting, its tone more energetic, and its image not tarnished by thirty years of more or less ineffectual activity. It was, as the Parti

17. For a point-by-point comparison of their respective programs see *La Nation*, December 26, 1936.

18. *L'Ouvrier Libre*, November, 1938. A police report for late 1936 claimed that the executive committee of the PSF had concluded that the working class and white-collar workers were generally sceptical about the party and that those who did belong were probably not to be relied upon in the event of a *coup dur*. Report from the Ministry of the Interior in APP, 79.501–1108–5–B, December 5, 1936.

Démocrate Populaire suggested, "a rejuvenated Republican Federation." The PSF implied that the present deplorable state of France was in some measure the fault of the traditional conservatives and that only a new party could restore social and political order. Those *modérés* who were shaken out of their apolitical complacency by the great fear of 1936–1937 were far more likely to turn to the PSF than to an old party like the Federation. The PSF also made inroads among the *militants* of the Republican Federation. Octave Lavalette, the propaganda delegate of the Federation of the Rhône, complained about the gains that the new parties (particularly the PSF) had made among the rank and file of the party. He told a departmental congress in the Rhône in January, 1937, that the new parties "recruited abundantly from our ranks and . . . the mass of their adherents come, in large measure, from our *militants*." In comparison with the dynamic new parties, the Republican Federation appeared aged and ineffective. A bitter former member of the Federation wrote Marin in 1937: "You are a party of leaders without troops. You have voters but the people don't know about the Republican Federation. [You are] a headquarters without *militants*, without contact with the real people [and] even your electors will abandon you for younger and more energetically social parties." Delegates to the rather dismal 1937 congress of the Federation were preoccupied by the "hemorrhage" among the *militants* provoked by the recruitment of the PSF. One delegate reportedly claimed that 80 percent of the Federation's rank and file had passed over to the PSF.[19]

With a huge membership, a powerful organization, an extensive press, and a greater popular appeal than most conservative parties, the rising PSF was a serious rival to the Republican

19. *Le Petit Démocrate*, January 17, 1937; Pierre Barral, *Le Département de l'Isère sous la IIIe République, 1870–1940* (Paris, 1962), 335; *Rapport sur la propagande, congrès départemental de la Fédération Républicaine du Rhône*, January 9–10, 1937, in Marin Papers, carton 79; [?] to Marin, December 10, 1937, in Marin Papers, carton 88; *Vendémiaire*, June 6, 1936. Emile Buré, director of *Vendémiaire*, was an acute journalist with an extensive knowledge of the right-wing scene. But by the late 1930s he took a perverse pleasure in the problems of the Federation and may have exaggerated the extent of concern over the "hemorrhage."

Federation. The Federation, nevertheless, retained one enormous advantage over the PSF. With sixty deputies compared to eight for the PSF, the Federation was clearly superior to the new party in parliamentary strength. The Republican Federation had traditionally drawn its strength from the number of deputies it attracted, not from the number of *militants*. Conversely, the huge membership of the PSF hardly served the ambitions of the party's leaders unless it could be translated into parliamentary representation. Therefore, it was not surprising that a major struggle between the two parties arose over the issue of a parliamentary by-election.

Mortain, in the west Normand department of La Manche, was typical of the constituencies held by the Federation. It was one of the most solidly conservative seats in France, situated in that region of lower Normandy that had traditionally been strongly conservative and clerical.[20] During the nineteenth century the constituency had been a virtual fief of the Legrand family. Alexis Legrand, director of the department of *ponts et chaussées* and minister of public works under Thiers, represented the constituency from 1832 until 1848. His son, Arthur Legrand, represented Mortain almost continuously from 1871 until 1916. In 1919 Gustave Guerin, a local pharmacist and prominent member of the Federation, gained the seat. Although the Republican Federation performed well electorally in La Manche, it had virtually no organization there. A Republican Federation of La Manche theoretically existed, but in 1937 one disillusioned *militant* from the department wrote Marin complaining that he had been a member of the Federation for seven years and he had yet to see "the slightest sign of life from other members or leaders of the F.R. in my region." The PSF, by comparison, made a concerted effort to organize the department. The departmental president of the PSF of La Manche could claim by January, 1937, to have established sections of the new party in all

20. André Siegfried, *Tableau politique de la France de l'ouest sous la troisième République* (2nd ed.; Paris, 1963), 44–45. *Le Populaire* described the constituency as "one of the most difficult, one of the most reactionary, one of those in which the *chouannerie* exercises its domination." *Le Populaire*, April 12, 1937.

of the department's cantons and many of its communes. He boasted of having made La Manche within six months *"le département le plus PSF de France."* Consequently, in December, 1936, when Guerin was elected to the Senate and the seat fell vacant, the PSF sought to capture it.[21]

The first candidate to declare himself was Georges Normand, a local dairy farmer. Typically, Normand had not hitherto been a member of the Federation, but he promised to sit with the party's group if elected. On December 26, therefore, he received the endorsement of the Federation and its local supporting newspaper, *Le Glaneur de la Manche.*[22] The departmental branch of the PSF held a congress three weeks later and selected a Dr. A. Gautier as its candidate. Gustave Guerin, the retiring deputy, attended the congress and announced his support for the candidate of the PSF. Guerin, who was still unaware of the candidacy of Normand, acknowledged his firm allegiance to the Republican Federation and to Louis Marin. However, he felt that he could support Gautier because he was a personal friend and because the PSF and the Federation had, in his eyes, "the same desires, the same aspirations and the same goals."[23]

Le Glaneur de la Manche, supporting the candidate of the Federation, received the news of Gautier's candidacy with considerable ill humor and pointedly asked why the PSF was contesting a seat that had always been safely in the hands of the Federation. One commentator wondered what a party that prided itself on being "the party of reconciliation" hoped to achieve in a region that always voted for the *modérés.* The PSF (*"parti sans franchise"*) was characterized as a "Parisian party," its candidate a city slicker imposing himself on the good farmers of Mortain. Guerin's behavior also annoyed *Le Glaneur,* which

21. Adolphe Robert and Gaston Cougny (eds.), *Dictionnaire des parlementaires françaises* (5 vols.; Paris, 1889–91), IV, 70–72; Guiter's records for 1939, in Marin Papers, carton 75; [?] to Marin, December 10, 1937, in Marin Papers, carton 88; *Le Mortainais,* January 22, 1937.

22. *Le Glaneur de la Manche,* April 10, 1937. Although not officially affiliated with the Federation, *Le Glaneur* was openly sympathetic and during the Mortain election faithfully echoed the latest declarations of the Federation's central office.

23. *Le Mortainais,* January 22, 1937; *Le Glaneur de la Manche,* January 23, 1937.

publicly wondered why he was supporting a candidate of another party. The central office of the Federation found Guerin's position awkward and dispatched an executive member. His presence, however, did not deter Guerin from supporting Gautier, nor *Le Glaneur* from castigating Guerin. Ultimately, Marin summoned Guerin to Paris and demanded an explanation. Guerin explained, plausibly enough, that he had supported Gautier because he had no idea that Georges Normand was a member of the Republican Federation. He added that he would only adopt a more neutral stance if *Le Glaneur* ceased its vitriolic attacks on the PSF. Jean Guiter formally requested that *Le Glaneur* moderate its election commentary, but the tone of the campaign did not change significantly.[24]

By this time a second candidate of the Republican Federation had entered the contest. At the end of February, *Le Glaneur* announced that "a number of important personalities in the electoral constituency of Mortain, anxious to preserve this constituency for that great national party, the Republican Federation, of which M. Guerin is a member . . . have solicited M. Jacques Legrand to present himself as a candidate." Legrand, the grandson of Arthur Legrand (the former deputy in the constituency), conducted a personal inquiry among the *notables* of the region and declared himself a candidate on March 17. The executive of the Federation, faced with two candidates, initially decided to support "all candidates who declare themselves to be of the party of Louis Marin and in favor of his program." It was soon apparent, however, that the Federation's representative, Bouteille, favored the more promising candidate, Legrand. Normand offered to withdraw in favor of Legrand if Gautier did as well. Understandably, the candidate of the PSF refused, and Normand remained a candidate. The presence of two candidates representing the same party finally became so embarrassing that the Federation, at the last minute, abandoned Normand.[25]

24. *Le Glaneur de la Manche*, February 1, 26, March 6, April 17, 1937; *Le Mortainais*, March 13, 1937.

25. *Le Glaneur de la Manche*, February 27, March 20, April 10, 17, 1937.

During the campaign, Bouteille and *Le Glaneur* mounted a sustained assault on the PSF and its candidate. They emphasized that, whereas Normand and Legrand were of old Mortainais stock, Gautier (like his party) was a newcomer and an interloper. (Gautier had in fact lived in Mortain for fifteen years.) Representatives of the Federation played on the supposedly totalitarian character of the PSF. Legrand spoke of "the PSF which envisages taking power by force and if necessary by bloodshed." Bouteille raised the issue of the PSF's changed image. At an election rally he goaded his opponents: "I remind you that for two years you harped on your D day and your H hour, your conquest of power by force, your affirmations that all parliamentarians were worthless. Today you want to elect deputies. When were you sincere? Two years ago or now?" At one point *Le Glaneur* claimed that the PSF had adopted Hitlerian tactics by drawing up a list of possible hostages in preparation for the proposed seizure of power—a list that was remarkably similar to the one the Communists were known to have. *Le Glaneur* also declared the PSF's position on religious and social questions to be equivocal and the party's celebrated formula, *ni à droite, ni à gauche*, to be a cheap trick which proved only that it was afraid to declare itself.[26]

There were seven candidates on the first ballot: Gautier; Legrand; Dr. Emile Malon, representing the Alliance Démocratique; Leroux, independent; Grandin, Socialist; and Longle, Communist. The results were: Gautier—4,917; Malon—3,071; Legrand—1,161; Grandin—825; Normand—773; Leroux—282; Longle—129. In the face of Gautier's overwhelmingly superior performance and in accordance with a preelection agreement between the two parties, both Legrand and Normand withdrew in favor of Gautier—but with such obvious bad grace as to leave little doubt as to their indifference to Gautier's fate on the second ballot.[27]

On the second ballot Gautier received a total of 5,718 votes;

26. *Ibid.*, March 10, April 3, 10, 1937.
27. *Ibid.*, April 3, 1937.

but Dr. Malon, the only remaining candidate, pulled ahead with some 5,784 votes. It was apparent that even after the candidates of the Left rallied behind Dr. Malon, he could not have won without receiving a substantial portion of the votes that had gone to Legrand and Normand on the first ballot. Since Gautier received only 800 additional votes on the second ballot, even had all of Normand's votes gone to Malon, a good 300 supporters of the official candidate of the Republican Federation must have broken discipline and helped deliver the constituency to the Alliance Démocratique. In a strongly Catholic constituency like Mortain, a victory for the traditionally laic Alliance represented a substantial shift to the Left.

The PSF was furious with the results of the election. The party expressed its outrage at the "treason" of the Federation and the vile campaign of *Le Glaneur* and Désiré Bouteille. The formal withdrawals of Legrand and Normand were inadequate compensation for two months of abuse. The presence of two candidates representing the same party made a mockery of the Federation's claim to be united and disciplined. For Colonel de la Rocque, the Mortain election proved that the old parties were composed of "sectarian fossils who are disturbed by [the PSF's] social program and dynamism." One local journal of the PSF bitterly commented that the Federation seemed to assume that parliamentary seats belonged to a party "by virtue of age or by a kind of predestination." It was not only the parties of the Left, the journal concluded, that felt at home in *"la république des camarades."*[28]

The Mortain election had disturbing implications for the Federation. It placed the party in the unenviable position of appearing as an undisciplined and disruptive force on the Right. More important, it revealed the threat represented by the electoral appeal of the PSF. In what had hitherto been a safe seat for the Federation, the candidate of the PSF had performed significantly better than Legrand and Normand combined. Official-

28. *Le Flambeau*, April 24, 1937; *Le Ralliement du Nord*, May 20, 1937.

ly, the Federation countered that the real disruptive force was the PSF, which instead of contesting seats held by representatives of the Popular Front, specialized in besieging seats that were safely in the hands of the *modérés*. The party attributed the strong showing of the PSF on the first ballot, not to the intrinsic appeal of the new party but to the support of Gustave Guerin. More significant, it argued, were the second-ballot figures, which showed the PSF to be incapable of gaining the support of a critical percentage of the *modérés*. Xavier Vallat noted: "Not only has the PSF not made inroads on the troops of the Left—as it so proudly boasts—but it can't even succeed in gathering all the votes of the *modérés* behind its candidates." Party spokesmen repeatedly asserted that Gautier would have won easily as a candidate of the Republican Federation, but many potential voters "could not understand why he associated himself with a formation which . . . gives the impression of being the party of a man who serves an authoritarian and dictatorial mystique." Although several members of the Federation questioned this self-righteous explanation, the bulk of the party accepted the official interpretation of the Mortain election.[29]

The Mortain election elucidated several critical aspects of the relationship between the Federation and the PSF. To *Le Glaneur* and the party faithful in Mortain, the Republican Federation was not so much a political party (and still less an organization) as it was a political tradition. In defending the Federation against the PSF they were defending a traditional style of politics, in which the candidates were selected by the local *notables* (if not by virtual inheritance) and not by party congresses. For them the Republican Federation represented a traditional and unequivocal Catholic conservatism. The new parties with their strange slogans, such as *ni à droite, ni à gauche*, smacked of

29. *L'Union Républicaine du Rhône*, April 25, May 9, 1937. At the party congress in June, Edouard Frédéric-Dupont challenged the executive's handling of the election, and the congress temporarily fell into an uproar. Most delegates, however, appear to have approved the actions of the executive. *Le Temps*, June 6, 1937; *L'Ordre*, June 5, 1937; *Le Flambeau*, June 12, 1937.

something foreign, not only to La Manche but to France. Certainly, most of the references to the dictatorial and authoritarian quality of the PSF were simply campaign rhetoric.[30] But in the eyes of its supporters, the Republican Federation stood for the grandson of a nineteenth-century deputy, whereas the PSF implied an *arriviste* town dweller with unreliable big-city friends.

Yet many *modérés* did not react to the PSF in the same fashion. Over half of Guerin's 1936 voters found Gautier to be acceptable, notwithstanding his PSF label. Guerin was in no sense a rebel within the Federation; he had, in fact, been one of Marin's closest supporters. His statements at the time reflect an honest bewilderment. Since the PSF and the Federation had, in his opinion, essentially the same program, he could not see that it mattered very much which of the two parties represented Mortain.

The reason it mattered, of course, was that the PSF was a young party trying to grow and the Federation was an old party trying to hold on to its parliamentary strength. The Mortain election clearly demonstrated the weakness of the Republican Federation when confronted with the energetic new party. Guerin could probably have turned the election any way he wished, but the Republican Federation itself proved that it could do little. Judging by the activity of its Paris headquarters, the party obviously wanted to win this contest yet was unable even to achieve a single candidacy until three days before the election. The PSF had a genuine party organization in the department; the Federation did not. Consequently, when Gustave Guerin went to the PSF congress (as a man of the Federation) to nominate his friend, he did not know that Normand had been nominated by a group of village mayors and had been a candi-

30. During the campaign, *Le Glaneur* raked far and wide for dirt to sling at the PSF and its supporters. It printed a letter from a diligent reader who, having leafed through back issues of the newspaper, discovered that while running for the departmental general council in 1907 Guerin had complained of the excessive influence of the Jews in Paris. The reader wondered why, thirty years later, Guerin was supporting the candidate of a party whose leader, de la Rocque, had recently announced that the PSF was open to Jews. *Le Glaneur de la Manche*, March 6, 1937.

date of the Republican Federation for three weeks. Faced with an ambitious rival on the Right, the Republican Federation was hard pressed to defend itself. The mobilization of the conservative masses, theoretically so desirable given the danger from the Left, threatened to work against an elite party like the Federation. The recently aroused *modérés* should have furnished the conservative elite with reliable troops to counter an eventual Communist insurrection and to improve the electoral fortunes of the conservative parties. Instead, in the hands of the PSF they were being used to displace the Federation from its dominant position on the far Right. It was this that permanently poisoned relations between the two parties.

In fact, electoral rivalries (rather than ideological or programmatic differences) governed the relations between the Republican Federation and the new parties. Unorthodox political programs disturbed the Federation far less than did threats to its parliamentary strength. Although the Federation feuded bitterly with the PSF (whose program so resembled its own), it was prepared to collaborate closely with a party with distinctly fascist qualities—Jacques Doriot's Parti Populaire Français.

The leaders of the Parti Populaire Français (PPF) came from much less respectable political backgrounds than did their counterparts in the PSF and held far less orthodox political and social views. A *modéré* would feel far more at home with a journal of the PSF than with one of the Parti Populaire Français. The latter, reflecting the former communism of many of the new party's leaders, clearly appealed to a lower-class clientele, denounced the betrayal of the Communists, and expressed relatively little concern for the problem of order. A number of the directors of the PPF, led by Pierre Pucheu, had come to the party from the PSF precisely because de la Rocque's party proved to be so conservative. Initially, the Republican Federation was unenthusiastic about the formation of yet another right-wing party headed by a former Communist and grumbled about the phenomenon of "wolves become shepherds." But Doriot's PPF, like Taittinger's Parti Républicain National et Social, never became a serious electoral rival of the Federation and did not stridently abuse the old parties. Indeed, the PPF accorded the Federation a certain deference, recognized it as "the principal party of the opposition," and admitted that "the Republican Federation is rich in talent and particularly rich in young talent." In the Rhône the local branch of the PPF openly sympathized with the Republican Federation and wrote enthusiastically about the work of Victor Perret.[31]

In April, 1937, when Doriot proposed a union of all non-Marxist parties to be known as the Front de la Liberté, the Federation, followed almost immediately by the Parti Républicain National et Social, expressed unqualified approval. Louis Marin welcomed the plan, regretting only that the minimum program of the Front, the defense of civil liberties, could not be extended to cover other issues. The prospect of entering into an alliance with a former Communist of doubtful republicanism did not perturb the leaders of the Federation. When asked why he was willing to work with a "former Communist enragé," Xavier Vallat replied that had he, like Doriot, been thrown at an early age into the slums of Paris instead of growing up in a patriotic environment, he would "doubtlessly have acted as Doriot did and would perhaps not have the courage he has shown today." Jacques Poitou-Duplessy suddenly remembered that as far back as 1927 he "couldn't help being struck by the sincerity that emanated from his person . . . and began to hope that one day, repentant of his errors, he would join us."[32] Undeterred by the fascist sentiments expressed by some members of the PPF, the Federation eagerly sought an alliance with its new neighbor.

In this the Republican Federation was virtually alone, for neither the Alliance Démocratique nor the Parti Démocrate Populaire seriously contemplated joining the Front de la Liberté.

31. Dieter Wolf, *Doriot, du communisme à la collaboration* (Paris, 1969), 168–69; Jean Baudouin, *La Nation*, July 18, 1936; *La Liberté*, November 17, 1938; *L'Attaque*, August 7, 1937.

32. *Gringoire*, April 30, 1937; *La Gazette d'Annonay*, July 14, 1937; *Le Réveil Charentais*, August 22, 1937.

Not only did it involve "the politics of two blocs," which they were determined to avoid, but it also represented a highly unsavory union. The Alliance lumped together the Federation and the new parties as representatives of "a reactionary conservatism." The PDP rejected the Front because it contained "all of the adversaries, inadvertent and otherwise, of democracy." The Federation's eagerness to ally with the most sordid elements of the extreme, antirepublican Right was indicative of the anxiety of some conservatives during the year of the Popular Front. Faced with the need to preserve the social order from the threat of revolution or even sweeping reform, the Federation effectively concluded that it had no enemies on its right. As Emile Buré, a perceptive and critical commentator on the French Right, observed in 1937: "What a curious state of mind these bourgeois of the Front de la Liberté have; they pay so that a counter-revolution may take from them what the Revolution left to them."[33]

The Republican Federation had a further reason for supporting the Front de la Liberté. The substantive content of the Front—defense of liberty in all its forms—was so vague that the Front had little meaning except insofar as it provided for a truce between the parties of the Right.[34] Victor Perret emphasized that the essential feature of the Front was "mutual respect for the established position [of parties] and unconditional support for all deputies who . . . have not proved unworthy." He added that the Front would have to leave "each deputy with . . . the complete freedom to rejoin [in the Chamber] . . . the formation of his party." Seen in this light, the Front de la Liberté presented the Federation with an opportunity to defend itself from

33. L'Alliance Démocratique, April 23, 1937; Le Petit Démocrate, May 5, 1937; Vendémiaire, August 25, 1937.

34. The minimum program of the Front was: (1) defense of the freedoms of association, thought, work, commerce, and the press; (2) defense of republican institutions; (3) prohibition against attacks on parties which, although belonging to the Popular Front, had protested against the attacks on freedom; (4) prohibition against mutual criticism among the parties belonging to the Front de la Liberté during the period of common action; (5) the right of the concerned groups and parties to expose their programs in their entirety at their individual meetings. Wolf, Doriot, 256.

the attacks of its too ambitious rival, the Parti Social Français. Others thought so too. One commentator for the Parti Démocrate Populaire noted: "The Republican Federation, whose parliamentary representation remains important, but whose troops have begun to desert can, by adhering to the Front de la Liberté, gain back many of those who now follow the PSF." He considered the Front to be "above all a committee for electoral coordination where, by virtue of the number of its deputies, the Republican Federation would regain the advantage *vis-à-vis* the new formations."[35]

The attitude of the PSF toward the Front was therefore critical. The PSF began negotiations with Doriot but nonetheless expressed serious reservations about the Front de la Liberté. De la Rocque distrusted Doriot, whom he correctly suspected of designs on the PSF.[36] Furthermore, the PSF felt that the formation of a right-wing union was incompatible with its task of national reconciliation and would only consolidate a Popular Front that appeared to be falling apart. Most important, the PSF protested that the Front, by providing for a political truce between adhering parties and for the preservation of the electoral status quo, constituted a trap for the PSF set by parties like the Federation. The PSF, de la Rocque announced, did not wish "to be reduced to the role of a 'league' at the disposal of the conservatives and *modérés*."[37] In fact, the PSF understood exactly what the Republican Federation expected from the Front de la Liberté. In 1938 when the question of an eventual Front de la Liberté was briefly reopened, the leader of the PSF explained his fears to a meeting in Lille.

> Let us examine only one of the parties that make up [the Front], the most important, the Republican Federation. It insists on principle that all political offices presently held by candidates belonging to the

35. *La Nation*, May 22, 1937; *Le Petit Démocrate*, May 30, 1937.
36. Machefer, "L'Union des droites," 112–26; Wolf, *Doriot*, 255.
37. *Le Flambeau*, June 12, 1937; see also the assessment of the Parisian journal of the PSF, *Les Libertés Républicaines du XIXe*, September, 1937. It charged the organizers of the Front with seeking "to incorporate the PSF into the Front in order to constrain its magnificent forces and to neutralize its president by submerging him in an assembly of leaders without troops."

parties of the Front must be maintained for them at the next election. What then? We who are newcomers to politics would content ourselves with giving the old parties the support of our considerable membership without being able to try our luck at the elections. We would become, in reality, a troop at the service of the other parties; we would no longer be a party in the real sense, but a league.[38]

The national council of the PSF ultimately rejected the Front de la Liberté, arguing that it would mean "the complete protection in the next election, of certain deputies who represent only conservatism and a condemned style of parliamentarianism" and would consequently "provoke the legitimate discontent of our *militants*."[39]

This pointed rejection, coming on the heels of the Mortain debacle, provoked a series of savage swipes by the Federation. The PSF, it announced, had become "the greatest common divider" of the forces of the Right and had succeeded only in giving comfort to the Popular Front. The "reconciliation" of which the PSF boasted had given way to disruption, and, as Henriot observed, the eternal flame of the Croix de Feu had become the torch of the PSF. Some, like Victor Perret, patronizingly urged "wisdom, prudence and moderation" on the PSF.[40] Others, like Vallat and Henriot, launched a series of vicious *ad hominum* attacks against Colonel de la Rocque. In this they were aided by the embarrassing revelations of the former member of the Croix de Feu, Pozzo di Borgo, which began to appear shortly after the failure of the Front de la Liberté. Pozzo di Borgo contended, among other things, that de la Rocque, the great exponent of independence, had for years been on the payroll of André Tardieu. Vallat and Henriot seized upon these charges and predicted the imminent demise of the leader of the PSF.[41]

38. *Le Flambeau de Flandre, Artois et Picardie*, May 22, 1938. De la Rocque made a similar speech in the Savoie in 1937; see *Volontaire 36*, June 18, 1937.

39. Fernand Robbe, *Le Parti Social Français et le Front de la Liberté* (Paris, 1937), 20.

40. Xavier Vallat, *La Gazette d'Annonay*, August 21, 1937; *Jeunesse 37*, May 1, 1937; *L'Union Républicaine du Rhône*, June 20, 1937.

41. Pozzo di Borgo's revelations and much of the subsequent confused debate ap-

Spokesmen for the Federation often struck at the PSF's political vagueness, in particular its claim to be *ni à droite, ni à gauche.* No one interpreted this slogan as a vague fascistic longing for a "third way." In the eyes of the Federation the slogan *ni à droite, ni à gauche* was simply a cheap (and unsuccessful) electoral trick and a new formula for a very old form of centrism. Significantly, the Federation charged the PSF, not with being an extremist group beyond the fringes of republican respectability, but with opportunistically taking refuge in the realm of the political Center. Indeed, by 1937 representatives of the Federation repeatedly berated the PSF for acting like the centrist Alliance Démocratique and perhaps even standing to that party's left.[42] Like so many groups before it, the Federation concluded, the PSF was trying to improve its electoral and parliamentary position by posing as something other than what it was—a party of the Right.

Ultimately the Republican Federation reproached the PSF, not for being merely the Croix de Feu under another name, but on the contrary for being the negation of the former league. Xavier Vallat complained that he could find in the PSF "neither the spirit nor the renovating methods of the Croix de Feu." Victor Perret wrote: "The Parti Social Français was born from the Croix de Feu, magnificent association in which we had put so much hope. . . . Faithful to the union and the spirit of the trenches . . . and sitting above all the political parties it could exercise a powerful influence on national life. Once it had become a political party, the great association found itself surrounded by problems." Once in the political arena the PSF hindered rather than helped the conservative forces, and "the

---

peared in the pages of *Choc*, a right-wing weekly. Among the numerous contemporary polemical works on the question see: Duc Pozzo di Borgo, *La Rocque: fantome à vendre* (Paris, 1938); François Veuillot, *La Rocque et son parti* (Paris, 1938); Paul Creyssel, *La Rocque contre Tardieu* (Paris, 1938); Maurice Pujo, *Comment la Rocque a trahi* (Paris, 1938); Pierre Dominique, *Vente et achat* (Paris, 1937). *Jeunesse 37*, August 14, 28, 1937.

42. *La Nation*, February 6, 1937; *La Gazette d'Annonay*, October 2, 18, 1937; *Le Glaneur de la Manche*, December 11, 1937; *Jeunesse 37*, May 1, 1937; *L'Union Républicaine du Rhône*, March 3, 1937.

principal victim was the Republican Federation." The Croix de Feu never appeared as attractive as it did in the era of the PSF.[43]

Relations between the Federation and the PSF remained tense throughout 1937 and 1938. Personal issues exacerbated the interparty feuding. The attacks of Vallat and Henriot on de la Rocque and Vallat's defense of Pozzo di Borgo provoked violent reaction from the PSF rank and file.[44] In 1938 when Vallat and Henriot attempted to speak in Lyon, their meetings were broken up by hooting bands of the PSF. The provocative demeanor of Vallat and Henriot upset some members of the Federation and prompted a few resignations. Some deputies disapproved of their offensive against de la Rocque. Deputies like André Daher, who had managed to stay on reasonably cordial terms with the PSF in Marseilles, resented the disruption in relations caused by the virulence of their colleagues.[45]

But the rivalry between the two parties went further than questions of personalities. The PSF made a concerted effort to displace what it considered to be an "antique formation," confident (as one of its local branches expressed it) that few Frenchmen would prefer the *eau de guimauve* of the Federation to our hearty wine." It continued to pressure those deputies of the Federation who had formerly been associated with the Croix de Feu to join the PSF. In 1938, for example, Pierre Burgeot in

43. *La Gazette d'Annonay*, October 18, 1937; *L'Union Républicaine du Rhône*, November 28, 1937.

44. Pozzo di Borgo was implicated in the so-called Cagoule, a 1937 plot against the state led by a small group of right-wing extremists. Since Pozzo had begun the intensive personal attack on de la Rocque, the PSF was furious when Vallat, a lawyer and personal friend of Borgo's, offered to act as his defense counsel. The Federation was in no way connected with the Cagoule, and most of the party observed a discreet silence on the subject. Vallat admitted that "half a dozen fools or *agents provocateurs*" had been guilty of reckless action but insisted that Pozzo di Borgo was innocent. He saw the Cagoule as a minor incident exploited by a Popular Front that needed a new issue to cement it back together again. *L'Union Républicaine du Rhône*, April 3, 1937. Henriot also dismissed the Cagoule as the work of "a few unstable types, certainly more naive than dangerous" and "gifted with more ingenuousness than common sense." *Jeunesse 37*, December 1, 1937.

45. *L'Union Républicaine du Rhône*, February 27, 1938; [?] to Marin in late 1937, in Marin Papers, carton 88; Pierre Renouard to Marin, September 1, 1936, in Marin Papers, carton 85; Guiter to Marin, November 25, 1937, 317 AP 79.

the Rhône and André Daher in Marseilles received ultimatums from the local branches of the PSF ordering them to join the new party or face opposition in the 1940 election. Despite the undeniable electoral assistance they had received from the Croix de Feu in 1936, both refused, insisting that their first allegiance was to the Federation.[46]

Local branches of the Republican Federation resented the invasion of a rival PSF organization. The president of the Federation's branch in the Hazebrouck, Eugène Warein, had appreciated the role of the Croix de Feu, who were "valiantly serving the national cause by demanding the most difficult and thankless assignments." He became less enthusiastic after the founding of the local section of the PSF and firmly requested that the new organization "respect our situation in the *arrondissement*" and "organize only in those communes that have as yet no nationalist political organization." The PSF, he hoped, would "not disrupt the [Federation's] troops who are already seasoned by numerous struggles." The Federation, Warein declared, would not let itself be "absorbed" by the PSF, and shortly afterward he published a detailed list of the areas of the arrondissement that the Federation considered to be its exclusive territory. Although a serious jurisdictional dispute was avoided, as late as March, 1938, the leaders of the Federation were still reminding the PSF not to "duplicate" its organization.[47] The Federation of Hazebrouck was unconcerned by the programs or the aim of the PSF but did regard the new party as a superfluous rival, competing for the same electoral clientele.

In the Rhône Victor Perret strove to avoid an open rift with

46. *Réalité*, March 6, 1937; Pierre Burgeot to Marin, May 13, 1938, Burgeot to the president of the PSF of the sixth arrondissement of Lyon, May 12, 1938, André Daher to Jacques Arnoult (president of the PSF of Marseilles), April 22, 1938, all in Marin Papers, carton 88.

47. *L'Entente Républicaine Démocratique de Hazebrouck*, June, October, November, 1936, March, 1938. Warein wrote: "On this matter I hereby inform you that we have created a section of the Entente in each of the villages of the two cantons of Hazebrouck with the exception of Blaringhem and Renescure, where, however, our women's section has already begun to organize, and Bine, Pradelles and Strazeele. Furthermore, we have sections at Steenvoorde and at Vieux-Berguin."

the PSF, but here too the aggressive attitude of the younger party rendered cooperation difficult. Prior to the 1937 cantonal elections, the Federation of the Rhône and the PSF reached an accord which involved, as Perret noted, "the most painful sacrifices" for the Federation. In 1934 the Federation had presented thirty candidates; in 1937 it presented only fourteen, the PSF ten, and the PPF two. But the PSF was unimpressed by the "sacrifices" of the Federation and assured its members that it could have presented candidates everywhere and done very well. The party boasted: "We abandoned to the Republican Federation . . . those constituencies where we had the best chance of capturing seats. For ourselves we reserved those where the struggle was desperate."[48] Not content even with the substantial concessions by the Federation, the Parisian headquarters of the PSF at the last minute demanded parity with the Federation and insisted that two of its candidates withdraw in favor of the new party. Two candidates of the Federation reluctantly agreed to retire, and one of them even agreed to campaign for the PSF.

In one of these two constituencies, however, the local supporters of the Federation refused to accept such an abrupt change. In St. Laurent de Chamousset a group of local mayors who belonged to the Federation and who had traditionally nominated the candidates announced that it "could not accept that such brutal discipline should be imposed upon them from Paris in the name of a new party." Consequently, the group nominated one of its members, Colonel La Batie, to oppose the newly appointed candidate of the PSF. La Batie dutifully submitted his resignation from the Federation, whose leaders accepted it "with tears in their eyes." After a vituperative campaign by both sides, La Batie outdistanced the candidate of the PSF by a handful of votes on the first ballot. His rival formally withdrew in favor of La Batie but not before asking his electors to "forget their disgust." In the exchange of insults that followed this elec-

48. *L'Union Républicaine du Rhône*, September 26, 1937; *Volontaire 36*, December 3, 1937.

tion, Alexandre Bosse-Platière countered the accusations of indiscipline that emanated from the PSF: "With us there is no chief who dominates: there is a leader who treats us as collaborators and friends. We of the Republican Federation don't wear uniforms, we have never paraded. We are not *sans-culottes*, we are *sans-chemises*." Slightly disrespectful newcomers like the PSF, Bosse-Platière suggested, ought to refrain from lecturing a party of the stature of the Federation.[49]

Tensions arising from the designation of conservative candidates often lay at the root of the animosity between the Federation and the PSF. The relative political neophytes in the PSF eagerly sought to break the monopoly of the traditional political elites over conservative politics. In a 1938 by-election in La Roche sur Yon in the Vendée, an assembly of mayors chose Pierre de Chabot as a candidate of the Republican Federation to replace the recently deceased Jean de Suzannet, also of the Federation. The local section of the PSF objected to such a nominating procedure. It felt that by relying exclusively on the mayors the local *notables* had ignored the wishes of the rank and file of the PSF, who were not as yet well represented in the *mairies* of the constituency. The president of the local section of the PSF recommended that his followers submit blank ballots in the election. In the Vendée a *modéré* did not really need the support of the PSF, and de Chabot won without difficulty despite a total of 2,250 blank ballots. The national office of the PSF disavowed the actions of the local president. However, shortly afterward the political director of the party, Edmond Barrachin, assured a meeting of the PSF in the department that the time was past when the local *notables* could manage an election without consulting the powerful PSF.[50]

Sometimes it was precisely those who felt themselves to be

49. *L'Union Républicaine du Rhône*, January 9, 1938; *Volontaire 36*, December 3, 1937. It would be tempting to make more of Bosse-Platière's apparent distaste for armbands and uniforms, but the ease with which he rallied to the National Revolution two years later suggests that his objections were essentially rhetorical ones.

50. *La Dépêche Vendéenne*, March 27, 1938; *La Province*, March 26, 1938; *Samedi*, May 14, 1938.

excluded from traditional conservative politics who were the most active leaders of the PSF. In the Loire-Inférieure the conservative candidate was nominated by a Comité de la Droite— an extremely powerful committee in that ultraconservative department since its nominee was certain of being elected. In 1937 when Jacques de Juingé (a deputy affiliated with the Federation) moved to the Senate, the Comité de la Droite selected a local supporter of the Federation, Augustin Dutertre de la Coudre, as his replacement. Another *modéré* attempted to contest the by-election, but the Comité forced him to withdraw, thus assuring Dutertre de la Coudre's election. The dissident conservative subsequently became president of the PSF of the Loire-Inférieure and an outspoken critic of both the Comité and the Federation.[51]

It was generally recognized that a final reckoning between the Federation and the PSF would come at the general elections of 1940, at which time, de la Rocque promised, the PSF would contest all seats including those of "certain veterans of old formations."[52] The PSF might well have gained a number of seats in 1940, mostly at the expense of the Republican Federation. How great the inroads of the PSF would have been is impossible to say. Without a revival of the Popular Front and the danger from the Left, it is difficult to see how the PSF could have sustained the enthusiasm of 1936–1937. The controversy surrounding de la Rocque, as well as the growing parliamentarianism of the PSF, might well have dampened the ardor of some of its adherents. Furthermore, the strength of the Federation lay not in numbers but in the allegiance of local elites and electorally secure deputies. Provided these remained faithful (and the behavior of some of them in the late 1930s suggests that they might have), the Federation could have retained many of its seats despite the inferiority of the party apparatus.

The social and political turmoil of the 1930s deeply frightened French conservatives and made them fear a drastic modification,

51. *La Province*, September 14, 1938.
52. *Le Petit Journal*, October 9, 1938.

if not the total collapse, of the existing social order. The more moderate conservatives in the Alliance Démocratique and the Parti Démocrate Populaire were disturbed by the Popular Front but recognized the fragility of the left-wing alliance and placed their hopes on a centrist coalition with the Radicals. The more extreme conservatives, particularly those of the Republican Federation, had less faith in the stability of the social and political order and sought new and more potent allies in order to ward off an impending social upheaval. The pre-1936 leagues had a special appeal for an elite party like the Republican Federation because they could attract a mass membership, which conservative parties did not command. They provided invaluable allies for the Federation, both as electoral auxiliaries and as counterrevolutionary shock troops. Despite its formal republican and democratic scruples, the Federation did not look too closely at the political coloration of its prospective allies. In any case, programmatically the leagues borrowed most of their ideas from the *modérés*. Although more skeptical of parliament than most *modérés* and more authoritarian in outlook, the leagues were close enough to the traditional conservatives to permit a substantial overlapping of membership. Insofar as the conservatives in the Republican Federation worried about the violent and extralegal character of the leagues, their chief concern was that irresponsible or restless elements in the leagues might prompt a left-wing counterattack with revolutionary consequences. The possibility of a fascist seizure of power worried the Federation far less than either a Communist or even a radically reformist victory.

Inevitably, there were strains in the partnership between the leagues and the Republican Federation. The leagues arose as a reaction against the threat from the Left and the chaos and impotence of parliament. But they also represented a protest against the sterile and ineffectual conservatism of parties like the Republican Federation. During the 1930s it was tempting for the leagues to blame the sad state of France on the repeated failures of the *modérés*. Such charges were often unfair. Louis Marin's record during the previous twenty years compared favorably to that of a Taittinger or an Ybarnegaray. But by 1935 it was galling for a man like Colonel de la Rocque to see a political formation that had in some sense failed acting as if it were still the guiding light of the French Right. As the leagues grew, they became less willing to play a purely supportive and subordinate role. Nevertheless, prior to June, 1936, the tension between the "new" and the "old" Right did not prevent them from cooperating closely in the struggle against the Popular Front.

Right-wing extraparliamentary formations could be of value to the Republican Federation, but rival right-wing parties could not. The Federation cooperated harmoniously with the Parti Républicain National et Social and the Parti Populaire Français because these parties did not seek to challenge the position of the older party. The Parti Social Français, however, took its role as a political party seriously and immediately conflicted with the Republican Federation. The Federation still sought allies, as its reaction to the Front de la Liberté indicated, but it could see no value in a right-wing party that competed for an identical electoral clientele and that merely sought to replace the Federation's deputies with ones of its own. The Federation sometimes leveled the charge of authoritarianism against the Parti Social Français, but these references were almost always made in the larger context of electoral struggles and were simply part of the lexicon of insults to be used against the disrupters of traditional conservative politics. The Federation saw the PSF as a threat, not to French democracy but to its own political fortunes.

Although the so-called "new" Right and the traditional conservatives had much in common, the founders of the Republican Federation would have felt ill at ease in the company of Pierre Taittinger, Colonel de la Rocque, and Jacques Doriot. However, they had lived in a more stable age, less haunted by the specter of revolution. Republican purity was a luxury the beleaguered conservatives of the 1930s could not afford. Indeed, as the next chapter shows, so traumatic was the experience of the 1930s that the Republican Federation not only compromised its republican loyalty but temporarily abandoned one of its fundamental conservative attributes—its firm and Germanophobic nationalism.

VI. *From Nationalism to Appeasement*

The same social and political crises that forced the Republican Federation to reexamine its attitude toward the forces of the "new" Right also provoked a fundamental reassessment of the party's intransigent nationalism. During the 1920s and 1930s the Republican Federation had been the most nationalistic political party in France—the party that had posed as watchdog over French security and had routinely excoriated French governments for their naïve or cowardly concessions to the Germans. It had been the party that was least sympathetic to international organizations, to detente with Germany, or to any revision of the Treaty of Versailles. To be sure, the Federation was inconsistent in the application of its principles. The party's foreign policy program, faithfully echoed at annual congresses, was occasionally ignored in parliament; and at times only a small minority led by Louis Marin remained true to the Federation's nationalistic doctrine. But the internal differences over foreign policy stemmed primarily from questions of expediency, not principles. Between 1928 and 1932 most members of the Federation concluded, sometimes reluctantly, that root and branch opposition to *Briandisme* would succeed only in driving the Federation from the moderately conservative coalition. Although most had reservations about the wisdom of Aristide Briand's approach to foreign policy, they accepted it as long as Briand was part of a conservative government whose domestic policy they approved. The divergence between theory and practice was greatest during the debate on the ratification of the Young Plan in the spring of 1930. After that, more and more deputies of the party became disillusioned with Briand and began to join Marin in voting against the government of the day. By the time of the vote on the Hoover Moratorium in 1931, a majority of the deputies followed Marin in rejecting the policy of the government.

After 1932 the Federation, now in the opposition, was once again free to pursue its traditionally nationalistic demands. Its deputies no longer had to restrain their nationalistic impulses in order to maintain sympathetic governments in power. Briand was dead, and the mystique of international reconciliation died with him. Illusions about Germany, which had arisen during the Stresemann era, were readily dissipated by Hitler's accession to power. Consequently, the Federation was in a position to consolidate its unbending defense of the international status quo and to place a solid obstacle in the way of any further concessions to Germany.

Yet it was precisely the threat to the domestic status quo that rendered the Republican Federation less, rather than more, firm in its resistance to Hitler and to changes in the political map of Europe. Because of domestic social and political upheaval, the Federation faltered in its defense of French security and became a more or less willing adherent to the policy of appeasement. The Federation's deviations from the nationalist doctrine during the middle and late 1930s were far more fundamental than the divergences of the late 1920s and early 1930s. Yet, whereas disagreements over foreign policy had severely disrupted the internal life of the Republican Federation between 1929 and 1932, a broad consensus among the leaders and the rank and file supported the party's dramatic reversal of position between 1935 and 1939. So real did the threat to domestic social peace seem that even the most vigorous nationalist in the Federation did not dissent as the party gradually discarded its traditional stance for a policy of appeasement and neopacifism.

Until 1935 the Federation's position on foreign policy remained substantially what it had been for twenty years. Hitler's rise to power simply demonstrated to the leaders of the Federa-

tion that Germany was as inherently duplicitous as they had
maintained all along. Nazi Germany was only the logical continuation of the eternally aggressive Germany, which had
masked its true character under the Weimar Republic. According to Camille Blaisot, Hitler's methods were "part of the German tradition . . . from Attila to von Bernhardi." Germany was
"the same incorrigible and warlike Germany, be she the Germany of Attila's Huns or the Germany of Hitler's Nazis." The
Federation still insisted that France should consider establishing
cordial relations with Germany "only after she had given con-
vincing proof of her faithfulness by paying reparations to those
countries that she attacked and by disarming herself." The party
remained adamant about revising the peace treaties. "Revision
means war," Jean Ybarnegaray declared at the 1933 congress. As
always the Federation suspected the statesmen of the Left of
naïve plans for disarming France and angrily condemned Joseph
Paul-Boncour's "concessions" at the Geneva disarmament talks.
At the same time it attacked the 1934 Four Power Pact as a disguised attempt to revise the peace treaties and weaken the alliance system of France.[1]

The Federation emphasized that the nature of the German
peril had not altered with the change of regime in Germany. It
was the entire German nation, not any particular regime, which
threatened France. Those on the Left who had begun to worry
about Germany only after Hitler came to power had completely
misunderstood the German problem. By distrusting only *Nazi*
Germany, they had not demonstrated a return to their senses
but simply manifested an ideological antagonism to fascism. In
the event of a German invasion of France, Camille Blaisot remarked, "there would be little point in trying to identify the
more or less Hitlerian character of the invasion: the invasion
would be there, exactly like those we have already experienced." Blaisot clearly felt that not all reasons for distrusting
Germany were equally valid. In early 1935 he simultaneously

1. *La Nation*, August 5, 1933, January 27, July 7, August 4, 1934.

branded the Germans as "incorrigible people whose militarism poisons the brains of its men and the hearts of its women" and warned "let us not make the mistake . . . of endlessly insulting Hitler, as we formerly insulted Mussolini without achieving anything . . . for the cause of peace." Apparently, to distrust Germany because Germans were a race of aggressors was the mark of realistic nationalism, but to oppose Germany because Hitler was a fascist dictator constituted a threat to the peace. Occasionally, some members of the Federation reflected uneasily about a possible shift in the position of the French Left because of the rise of Nazism. Shortly after Hitler became chancellor the blunt-spoken Xavier Vallat wrote: "I await with some curiosity the declarations of the frenzied partisans of Franco-German *rapprochement*; those for whom France never made enough concessions. . . . Will they tomorrow propose a holy war against Hitler's Germany in the name of democratic principles?" Vallat's fears would be widespread within a few years; but for the first two years of Hitler's rule, most members of the Federation continued to attack the militarism of the Germans and the pacifism of the Left very much as they always had.[2]

Until well into 1935 the Federation's attitude toward Italy and Soviet Russia remained in line with orthodox French nationalism. With the rise of Nazi Germany, both nations sought closer relations with France, and the Federation welcomed the possibility. At its 1933 congress it declared that reestablishing friendship with Russia was "of capital importance for the future," although it insisted that any pact with the Soviets must be accompanied by a recognition of the prewar debt to France and by the cessation of the subversive activities of the Third International. The party was naturally more enthusiastic about an alliance with its former ally and Catholic neighbor, Italy. It saw an alliance with Italy as being "in the nature of things," thus far prevented only by the Left's sectarian hatred of Mussolini.

2. *La Nation*, December 22, 1934, January 19, 1935; *La Gazette d'Annonay*, February 11, 1933.

Although the Federation wanted closer relations with Italy, it would not pay the price of territorial concessions in the Adriatic since this would necessarily weaken Yugoslavia and her eastern allies. As Marin declared in 1934, the Federation could not "consent to friendship with Italy at the price of loosening our ties with the Little Entente." Party spokesmen still expressed certain reservations about the attitude of France's southern neighbor. Camille Blaisot early in 1935 contrasted the French "thirst for peace" with the "military arrogance" of her neighbors and spoke of the "gulf which, today more than ever, separates the French mentality from the Italian mentality." Despite these reservations, the Federation still approved the Laval-Mussolini conversations in January, 1935, and the Stresa Pact of April, 1935. At this time, however, neither the prospect of a Franco-Russian rapprochement nor that of a Franco-Italian alliance stirred up the violent emotions that they would by the end of 1935. The one had not yet become a menace to the peace of Europe, and the other had not yet become the universal panacea for all the diplomatic problems of France. Until the late spring of 1935 neither the mutual assistance pact with the Soviet Union, which the Federation approved with reservations, nor the Stresa Pact, which the party welcomed, was the object of much concern.[3]

The Federation's outlook began to change in the spring of 1935 in response to events within and outside of France. At home the municipal elections of May 5 and 12 revealed the potency of the emerging alliance between the parties of the Left. Still more disturbing, the Communist party, which doubled the number of seats it held, seemed to be gaining the most from the embryonic Popular Front. For conservatives, the municipal elections were a premonition of future radical and possibly revolutionary changes in France. At the same time, while the French Left celebrated the baptism of the Popular Front on July 14, 1935, Italy began mobilizing for war against

3. *La Nation*, June 24, August 5, 1933, January 5, 1934.

Ethiopia. This particular conjuncture of domestic and foreign events was not lost on the Republican Federation and governed its response to the Ethiopian crisis.

Initially, some members of the Federation expressed some misgivings about a rival Italian imperialism, which could conceivably harm French interests in North Africa. Most members of the party, however, sympathized with Italy's imperial ambitions and commented favorably on Mussolini's "civilizing mission." For them the Italo-Ethiopian conflict represented the struggle between "civilization" and "a petty negro king, a slave dealer and a bloody hangman." The colonial expansion of "France's great Latin sister" was a "vital necessity" and an "act of human liberation." The Federation protested angrily, therefore, when the Laval government, under pressure from Great Britain and the domestic Left, began to apply the sanctions of the League of Nations. It seemed utterly hypocritical for two colonial powers like Britain and France to oppose the legitimate colonial ambitions of their former ally. Britain's righteous indignation merely masked her desire to retain an economic monopoly over East Africa, and the League's sanctions appeared only to serve "the interests of the oil industry and the British colonialists." Economic sanctions were in any case pointless since they would hurt France more than Italy and would end by giving Germany control over the Italian market.[4]

The attempt to impose sanctions seemed to be all the more foolish since only a few months earlier Franco-Italian relations had been better than at any time since the end of the war and Italy appeared to be secured as an ally against Germany. When this invaluable entente was threatened for the sake of a backward African kingdom, the Stresa Pact acquired a significance it had not possessed the previous spring. Then it had seemed to be a desirable, but not momentous addition to the French alliance

4. Xavier Vallat, *La Gazette d'Annonay*, July 31, September 14, 1935; Jacques Poitou-Duplessy, *Le Réveil Charentais*, October 20, 1935; *L'Union Républicaine du Rhône*, September 29, October 27, 1935; *Le Réveil Charentais*, October 20, 1935; *La Gazette d'Annonay*, October 12, 1935.

system. Now a working alliance with Italy increasingly appeared as the critical precondition for any effective diplomacy. Arguing that the application of sanctions would lead to war, the Federation lauded the efforts of Pierre Laval and the British foreign minister, Sir Samuel Hoare, to reach a compromise with Mussolini. The Hoare-Laval Plan, far from simply conceding the Italian dictator the fruits of his aggression, became a statesmanlike attempt to preserve the peace.[5]

Officially, the party continued to couch its foreign policy in traditional and pragmatic terms: the policy of economic sanctions was diplomatically disastrous and economically unsound. Privately, however, the Federation preoccupied itself with what it perceived to be the sudden and uncharacteristic bellicosity of the French Left. The former "spineless pacifists" had now become "frenzied warriors." Perret commented, "The men who, today, wish to lead us into war are the same ones who, before 1914, wanted to disarm us with their utopias." For the most part the Federation assigned this unsettling about-face to the tendency of the Left to conduct foreign policy in the light of ideological rather than national considerations. Mussolini was the bête noire of the Socialists and the Communists; even the Radicals sought revenge on the regime that deprived the Freemasons of their occult influence.[6]

Occasionally, members of the Federation hinted at deeper and more Machiavellian motives behind the *volte-face* of the Left. The recent union of the forces of the Left and the possibility of an electoral victory of the Marxists had made the Federation acutely sensitive to problems of internal stability. With the domestic front threatened by a revolutionary coalition, France could not safely become involved in a foreign war. From

5. On the general feeling of rapprochement that pervaded France in the spring of 1935, see Franklin D. Laurens, *France and the Italo-Ethiopian Crisis, 1933–1936* (The Hague, 1967), 51–55. Alfred Oberkirch, *Journal Officiel*, December 28, 1935, p. 2867.

6. *La Nation*, October 20, November 30, 1935; Xavier Vallat, *La Gazette d'Annonay*, August 24, 1935; Victor Perret, *La Nation*, September 28, 1935; Jacques Poitou-Duplessy, *Le Réveil Charentais*, December 22, 1935; Victor Perret, *L'Union Républicaine du Rhône*, September 29, 1935.

this position it was but a short step to the assumption that the revolutionary elements within the Popular Front sought war precisely because they recognized that an external conflict would create ideal conditions for a revolutionary seizure of power. Victor Perret asked: "When Messieurs Blum and Cachin are at the head of those who want to push us into war, what better proof is there that the question at stake is less one of justice than of revolution?" He repeatedly reminded his readers that war had always been "the best auxiliary of revolutions" and that the foreign policy of the Popular Front could only be understood in those terms.[7]

The Ethiopian crisis marked the beginning of the automatic association of war with revolution that was to haunt the Federation for the next three years. The conjuncture of international tensions and the formation of a revolutionary front at home heightened the party's awareness of the domestic causes and consequences of war. Because the Federation assumed that the nonrevolutionary groups (like the Radicals) had fallen under the sway of the Communists, it suspected even the diplomatic initiatives of the liberal Left. Once convinced that the Communists would use a war to provoke a revolution at home, the party began to regard as suspect any act of diplomatic firmness that could conceivably lead to war.

The Federation's uncertainties over foreign policy surfaced again in the debate over the ratification of the Franco-Soviet pact of mutual assistance. When the pact was signed in May, 1935, it had aroused comparatively little domestic reaction. Officially, the Federation merely issued a ritualistic warning about the danger of Soviet propaganda. Xavier Vallat worried that France might be drawn into a war because Germany claimed some town in eastern Europe "whose name we cannot pronounce," but most members of the party regarded the possibility as slight. However, by February, 1936, when the pact

7. *La Nation*, December 21, 1935, January 25, 1936. Marcel Cachin was the secretary-general of the Communist party. *L'Union Républicaine du Rhône*, September 29, 1935.

came before the Chamber for ratification, the cautious approval of the previous spring had changed to open hostility. Many conservatives had accepted the Russian alliance because it had been complemented by an understanding with Italy; after the diplomatic rupture with Italy, provoked by the Italo-Ethiopian war, a number of them began to see the Soviet pact in a new and less favorable light.[8] Moreover, the domestic situation had changed drastically since the mutual assistance pact had first been signed. The Communists, who had seemed relatively weak and isolated at the beginning of 1935, had demonstrated their growing strength in the intervening municipal elections. With the Communists an increasingly important political force, a pact with the Soviet Union seemed more dangerous, and its ratification risked giving the domestic Communists a newfound respectability. A final factor that influenced many on the Right was the fact that the mildly conservative Flandin and Laval governments, which had sponsored the mutual assistance pact, had been replaced by the more left-wing, caretaker Sarraut government. The Federation no longer had any representatives in the government and could feel free to vote against ratification.

Some held that one simply could not do business with the Communists. The branch in Calais contended that "it was monstrous to deal with people who stabbed us in the back during the war, who stole our money and who are organizing a revolution at home." For the most part, however, spokesmen for the Federation attempted to avoid purely ideological objections to the pact, particularly since the party condemned the Left for allowing ideological considerations to dictate foreign policy. Xavier Vallat told the Chamber that, if necessary, he was prepared to emulate François I and make a treaty with the twentieth-century equivalent of the Grand Turk, although he observed that in the sixteenth century the Grand Turk did not maintain in France "a Moslem party whose efforts were directed towards overthrowing the monarchy and substituting the Koran

8. *La Gazette d'Annonay*, May 4, 1935; William Evans Scott, *Alliance Against Hitler* (Durham, N.C., 1965), 263.

for the Gospels." Like most members of the Federation, he preferred to stress the practical objections to the pact and argued
that it was not militarily feasible. He questioned the military
effectiveness of the Soviet Army and suggested that the glowing
press reports about Russian aviation sounded suspiciously like
those that had promised a Russian steamroller in 1914. Since
Russia had no common military border with Germany, in the
event of war she would have to pass through one or more unfriendly countries in order to aid France. This posed, Vallat
asserted, impossible diplomatic and logistical problems and
rendered an alliance with Russia of limited value. Pierre Taittinger noted that France had adopted a purely defensive military policy suited to the Maginot Line; to adjust to a foreign
policy requiring aid to the Soviet Union, she would need to
carry out a drastic and possibly crippling reorganization of military policy.[9] Most of the Federation's critique of the proposed
military cooperation with the Soviet Union involved such practical considerations.

Nonetheless, some were also apprehensive about the consequences of the Franco-Soviet pact for Franco-German relations.
In the Chamber, Alfred Oberkirch (deputy from Mulhouse)
admitted to being skeptical about negotiations with Germany
but nonetheless warned that the proposed pact could only im-
pede "a courteous, sincere and loyal conversation" with France's
eastern neighbor. This was a strange choice of words for a
deputy of a party that had once been so suspicious of Aristide
Briand. Furthermore, concern over Germany's reaction could
lead to a more drastic reassessment of the European diplomatic
situation. The Soviet Union's desire for military cooperation
was obviously conditioned by her fear of the eastern ambitions
of Nazi Germany. It might follow that German territorial ambitions were primarily limited to eastern Europe, in which case
an alliance with the Soviet Union could be diplomatic folly.
Octave Lavalette concluded:

9. *Le Réveil du Calaisis*, February, 1936; *Journal Officiel*, February 18, 1936, pp.
453–56.

Germany appears to be more inclined towards expanding into the East where she would find territory for colonization, territory which she presently lacks, than she is towards seeking revenge in the West where she would once again face the alliance of the former allies and where she could hardly, in the event of victory, conserve her conquests. The ratification of the Franco-Soviet treaty could change her attitude and predispose her, in order to avoid being caught between two opponents, first to regulate her account with France . . . before beginning her expansion towards the East.

If the goals of German foreign policy had altered, then she ceased to represent the traditional threat; and France was no longer obliged to take her allies where she could find them. Implicit in this view was the assumption that France's eastern allies—particularly Poland and Czechoslovakia—were more or less expendable and that the annihilation of the Soviet Union by Nazi Germany might not be altogether undesirable. Although few were as outspoken as Lavalette in 1936, within his analysis lay the germ of the complete abandonment of the Federation's traditional foreign policy and a concomitant willingness to give Hitler a free hand in the east.[10]

On February 27, 1936, the Chamber voted to ratify the Franco-Russian pact of mutual assistance, over the objections of most of the Right and all the Republican Federation. Within a week, events appeared to have justified many of their fears. When Germany reoccupied the Rhineland on March 7, 1936, effectively tearing up the Treaty of Versailles and the Locarno Pact, she began the first of a series of military actions that would seriously weaken the strategic position of France. The reactions of the Federation varied: all agreed that the reoccupation was the fault of the statesmen of the Left, but individuals differed as to exactly how to lay the blame. Some viewed the reoccupation as the inevitable consequence of the concessions made to Germany during the Briand era, the end result of the naïve internationalism of the 1920s. Others saw Germany's aggression

10. *Journal Officiel*, February 18, 1936, pp. 456, 466–67; *L'Union Républicaine du Rhône*, February 16, 1936.

as the first fruits of the Franco-Soviet pact, the predictable outcome of a provocative alliance.[11] The Federation simultaneously
condemned the Left for having granted too much to Germany in
the past and for unnecessarily provoking her at the present moment. While France could easily have restrained Germany, the
Left had made dangerous concessions. Now that Germany was a
major military power, the former exponents of international cooperation wanted to provoke a war. By emphasizing what they
felt to be the dangerous inconsistencies of their political enemies, the leaders of the Federation sought to disguise the increasingly apparent anomalies in their own view of the German
problem.

These anomalies appeared even in the reaction of the party's
most traditional nationalist, Louis Marin. Marin's reaction to the
German coup was very much like the countless other protests
he had made against the Germans during the preceding seventeen years. Two weeks before the reoccupation of the Rhine,
Marin had signaled the presence of German troop concentra-
tions and dourly predicted that as soon as the Franco-Soviet
pact was ratified the Germans would invade. Having predicted
the event, he had more scope than ever for developing his indignation, and he thundered his disgust for a government that
could not foresee what should have been obvious to everyone.
Albert Sarraut, then premier, later recognized that Marin had
been one of the few conservatives who had been prepared to
respond with force to Hitler's Rhineland provocation. Marin
recognized the Franco-Soviet pact as the pretext and not the
cause of the most recent German outrage; the cause was the immutable Germanic spirit of aggression. Utterly suspicious of
German pacifistic utterances, he scoffed at Hitler's famous interview with Bertrand de Jouvenel, in which the former indicated
his hopes for a Franco-German rapprochement. Marin branded
as "imbeciles" those parliamentary colleagues who were im-

11. Jean Baudouin, *Voir Clair en Politique*, April 1, 1936; *Le Réveil du Beaujolais*,
March 11, 1936; *L'Union Républicaine du Rhône*, March 15, 1936.

pressed by Hitler's declarations. In short, Marin's response was a restatement of his firmly rooted anti-German nationalism.[12]

Yet Louis Marin obscured an otherwise clear and unequivocal position by making several strange, incidental references. While denying the value of Hitler's interview with de Jouvenel, he nonetheless reproached the authorities for having delayed its publication for a week in order to assure the ratification of the Franco-Soviet pact.[13] Considering that Marin thought the declarations of Hitler to be worthless and even dangerous, this was a strange accusation. Perhaps he hoped that the Chamber would have reacted to the interview by rejecting the pact, although had it done so it would most certainly have been for the wrong reasons. Marin's attitude prefigured a later campaign against "false news" and reflected the growing assumptions in the Federation that the Right distrusted German peace feelers out of realism, whereas a similar distrust on the part of the Left stemmed from more dangerous motives. In the same article he remarked: "The mentality which would like to drag us stupidly into war is the same as that which would like to bring us into a bloody revolution." Marin's writings abounded with stray sentences, and this one seems to have been thrown in primarily for rhetorical purposes. Nonetheless, it was a singular remark to make in an article devoted to denouncing the eternally warlike Germans and condemning a government that had been unwilling to resist the latest German aggression. While expounding his traditional views on Germany and on French diplomacy, Louis Marin allowed the equation of war with revolution to creep into his writings. Although still in its infancy, this formula would ultimately undermine his traditional views. In 1936 Marin was still trying to accommodate his perennial suspicions of Germany with his more recent but growing suspicions of the Left.

12. *La Nation*, February 22, March 14, 1936; *Chambre des Députés, Rapport fait au nom de la Commission chargée d'enquête sur les événements survenus en France de 1933 à 1944*, III, 603.

13. The article was published in *Paris-Midi* the day after the German action and about a week after the interview had been granted.

The task proved impossible; and over the next two years as the domestic situation grew more uncertain, his fear of revolution would gradually take precedence over his fear of the Reich.

The victory of the Popular Front and the frightening wave of strikes in the summer of 1936 greatly increased the Federation's sensitivity to the possibility of domestic upheaval. What had been an alarming prospect in the spring began to seem a distant possibility by the summer. A minimum condition for containing the revolutionary forces within France, the party came to believe, was the avoidance of any possible foreign entanglement. When the Spanish Civil War erupted in July, 1936, at the height of the social unrest in France, the Federation feared that France might be drawn into precisely the kind of war it was so essential to avoid. Although the Popular Front government played a relatively innocuous role in the Spanish conflict and although many on the non-Communist Left vigorously insisted that France remain neutral, the climate of suspicion within France was such that the Federation's anxieties about war and revolution were greatly increased by events in Spain.

The Republican Federation was not sympathetic to the Spanish Republic. The party was no more prepared to recognize the essential moderation of the Spanish Popular Front government elected in February, 1936, than it was to accept the defensive nature of its French counterpart. French conservatives sided with their opposite numbers in Spain, overemphasized the role of the Spanish Communists, and saw in the newly elected government only revolutionary chaos, anticlerical outrages, and total disrespect for private property. Consequently, when General Francisco Franco (backed by the army, the Church, and the conservative forces in Spanish society) led an armed insurrection against the government, the Republican Federation did not protest. No one was troubled by the fact that Franco was revolting against the legally elected government of Spain or that the Federation was, in principle, opposed to insurrectionary politics. The Federation considered the legality of the Spanish republican government to be more apparent than real and accepted the view that Franco had "risen legitimately against the Communist brutality and the tyranny of Moscow."[14]

What worried the leaders of the Federation was the possibility that the government of the Popular Front would intervene in the conflict by supplying arms to its ideological brethren in Spain. Such an intervention greatly increased the risk both of war and of revolution. Félix Grat, the newly elected deputy from the Mayenne, believed that intervention would mean war with Germany. He also insisted that the Soviet Union and its agents in France were pushing France toward intervention and war because the ensuing "complications" would lead to war "here in France."[15] He granted that the Soviet Union also advocated intervention in order to save Spain from fascism, but he persistently returned to the view that the forces of the Left sought war over Spain as a means for fomenting revolution at home. There were plenty of reasons for demanding neutrality in the Spanish Civil War. The need to restore order on the Iberian peninsula or the lack of support from Great Britain could have been sufficient grounds for nonintervention. Yet Grat and others in the party persisted in viewing the question of intervention through the optic of revolution.

By the beginning of 1937 it became obvious that only Britain and France were taking nonintervention seriously. Germany, Italy, and the Soviet Union were sending men and war materials in substantial quantities. The possibility that Germany might derive considerable strategic advantage from her increased influence in Nationalist Spain did not move the Federation to reconsider its unqualified support for Franco. Jacques Poitou-Duplessy, one of five members of the Federation who visited Nationalist Spain in December, 1936, denied that the Germans stood to gain a potential ally west of the Pyrenees.[16] France,

14. Octave Lavalette, *L'Union Républicaine du Rhône*, August 9, 1936.
15. *Jeunesse 36*, December 1, 1936.
16. The other four included Edouard Soulier, Bernard d'Aillières, François de Saint-Just, and Augustin Michel. Along with independent conservatives Henri de Kerillis and Jean-Louis Tixier-Vignancour, they gained a brief notoriety in the left-wing press as "the seven traitors." *Le Jour*, December 19, 1936; *Jeunesse 37*, January 15, 1937.

he argued, was too much of a nationalist to allow any foreign power to dominate in Spain. The real threat to France came not from Franco but from Republican Spain, which remained in the grip of the Red dictatorship. In any case, the intervention by the Axis powers came only in response to repeated French violations of the nonintervention agreement and to the huge influx of eastern European Communists into Spain. Philippe Henriot, who visited Franco in March, 1937, echoed these sentiments and insisted that Franco's use of Axis forces was acceptable to anyone who understood "the struggle of civilization and the faith against the destructive forces of Bolshevism." The Popular Front, he contended, deliberately magnified the German role in Spain in its search for a new "Ems dispatch" that might help provoke war.[17]

During the eighteen months between the outbreak of the Spanish Civil War and the Austrian Anschluss, the earlier doubts and anxieties crystallized into a radically altered perspective on foreign affairs. Officially, the Federation retained some of the traditional position, but under the altered circumstances of the late 1930s, its earlier arguments lost much of their force. The party still complained of the debilitating effect of the forty-hour week on rearmament and bemoaned the low morale of military conscripts. Yet, even the Federation grudgingly admitted that the Popular Front government provided the army with whatever it requested. The party still railed against the territorial, financial, and military concessions made to Germany, but refighting the battles over Locarno and the Young Plan in the pages of *La Nation* hardly constituted a cogent position on the present international situation. The party's sole constructive alternative to the government's policy was to rebuild the Italian alliance. In its desire to regain her natural ally, so foolishly or so fiendishly alienated by the Left, the Federation made extravagant claims for the "millions of bayonets" at Rome. No one any longer questioned Italian good faith, still less Italian

17. *Jeunesse 37*, January 15, March 15, November 15, 1937.

military capability, or the impact of an Italian alliance on the relationship of France to the Little Entente.[18]

What obsessed the Federation during this period was the apparent about-face by leaders of the Popular Front on questions of military and foreign policy. Ignoring for once the numerous Radicals and Socialists who retained their pacifist outlook, the Federation concentrated on those of the Left who increasingly demanded that France stand up to Hitler. There were two distinct thrusts to the Federation's analysis of the changed stance of the Left, with very different implications.

The more obvious (and more innocuous) interpretation of this sudden change by the Left was that its leaders were moved by an ideologically conditioned hatred for Hitler and Mussolini, which could only be satisfied by an antifascist crusade. Unlike conservatives, who could accept military action only in "the defense of the soil and the primordial interests of the country," the French Left sought "a bloody 'crusade' for a political or philosophic cause."[19] To the sectarian zeal of the Left could be added the more pragmatic desire of the Communists to serve the material and strategic interests of Moscow. The changed attitude of the Left represented not a sudden recognition of the realities of international politics but a perverse desire to destroy foreign ideological enemies. Seen in this perspective, the turnabout by the Left might be thoroughly exasperating but not particularly menacing. The fascist threat for the Left could converge with the eternal German menace for the conservatives, and the two could support a common policy, albeit for fundamentally different reasons.

The Republican Federation, however, also came to believe that the Popular Front, or critical segments of it, sought not just revenge against fascism or defense of the Soviet Union, but world revolution. Since the Federation assumed that the liberal, nonrevolutionary elements in the Popular Front had fallen

18. *La Nation*, April 11, September 19, 1936.
19. *Ibid.*, October 3, 1936.

under the sway of the Communists and the radical wing of the Socialists, many suspected that the Popular Front was part of a grand design for revolution. The foreign policy of the revolutionary Left thus seemed to complement its obvious domestic objectives. Just as the Russian Revolution and the wave of upheavals that followed it had arisen from the chaos of the First World War, the Federation believed that war would once again be the vehicle of revolution. Jacques Poitou-Duplessy insisted that, in the event of war, the Communists would "profit from these complications and declare civil war to overthrow capitalism and crush the bourgeoisie so that they could be replaced with the dictatorship of the proletariat and by socialism." The rest of the party, from Gustave Gautherot to Louis Marin, echoed the same theme.[20]

One must treat these public statements with caution. In the emotionally charged atmosphere of the late 1930s, extravagant slogans were on everyone's lips, and members of the Federation did not always mean what they said about the Popular Front. It is hard to believe that all members of the Federation actually thought that the French Left was deliberately plotting war in order to make revolution. There were, after all, some logical difficulties with such a proposition. If Russia really did feel threatened by Germany and desperately wanted the support of the brave little French *poilus*, then it was unlikely that she and her agents would deliberately foment a revolution in France. No one in the Federation satisfactorily explained how a France that was convulsed in civil war and revolution could be of much use to the Soviet Union should she be invaded by the German legions. Because the Federation assumed that the Communists sought to make the Popular Front into a revolutionary enterprise, it was difficult simultaneously to admit that Moscow had postponed its world revolutionary ambitions to assure itself a sound ally. Louis Marin once admitted that the comparative moderation of French Communists since 1934 was dictated by Russia's fear of Hitler, but he persisted in referring to the fruits

20. *Le Réveil Charentais*, January 12, 1936; *La Nation*, April 11, October 9, 1936.

of this moderation as a "revolutionary front." The relative "reasonableness" of French Communists was occasionally interpreted as a maneuver to increase their influence in government. In early 1938 Joseph Denais reasoned that the Communists were even prepared to enter a government, not out of moderation, but in order to hinder any peaceful resolution of the international crisis.[21]

No one yet spoke of defeat. The Federation assumed that even in the event of a victorious war or a stalemate, domestic revolutionary forces (presently so strong and benefiting from the benevolent neutrality of the Popular Front government) would take advantage of the inevitable complications to overthrow the government. Even if the revolutionaries did not deliberately plot war to ignite revolution, they could be expected to exploit the confusion that would certainly exist in a modern society at war. Whether intended or not, under existing conditions revolution would be the highly probable outcome of war.

Viewed in this light the Soviet Union represented as great a menace to France as did Nazi Germany. By 1937 the Federation repeatedly warned that, despite their obvious ideological differences, both Germany and the Soviet Union were united in their desire to destroy the France that conservatives cherished. Bolsheviks and Hitlerians, Teutons and Slavs were determined to push France into "civil and foreign war." The prevailing anxiety about domestic upheaval even led some members of the party to suggest that the Soviet threat was the greater of the two. One could arrive at this position by assuming that Nazi Germany was primarily interested in eastward expansion. Jacques Poitou-Duplessy, one of the most hysterical anti-Communists in the party, analyzed the international situation in a way that minimized the German peril and maximized the threat of the Soviet Union.[22] Arguing that the principal dynamic behind German foreign policy was a desire to "take up the ancient

21. *La Nation*, May 16, 1936; *L'Union Républicaine du Rhône*, February 13, 1938.
22. In December, 1936, for example, he reported that thousands of revolutionary Arabs were invading France, armed with grenades manufactured by the hundreds of thousands in clandestine Communist factories in Lyon. *Le Jour*, December 13, 1936.

mission of the Knights of the Teutonic order" and expand into the east, he asserted that France at all costs ought to stay clear of the consequent Russo-German struggle: "Between the neo-Asiatic Slavism of Moscow and the Germanism of the Aryans a duel to the death is being prepared. It is truly maddening that we should give the whole world the impression of being allied body and soul with the first against the second in a quarrel in which we really do not belong." As long as Germany was content to expand into the obscure realms of eastern Europe where France "really did not belong," the only loser, apart from the recently created eastern European states, would be Stalinist Russia. Under these circumstances France, far from "brandishing the Red Flag" under the nose of Germany, ought to leave the Soviet Union to its fate.[23]

Not everyone in the Federation shared Poitou-Duplessy's penchant for seeing the Soviet Union as the real threat to the peace.[24] There can be little doubt that Louis Marin was never seduced by the possibility of Germany limiting her aggression to the east. Although he repeatedly condemned the cynical designs of the Soviets, he still insisted that "for Europe and the world, the German peril is, without question, the primary menace." But Marin did not make that kind of unambiguous statement very often, nor did he express his views on the subject very clearly. Neither did his principal lieutenants. François Valentin, a young deputy from the Meurthe-et-Moselle and a protégé of Marin, presented a report at the Federation's 1937 congress designed to expose the illusion that Hitler had designs exclusively on the east. Although he made a cogent case for the anti-French thrust of German foreign policy and warned against expecting a Franco-German rapprochement, he nevertheless weakened the impact of his message by a long diatribe against the Soviet Union. He concluded by admonishing the Quai d'Orsay against any alliance with "a state confounded with an international or-

23. Louis Marin and Jean Baudouin, *La Nation*, September 5, October 3, 1936; *Le Réveil Charentais*, September 20, 1936.

24. Poitou-Duplessis himself admitted that conservatives were divided as to whether Hitler or Stalin was the principal enemy. *Jeunesse* 37, January 15, 1937.

ganization whose goal is that of triggering the outbreak of world revolution by any means including war." His relatively firm position on the German question was thus undermined by his focus on the war-revolution nexus that was increasingly the bane of French conservatives. Similarly, Henri Becquart, the newly elected deputy from Lille, in an article in *La Nation* gave sound reasons why a reconciliation with Germany was both unlikely and undesirable. Yet Becquart, who was close to Marin, devoted a disconcerting amout of space to defending the partisans of rapprochement with Germany against the charge of being "French Hitlerians." Such charges, moreover, had been leveled, not by the Left but by unequivocally anti-German conservatives like Henri de Kerillis, Pertinax, and Emile Buré.[25]

The absence of any open debate within the Federation on the direction in which it was moving indicated the extent of the consensus that had developed. In sharp contrast to the early 1930s, questions of foreign policy no longer divided the Federation. Although most members of the Federation probably were reluctant to go as far as Poitou-Duplessy and give Hitler a free hand in the east, they permitted a shadow of doubt to come over their position and became so transfixed by the specter of Communism that at times they allowed Hitler to drop into the background. Jacques Debû-Bridel recalled that by the time of the annual congress of the Republican Federation of the Rhône in early 1938, "one would have thought, to hear the speakers, that France was really being threatened by Russia and that a raid on Paris by Cossacks was imminent."[26]

However much the machinations of Soviet Russia might have preoccupied them, by early 1938 the leaders of the Federation could not ignore the renewed threats from Nazi Germany. The changes in German military and diplomatic personnel presaged a new move by Germany. They had, as Marin observed, "the character of a sinister warning." During the first weeks of the year, *La Nation* warned that both France and Britain would be

25. *La Nation*, August 21, October 9, 1937; Marin Papers, carton 88.
26. Jacques Debû-Bridel, *L'Agonie de la Troisième République* (Paris, 1948), 456.

in a better position to face an eventual German challenge if they were led by firm and energetic governments. At the same time, it repeated that in the event of an international crisis Hitler's strongest card would be the powerful forces of the Third International in France. The Communists were potential "collaborators with the German army whose operations they would facilitate by creating disorders at home."[27] No one in the Federation proposed any concrete action, but everyone deplored France's lack of preparation, hoped for a reconciliation with Italy, and expressed suspicion of Moscow.

Even before the Anschluss, some members of the party attempted to pin the responsibility for the imminent fall of Austria on the Left. Octave Lavalette remembered that four years previously Italy, now thoroughly alienated by the policies of subsequent French governments, had mobilized on the Brenner to deter a German attempt on the independence of Austria. Xavier Vallat set forth his pet panacea for central and southern Europe: the restoration of the Habsburgs and the creation of a Danubian Federation binding the diverse nationalities together. Vallat, a personal friend of the Habsburg pretender, realized that his ingenious scheme amounted to the restoration of a modified Habsburg Empire and would be wrecked both by the antimonarchism of the Left and the opposition of the Czechs or as he put it, "the fanaticism of the Hussite heretics." The notion that a federation of Austria, Hungary, and Czechoslovakia could stop Hitler was quixotic, but it found an echo with some members of the party and helped create the illusion that the selfish Czechs were responsible for the loss of Austria.[28]

When Austria fell, the Federation proposed no military action and had no concrete response except the time-honored government of national union. To Léon Blum's proposal of a government extending from the Communist Maurice Thorez to Louis Marin, the party retorted that a government of national salvation

27. *La Nation*, February 12, 19, 26, 1938.
28. *L'Union Républicaine du Rhône*, February 20, 1938; *La Gazette d'Annonay*, February 5, 27, 1938.

could hardly include the sworn agents of a foreign power. Louis Marin presented a dismal postmortem on events in Austria, stressing the severity of the blow to French security and predictably placing responsibility on the blunders of the 1920s. Members of the Federation took solace only in the hope that German aggression in Austria would shake Italy out of the German orbit. Austria, like France, was a Catholic country. Her loss filled many, like Philippe Henriot, with "a sentiment of sad humiliation" and the gloomy sense that France had sacrificed not only her Catholic sister but also her "honor and prestige." Some even charged that Austria had been sacrificed precisely "because she was Catholic" and noted ironically that by contrast "the leaders of the Popular Front will not hesitate for a moment to rush to the defense of the masonic Czechoslovak republic." Already one member of the Republican Federation had begun to wonder why, if France had been unwilling to fight for Catholic Austria, Frenchmen should die for Protestant and Masonic Czechoslovakia.[29]

No one doubted that Hitler would next strike at Czechoslovakia. In a series of articles on the Czech problem, *La Nation*'s staff writers noted the complexities of the minorities issue and observed that by their naïve *Briandisme* in the 1920s and their opposition to Habsburg restoration, the Czechs had been the authors of their present difficulties. The journal left no doubt, however, that the Sudeten problem had been magnified and largely stimulated by Germany, and it insisted that preserving the territorial integrity of Czechoslovakia was of the utmost strategic importance for France. In May, 1938, when the Czech army mobilized in response to a series of border incidents, Marin took this action as proof both of the viability of the Czech military force and of the solidarity of the nation. The diplomatic firmness of the Czechs and of the British seemed highly significant to Marin, since it marked the first time in fifteen years that

---

29. *La Nation*, March 19, 1938; *Jeunesse 38*, March 17, 1938; Raymond Silles (president of the Federation's branch in the Loir-et-Cher), *Le Petit Loir-et-Cher*, March 18, 1938.

the former victors had resisted German demands. He also reminded conservatives that the German army was not invincible
and cited the serious deficiencies of the German armored
divisions during their entry into Vienna. His lieutenant, François Valentin, echoed Marin's resolve when he told the National
Council that the party "solemnly reaffirms its attachment to the
principle of reciprocal respect for the given word and concluded
agreements." The obvious reference to the French treaty of
assistance with Czechoslovakia appeared to presage an inflexible
position with regard to German demands.[30]

Simultaneously, however, most members of the party began
to doubt the possibility and the wisdom of defending Czechoslovakia. Increasingly, they drew attention to the polyglot character of the Czech state. Their ally was, in Henriot's words, "a
motley and pock-marked collection of races and peoples," and "a
country so deprived of unity and so much the arbitrary creation of the sick brain of President Wilson." Such an ally, lacking internal cohesion, could hardly defend herself. "This strange
and fragile agglomeration of peoples," wrote Jacques Poitou-
Duplessy, "could not defend the Bohemian plateau for more
than twenty-four hours." In any case Poitou-Duplessy persisted
in seeing the Czech issue in the context of the "duel to the
death" between the "neo-Asiatic Slavism of Moscow and the
Germanism of the Aryans of Berlin," and he clearly implied that
France could abandon her worthless ally to whatever fate the
two dictators of the east decided for her. Long before the confused days of September, 1938, many in the Federation had
made up their minds about Czechoslovakia.[31]

The leadership of the party did little to dissipate this atmosphere of resignation. Even such traditional nationalists as Camille Blaisot filled *La Nation* with denunciations of the Soviet
Union as the foremost enemy of the peace and admonitions to
conservatives to "refuse to allow the Popular Front to precipitate

---

30. *La Nation*, April 2, May 7, 28, June 4, 11, 18, 1938; *Le Jour*, June 3, 1938.
31. *Jeunesse 38*, March 15, 1938; *Le National*, June 4, 1938; *La Gazette d'Annonay*,
May 7, 1938; *L'Union Républicaine*, May 1, 1938; *Le Réveil Charentais*, March 23, 1938.

us into a bloody catastrophe for the pleasure of Stalin and the revolutionary schemes of Moscow." Late in August, Henri Becquart submitted a thoroughly anti-German article to *La Nation*, invoking the values of the Christian west against the neopaganism of the eternally belligerent Germany. Yet his article was replete with attacks on the Czech president Edouard Beneš, on the crusading zeal of the French Left, and on the duplicitous schemes of Moscow. He now hinted that the minority of firmly anti-German conservatives led by Emile Buré were acting on orders from Moscow and admitted that "Europe can live without Czechoslovakia." Marin worried about the general drift of the Federation's foreign policy and the growing tendency to regard Soviet Russia as the principal enemy of France, but he made no effort to resolve the confusion and for once did not try to impose his views on his fellow deputies. No one in the Federation seemed interested in a frank discussion about foreign policy. Becquart claims to have demanded an exchange of views among the party's deputies about their respective attitudes toward Germany and Russia, but his suggestion was received with "reproachful silence."[32]

As the Czech crisis came to a head in early September, the Federation issued a statement expressing concern about the state of the nation's preparedness and denouncing the continued application of the forty hours legislation to the war industries. Louis Marin demanded the stockpiling of strategic materials and complained of a "campaign of false news" that rendered it difficult to make an objective assessment of the international situation. On September 21 the parliamentary group of the party reiterated its demands for increased armaments and insisted on the need for a return to law and order and the ruthless suppression of revolutionary organizations.[33]

As Hitler's demands on Czechoslovakia escalated, members

---

32. *La Nation*, July 9, 1938; Henri Becquart to Marin, August 27, 1938, in Marin Papers, carton 79; Debû-Bridel, *L'Agonie de la Troisième République*, 420; Henri Becquart, *Au temps du silence* (Paris, 1945), 156–57.

33. *La Nation*, September 10, 17, 24, 1938.

of the Federation began to panic. Marin insisted that France could not contemplate war "as long as fair and perfect order does not reign in our land, as long as the law is trampled underfoot, as long as contracts are not fully respected, as long as the government supports those who are responsible for trouble." Although Victor Perret retained some composure, praising the magnificent calm of the French and the "unreserved friendship" of the British (whom he thought had at last regained the spirit of the summer of 1914), Pierre Rossillion, the director and financial columnist for *La Nation*, reminded Perret that in 1914 the nation "did not have unemployment, the forty hour week or the high cost of living."[34]

La Nation's usually circumspect staff writers grew hysterical. Marcel Petitjean pilloried what he called the "war party," "a clan" that included "the Communists, the trade unionists who have sold their soul to Moscow, the decadent intellectuals and the tedious journalists." During recent years this clan had sought "to poison Franco-German relations," and he fully expected that once again "the efforts of statesmen of 'good will,' who seek to arrive at a solution of conciliation and peace" would be "disfigured, distorted and denounced." Petitjean reasoned that Stalin and his allies desired a general European conflict "simply because they assume that a world revolution might come out of it." In explaining why the majority of the working class followed the "doctrinaires" of the "war party," Petitjean produced a remarkable exercise in class hatred. Workers, he wrote, "assume, for the most part, that, as was the case twenty-four years ago, they will continue to get royal salaries in some factory or shop in the rear, as they tranquilly produce guns, ammunitions, rifles, machine guns, tanks or airplanes while the peasants, the small businessmen, the intellectuals and the middle classes are on the front lines withstanding the attacks of the enemy."[35]

The Munich crisis, in fact, brought the party's antipathy to-

34. *Ibid.*, September 24, 1938.
35. *Ibid.*

ward the working class to the surface. Hubert Bourgin,[36] another regular contributor, remarked on the excellent morale of the nation but excluded "what extremists insist on calling the 'working class.'"

> That class does not exist . . . the workers in France do not form a class; they have the same rights as all other citizens as well as a certain number of economic and social privileges. These ought not . . . to dissociate them from the nation but should cause them to express a particular zeal and attachment for it. The persistent and all too effective effort of their leaders tends to destroy in them any recognition of this fact, destroys their loyalty and effectively detaches them from their generous and great motherland to which they owe so much.[37]

This same passage twenty-four years earlier could have been used to upbraid the cowardly working class for refusing to defend the honor of its motherland. In 1938 it served to condemn a working class which Bourgin suspected of wanting to fight to save the Czech republic from Hitler.

Henri Becquart, in a long article entitled "Above All, No Crusades," revealed the misgivings of a conservative nationalist at the prospect of war in the ideological climate of the late 1930s. France, he believed, was in danger of repeating an earlier mistake: fighting the right enemy for the wrong reasons. During World War I France had erred in pretending that the war was being fought for democracy rather than for French national security. As a consequence, France obtained from her victory in 1918 not a secure eastern frontier but a brief promise of a democratic Germany. The rhetoric of democracy had blinded France to her material self-interest during one war, and he feared that the nation would repeat that mistake.

> Once again, certain people are preaching the idea of an ideological crusade. To believe them, it is not a question of saving France and her civilization from the German peril, but one of assuring the tri-

36. Bourgin, a former secretary of the Ligue des Patriotes and a collaborator with the fascist Georges Valois in the 1920s, began to contribute to *La Nation* in 1936.

37. *La Nation*, September 24, 1938.

umph of democracy—Stalinist democracy, for example—against fascism. In saying this, not only do they diminish our chances of saving the peace and separate us from necessary alliances, but they once again risk making our eventual victory a fruitless one. [38]

Becquart clearly suggested that unless France finally recognized that the real danger stemmed from Germany herself and not merely the Nazi regime, she might once again accept a change of regime as a substitute for the definitive elimination of Germany's aggressive capacity. He also feared that by making resistance to Hitler into an ideological crusade, France would attract the wrong kind of allies (both inside and outside of France), alienate more realistic allies, and ultimately render war inevitable. Even if France were victorious, a defeated Germany, in 1938 as in 1918, would undergo a profound social and political upheaval.[39] Given the mood of the late 1930s and the ideological composition of the anti-German camp, the chances of a successful revolution were far better than they had been after the First World War. Becquart obviously wanted none of this and conditioned his anti-German nationalism and his desire to resist German expansion on the restoration of a secure and stable political and social situation in France.

Virtually all members of the Federation whose immediate reactions to the crisis have been preserved[40] were unabashedly in favor of abandoning Czechoslovakia. François Boux de Casson, deputy from the Vendée, wrote that both Berlin and Moscow sought war, the latter in order to foment worldwide revolution. Early in September Philippe Henriot despaired of saving the Czechs. Xavier Vallat now decided that the German claims on the Sudetenland were consistent with the right of national self-determination so cherished by the Left. The impending war

38. *Le Petit Bleu*, September 27, 1938.

39. As early as 1935 Pierre Taittinger had insisted that even in the event of a victory over Germany, France would still be "gangrened" by Bolshevism. *Candide*, November 28, 1935.

40. Regrettably, neither *L'Union Républicaine du Rhône* nor *Le Réveil Charentais* is preserved for the second semester of 1938. *Jeunesse 38* is missing after the first week of September.

would be fought, not in defense of any valid principle, but "to please Stalin, the high priest of universal revolution and to avenge universal Jewry which cannot forgive Hitler his anti-semitism." When Louis Marin learned on the night of September 28 that the four major powers had agreed to meet in Munich, he expressed his intense relief that war seemed to have been avoided and gave vent to the extreme fears he had recently experienced: "An international clan wished diabolically to unleash a world war, at any price and at every opportunity. Under all circumstances the weight of the war would have been supported by the France that they are attempting to Bolshevize. The unquestionable purpose of that war was the triumph of the brutal revolution of Moscow; its assured result would have been the frightful ruin of Europe, of civilization and of our nation." In his diatribe against the party of war, Marin made no attempt to take account of the handful of conservatives—Georges Mandel, Paul Reynaud, Henri de Kerillis, or Emile Buré—who advocated resistance to Hitler. What preoccupied him was the international clan that wanted to Bolshevize France. Only at the end of his article did he reveal the essentially pacifist distaste for war which World War I had instilled in even the most nationalistic of French conservatives. As he reflected on the crisis that had just passed, Marin recalled Gabriel Hanataux's celebrated phrase: "We cannot at our own expense offer the world a battle of the Marne every twenty years."[41]

Once the crisis had passed, the Federation soberly reassessed what it understood as an inglorious but inevitable diplomatic defeat. There had been two games going simultaneously in September, Philippe Henriot reported: "a Franco-German prestige match" and a "match of the Soviets against civilization." Fortunately, France had shown the wisdom not to play in either game. Joseph Denais opined that those who had counseled resistance in September had done so either "to fill their pockets by stock market speculation or to make possible the world revo-

41. *La Dépêche Vendéenne*, September 25, 1938; *Jeunesse 38*, September 1–15, 1938; *La Gazette d'Annonay*, September 17, 1938; *La Nation*, October 1, 1938.

lution." Some even professed a certain satisfaction at the defeat of "that scheming shirker, Beneš."[42]

At the special parliamentary session of October 4, Louis Marin conceded that Hitler had gained an exceptional victory and that both French honor and French security had been seriously compromised. The Republican Federation, Marin claimed, had accepted the Munich accords only because it knew that the substance of the agreement had already been granted by England and France at Berchtesgaden and accepted reluctantly by the Czechs on September 22. A campaign of false news and a lack of government information had confused the public and made it difficult to make a wise decision during the crisis. France, he concluded, had been obliged to accept a humiliating settlement because of a long series of diplomatic errors, because of her military unpreparedness, and because of the existence of a "state within a state" in France, the Communist-dominated labor unions. His speech was unexceptional and unconvincing; it it hard to understand why an American reporter told Jacques Debû-Bridel that "Louis Marin has saved the honor of French parliament." Marin's address had none of the Churchillian indignations of Kerillis' biting indictment of the Munich accords. Neither Marin nor any other member of the Federation expressed any sympathy for Kerillis' position. The only reaction came from Augustin Michel, deputy from the Loire, who interrupted Kerillis to inform him that the French peasantry did not share his apparent desire to fight for Czechoslovakia. All deputies of the Federation voted to accept the decisions made at Munich; and as Henri Becquart later observed, "After Munich, it was the rare member of the Federation who did not treat the accords as a triumph."[43]

In the aftermath of Munich, however, the Federation's tone changed. The hysterical rhetoric gave way to more moderate

42. *Le Petit Bleu*, October 1, 4, 1938; Raymond Silles, *Le Petit Loir-et-Cher*, September 30, 1938.

43. *Journal Officiel*, October 4, 1938, pp. 1932–35, 1937; Debû-Bridel, *L'Agonie de la Troisième République*, 490; Becquart, *Au temps du silence*, 157.

language, and the more paranoid theories were conveniently forgotten. Marcel Petitjean gave a very conventional explanation of the present dilemma, assigning responsibility to Briand, the Left, and the original inadequacies of the peace treaties. He now concentrated on past mistakes and present unpreparedness and completely omitted any reference to the "war party," to plots by Stalin, or to the betrayal of the working class, which had so preoccupied him a week before.[44]

The Federation was obviously uncomfortable about its stance during the crisis. In order to explain its present feebleness, the party fell back on its past intransigence. France had been forced to abandon the Czechs because the Federation had not been heeded for the first fifteen years after 1919, and the party's earlier wisdom exempted it from any present blame. Xavier Vallat, the Judeo-Masonic conspiracy now forgotten, insisted that the Federation was the only party that "in the face of the recent internal and external events, does not have to say a *mea culpa*." The party's struggles against the Locarno Pact and the Young Plan "could permit Louis Marin and his friends to subscribe to the Munich compromise as the unfortunate but inevitable consequence of errors we had condemned."[45]

At the annual congress in October, François Valentin presented the official report on the party's foreign policy. He admitted that Munich had been a disaster and attempted to justify the Federation's behavior during the crisis. The crux of his defense lay in his interpretation of the Berchtesgaden agreement of September 19. He argued that it had granted most of the Sudetenland to Germany and had been accepted, albeit reluctantly, by all parties. Consequently, all further disagreement appeared to concern only the modalities of the settlement and hardly justified resorting to war.[46] He asserted that the Berchtesgaden agreement had horrified the Federation, which

44. *La Nation*, October 1, 1938.
45. *La Gazette d'Annonay*, November 26, 1938.
46. This had been the substance of the communiqués by the party's deputies on September 28.

"doubtlessly" would have opposed it had parliament been in session. Since the Czechs had conceded the principle of territorial cession, however, the Federation merely bowed to a *fait accompli*. Without precise information about the difference between the Berchtesgaden agreement and Hitler's subsequent Godesburg demands, the Federation had been forced to conclude that the crisis of late September had been over technicalities. Valentin, nonetheless, cherished no illusions about Munich and warned that German imperialism was now insatiable.[47]

The Federation's *post-facto* justification of its position during the Munich crisis differed sharply from those given in September. In October all leaders of the Federation presented the Munich crisis as the regrettable, but unavoidable consequence of diplomatic and military weakness. The previous month, in contrast, the principal concern of all members of the party had been the threat of civil war and revolution. Their preoccupation with Communist, Masonic, or Jewish "plots," the machinations of "international clans," the "faults" of Beneš, and the "disloyal" attitude of the working class was more important than their assessment of the military potential of France. Once the crisis had passed, the leaders of the Federation might have been relieved to have escaped revolution, but they were not proud of the Munich settlement nor of their attitude in September. Therefore, it seemed more honorable to present the abandonment of Czechoslovakia as the result of France's strategic weakness and not as a necessary tactic for preserving the social order.

Contemporary political observers rarely remarked on the shift in the foreign policy of the Federation. By the late 1930s the Federation was of far less interest to the Left than "protofascist" movements like the Parti Social Français. Conservative nationalists like Emile Buré, Henri de Kerillis, and Pertinax were seriously concerned about the existence of French Hitlerians, but only infrequently did they single out specific individuals for attack. Buré once suggested that there were a number of members

47. *La Nation*, January 21, 1939.

of the Federation, including some leaders, who admired both
Mussolini and Hitler. He cited Philippe Henriot as an example.
But in an exchange of letters he was forced to admit that he had
no real evidence of the pro-German sentiments of Henriot, who
kept his personal attitudes well hidden. In his *Les Fossoyeurs*,
Pertinax made only one allusion to the Federation, and that was
to the party's opposition to sanctions during the Ethiopian crisis.
After Munich the wrath of the antiappeasers was directed toward the most notorious *munichois*: Jean Montigny, Gaston Bergery, and above all Pierre-Etienne Flandin. Newspapers of the
extreme Right concentrated on such *vendus aux Soviets* as Paul
Reynaud, Georges Mandel, and Auguste Champetier de Ribes.
The opponents of Munich could overlook the pro-Munich stance
of the Federation because in their eyes the Federation was
Louis Marin, and Louis Marin remained the symbol of French
nationalism. Two months after Munich the unyielding *anti-
munichois*, Emile Buré, asserted that Marin had always been a
traditional nationalist, not a *munichois*. Public attention focused
on the congress of the Alliance Démocratique and the struggle
between the appeaser, Flandin, and the archnationalist, Reynaud. The congress of the Federation, which took place at the
same time, was all but ignored.[48]

One reason for the absence of press coverage was the general
unanimity that prevailed within the Federation during the
Czech crisis. The Federation did not suffer the internal rifts
that the Munich accords provoked in most other parties. There
were differences of opinion about foreign policy but not fundamental ones. Jacques Debû-Bridel later divided the Republican
Federation into two camps: the *munichois* represented by Vallat
and Henriot and the *anti-munichois* represented by Marin and
Blaisot.[49] But Debû-Bridel viewed the Federation from the perspective of the postwar, and his portrait reflected the experience
of the occupation, not the reality of 1938. He was right about

48. *L'Ordre*, June 9, 13–14, 1937, November 12, 1938; Pertinax, *Les Fossoyeurs* (2
vols.; New York, 1943), I, 304n.
49. Debû-Bridel, *L'Agonie de la Troisième République*, 476.

the differences in the party but wrong about where they lay. In 1938 all members of the Federation were *munichois* in that they accepted, indeed welcomed, the Munich settlement. But there were nuances of thought on the problem—nuances that corresponded roughly to Charles Micaud's categories of "conditional" and "resigned" nationalists. The former continued to treat Germany as France's traditional enemy but were willing to resist her only on the condition that the threat of revolution posed by the Popular Front be eliminated. The latter viewed Soviet Russia as their principal enemy and resigned themselves to German expansion into eastern and central Europe.[50]

Louis Marin represented the conditional position. He always maintained a deep distrust for Germany. Although he sometimes appeared to get lost in his increasingly paranoid denunciation of the Soviet Union, he never quite lost sight of the fact that Germany was the major enemy. He refused to believe that the territorial ambitions of Germany were limited to eastern Europe, and he did not regard Czechoslovakia as expendable. In May, 1938, when others were pointing to the polyglot character of Czechoslovakia, Marin was praising the courage of the Czechs. In fact, Marin retained so many of his traditional nationalistic reflexes that many afterward remembered, erroneously, his position as having been that of an *anti-munichois*.[51]

For all his instinctive nationalism, Marin accepted the proposition that revolution would be the inevitable and intended consequence of war as long as the Popular Front remained in power. It is possible to question how sincerely Marin and the others in the party believed in the imminence of revolution. It

50. Charles A. Micaud, *The French Right and Nazi Germany, 1933–1939* (Durham, N.C., 1943). Micaud's pioneering work, based on a comprehensive examination of the Parisian press, is still the best study of the subject. In some respects, however, his analysis is unduly schematic, and his political topography is often imprecise. At different times he refers to "the Right," "the extreme Right," the "*modérés*," and the "Extremists" without clearly defining these categories or specifying which politicians and parties were in each.

51. Debû-Bridel is an example, but similar assessments were made by such diverse individuals as Lucien Rebatet, *Les Décombres* (Paris, 1942), 93, and René Rémond, *La Droite en France* (2 vols.; Paris, 1968), I, 234.

would have been tempting for them to use the specter of revolution as a cover for a reactionary domestic policy and a neo-pacifism born of latent sympathies for conservative authoritarian regimes. But in September, 1938, Marin and his colleagues had no need to draw upon the revolutionary threat to justify their opposition to war; it would have been enough to point to the military inferiority of France and to her lack of preparation for war. The fact that during the crisis Louis Marin chose to emphasize the revolutionary menace suggested that it was a fear he genuinely felt.

Between 1935 and 1938 Marin portrayed war, and more important, any diplomatic action that could conceivably lead to war, as at best a manifestation of the ideological fanaticism of the Left and at worst a cynical plot to trigger off a world revolution. He could not accept the fact that the left-wing forces in France now shared his fears for national security. Since he could see no fundamental change in the direction of German foreign policy since 1933, he suspected those who suddenly claimed that they could. Furthermore, the about-face of the Left, and particularly that of the Communists, seemed to coincide all too closely with the formation of what Marin believed to be a revolutionary front. He could not interpret the Popular Front as a defensive reaction to the threat of domestic and foreign fascism. From his perspective any electoral coalition that included the Communists had a revolutionary intent. Unlike Mandel, Reynaud, or Kerillis, Marin was unable to place the Popular Front in perspective and to recognize that Hitler threatened the France he wished to preserve far more than did Blum or Thorez.

Marin's friends in the Republican Federation liked to treat him as a French Cassandra in matters of foreign policy. Although his views had a persistent (if monomaniacal) lucidity during the 1920s and early 1930s, by the late 1930s Marin's position had become confused and uncertain. He asserted the primacy of the German peril over the Russian one, but he did so sotto voce and without condemning those who, even within his own party, feared Stalin more than Hitler. A few years earlier Marin had split the Federation because some of its members had been complacent about Germany. By 1938 when the German threat was immeasurably greater, he was no longer willing to be so categorical. In 1929 the issue had seemed relatively simple to him—either Germany had started the war or she had not; either she was bound by the peace treaties or she was not; either she had to pay or she did not. It seemed criminal to Marin for Frenchmen to forget these basic facts just because Stresemann had temporarily uttered some conciliatory phrases. By 1938 the issue seemed more complicated, clouded by the growing strength of the forces of revolution. Increasingly, Marin took refuge in empty phrases that masked his steadily dwindling resolve. Not only did he allow himself to forget about the Germans, but he allowed his journal to spew forth all the fear and hatred of a very frightened bourgeoisie. Although Marin was not entirely responsible for the sort of thing written by Petitjean and Bourgin, both men were regular contributors who had never before diverged from Marin's position. Since nothing appeared in *La Nation* that Louis Marin did not approve of, it is safe to assume that their fears were very like his own.

Other members of the Federation fell more readily into the camp of resigned nationalists. Poitou-Duplessy had implicitly given up on eastern and central Europe as early as 1936 and, in his belief that Nazism was a creed that was dangerous only to Communists, had been willing to give Hitler a free hand in the east. Few were as outspoken as Poitou-Duplessy; but Henriot, Vallat, and Lavalette all found reasons for France to abandon eastern Europe and all showed an early willingness to leave eastern Europe to its fate. For them Czechoslovakia was one of the more debatable products of the peace treaties, a polyglot state that would be difficult to defend and probably not worth defending. All were willing to admit that Hitler had a case for the destruction of Czechoslovakia. Perhaps some members of the Federation took their own rhetoric seriously and believed that if Hitler had to be challenged, France should have a more solid ally. Yet it is difficult to believe that Xavier Vallat, who had long advocated a federation of Hungarians, Austrians, and Czechs as the only means for resisting Germany, could really have thought that Czechoslovakia would have been such an impractical ally. It was impractical only because they had ceased to regard eastern Europe as critical to the security of France and because they did not care about what happened to the product of the "sick brain of President Wilson." Along with Marin and the rest of the party, they accepted the notion that war was a prelude to revolution. Their opposition to war rested on the assumption that eastern Europe had already been lost and was worth sacrificing to prevent war and revolution. Their opposition to fighting for Czechoslovakia was more shrill than Marin's and began earlier. The effect was about the same.

The differing opinions on foreign policy in 1938 were nuances rather than basic divergences. Most members of the Federation probably stood closer to Marin than to Poitou-Duplessy and would have found Marin's conditional nationalism easier to swallow than the more radical approach of the resigned nationalists. But on the Czech question the two approaches led to the same position, and it is doubtful that many in the Federation worried about which of the two *munichois* attitudes they held. Whatever regrets they may have felt afterward, every member of the party supported the Munich settlement, and no one showed any willingness to fight Hitler.

The reaction of the Republican Federation was that of a party of traditional conservatives in a confused and frightening world. The Federation's instinctive nationalism lost both its meaning and its legitimacy in the unstable climate of the late 1930s. A nationalism that flourished when it seemed consistent with, or even supportive of, the *ordre établi* became suspect when it seemed to play into the hands of the destructive forces in society. A contemporary commentator remarking on the neopacifism of French conservatives observed that "certain bourgeois abandon the patriotic sentiment insofar as the patriotic apparatus of the nation seems to be opposed to their class interests." Conservatives became reluctant to fight for "a France which increased their taxes, which obliged them to accept social legislation that they deemed to be ruinous and which, above all, stripped them of their authority and their prestige."[52] Not only did France no longer invite their loyalty, but they feared that war could only accelerate these disruptive changes. That war would inevitably lead to revolution became an axiom for much of the French Right.

Given the moderation of French Communists in the late 1930s and the fragile state of the Popular Front by 1938, conservative predictions about the imminent Bolshevization of France seem implausible and even dishonest. Conservatives after all are rarely reluctant to exaggerate the revolutionary tendencies of their opponents. Yet to the besieged *modérés* in the Federation, the threat of revolution was real enough. Not only did the balance of political power now seem to favor the working class, itself something of a revolutionary change, but during the previous two years the Communists had gained a substantial power base within the labor unions and within France. There was no reason for conservatives to believe that the temporary moderation of the Communists was anything but a tactical ruse; statements of the Communist leaders themselves assured French *modérés* that revolution was still very much their ultimate goal. Since war and defeat had given birth to revolution twenty years earlier, it seemed neither unreasonable nor unrealistic to predict a similar pattern in 1938.

Furthermore, the war-revolution hypothesis was not necessarily predicated either on defeat or on the strength of the French Communists. Even a successful war would produce chaos in central Europe, and the destruction of Nazism would leave the Soviet Union free to import revolution into that region. In her present condition, France could hardly enforce the *cordon sanitaire* as she had in 1919. More likely, a victorious and popular French army would serve as a conduit to bring the revolution home to a France that for two years had been condi-

52. Joseph Folliet, *Pacifisme de droite, bellicisme de gauche* (Paris, 1938), 40–41.

tioned to welcome it. French conservatives were not alone in making such calculations; their counterparts in England perceived a similar relation between war and revolution.[53] In the context of the "great fear" of the late 1930s, it was relatively easy for French conservatives to abandon a set of attitudes that had characterized them for over forty years. The same process that drove the once proudly *republican* Republican Federation into the arms of a Jacques Doriot also led the former bulwarks of French nationalism to welcome the Munich accords. The evolution is understandable since preservation of the existing social order meant more to conservatives than either republican purity or France's national glory. Conservatives rallied to the Republic when convinced that it could reliably defend their interests; they adopted an extreme nationalism, previously the preserve of the Left, when it seemed to strengthen internal political security. In the late 1930s neither of these conditions obtained, and conservatives like those in the Federation changed their stance accordingly.

On the eve of World War II, Louis Marin examined the path that led from the capitulation of Munich to the firm national resolve that he sensed in the summer of 1939. He saw two major steps in this evolution: the "victory of November 30" and the German aggression of March 15, 1939. Although the Popular Front had been in an advanced state of disintegration by September, 1938, the Confédération Générale du Travail (the potential shock troops of the Communists) remained powerful. Despite its distinctly nonrevolutionary tone, the CGT continued to worry the Federation as long as the government remained unwilling to curb its powers. As late as November 25, the Federation still issued press releases denouncing the Communist party "which, after having lost hope of precipitating France into a foreign war, today attempts to unleash civil war."[54]

The failure of the general strike of November 30 altered the

53. Margaret George, *The Warped Vision: British Foreign Policy, 1933–1939* (Pittsburgh, 1965); A. L. Rowse, *All Souls and Appeasement* (London, 1961).

54. *La Nation*, September 2, 1939; Marin Papers, carton 85.

domestic picture. Once the Daladier government dealt resolutely with the French workers and used its power to crush their protests, the revolutionary menace appeared to have abated. The government had at last stood up to the revolutionaries and deprived the Socialists and Communists of much of their former influence. With the Popular Front disrupted and the CGT critically weakened, the Federation slowly lost its grim view of the future. Jean Fernand-Laurent, the deputy from Paris who joined the Federation in 1938, remarked in March, 1939: "We have known some terrible and frightfully sad times. . . . But the country is reviving and is in the process of refinding its faith."[55]

The foreign policy pronouncements of the Federation gradually reflected this revival. During the first few months after Munich, La Nation retained some of the rhetoric of September. At the end of the year, Camille Blaisot still accused the Left of having plotted a revolution during the Czech crisis. He urged "patriots" to be "prudent in their recriminations against the Munich agreement so as not inadvertently to bring water to the mill of the revolutionaries." But the Federation made it clear that the era of concessions had ended, and the parliamentary group formally protested the Bonnet-Ribbentrop talks in December, 1938. The suggestion of possible colonial concessions to Germany and Italy elicited angry protests from the Federation. Louis Marin announced that he opposed any more international conferences to discuss colonies or anything else. He told the Chamber that the recent colonial demands of Italy were "monstrous," especially since France had already "given" the Italians far too much in 1935.[56]

Even the previously resigned wing of the Federation sounded more resolute. Vallat still insisted that France was not "the gendarme of Europe," and Henriot continued to urge concessions on the Czechs. In the Chamber, however, Henriot attacked the

55. La Nation, March 18, 1939.
56. La Nation, December 3, 24, 1938, February 11, 1939; Journal Officiel, January 24, 1939, p. 192.

"curious doctrine" of Gaston Bergery, the archappeaser, who advocated a free hand in the east for Hitler. Vallat affirmed that it was as necessary to contain Germany's eastward ambitions as to curtail the influence of the Soviet Union.[57]

The German coup in Czechoslovakia on March 15, 1939, made a profound impact on western opinion, and within France even some of the most frantic *munichois* reverted to a traditional nationalism. For the first time, the Federation was prepared to grant the Daladier government full powers to deal with the international crisis, on the condition that it show "the firmest determination to abandon the policy of weakness and return . . . to a foreign policy worthy of the name of France." Two weeks later when Britain guaranteed the integrity of Poland, Marin could hardly contain his joy; Britain had at last come to her senses, and this "historic date" marked the beginning of the revival of the western democracies. To those who worried that Britain's support had come too late, he reported: "It is never too late!" An element of reticence remained, although it was no longer based on the fear of revolution but on a profound horror of war. Victor Perret, while pleased that Britain now considered the Rhine to be her frontier, nonetheless noted anxiously that in the event of war it would still be France that absorbed the initial blow. Xavier Vallat predicted victory in a future war, as in the previous one, but he too wondered: "at the cost of what sacrifices!" No one relished the prospect of war, but their reservations were fundamentally different from those of the previous year.[58]

By the summer of 1939 Louis Marin had returned to his favorite role as a guardian of French interests around the world. He devoted no less than five articles to protesting France's cession to Turkey of the Sanjak of Alexandretta. As war loomed,

57. *La Gazette d'Annonay*, April, 1939; *La Liberté du Sud-Ouest*, October 25, 1939; *Journal Officiel*, January 20, 1939, p. 143, January 24, 1939, p. 170.
58. Micaud, *The French Right*, 206–21; Dieter Wolf, *Doriot* (Paris, 1969), 288–94; *La Nation*, March 24, April 8, 1939; *La Gazette d'Annonay*, April 14, 24, 1939.

Henri Becquart filled *La Nation* with accounts of the "Goths" and "Huns" whose "bellicose humor" and "appetite for domination" made them a threat to civilization. Since the eighteenth century there had been no "good" Germans. If France were forced in the near future to take up arms against her barbarian neighbor, Becquart warned that she would not put them down "until we have broken up Germany and made it peaceful and inclined, as formerly, only towards the arts and good living."[59]

Nonetheless, the Federation's increasing firmness against Hitler was not complemented by any willingness to improve relations with the Soviet Union. Although the menace of domestic Communists had dwindled, the Federation still opposed a military alliance with the Soviet Union and refused to consider her a potential partner in the struggle against Pan-Germanism. Alfred Oberkirch told the Chamber that he could see no value in the Soviet pact. It had alienated France from its conservative eastern neighbors, the quality of the Soviet military seemed questionable, and most important the Soviets could not be trusted. He warned of a possible rapprochement between Russia and Germany, observing that in spite of the constant verbal duel between the two powers there were signs of increased diplomatic and economic cooperation. He proposed that France turn her attention from Russia to her much more natural ally, Poland. In June, 1939, Camille Blaisot admitted that France ought not to exclude automatically any potential allies, but he argued that good faith was a necessary precondition for an effective alliance against Hitler. Consequently, he ruled out an alliance with Soviet Russia, who would almost certainly betray France at the first opportunity. Two months later Blaisot's prophecy fulfilled itself, and Russia and Germany signed a pact of nonaggression. Blaisot, recalling his earlier foresight, expressed no alarm and relatively little indignation. "The enemy," he said, "has been demasked, he will not strike us in the back." Marin too expressed relief that all of the known villains were now in the same

59. *La Nation*, August 9, 1939.

camp, and France was rid of her "unnatural alliance." Marin stated, "Without doubt, the Anglo-French bloc is more solid after the famous pact; the spirit of the two nations is calmer and more resolved in the face of the possible tempest." The prospect of Hitler now having his eastern flank protected or the possibility that the working class would now be less eager to fight against Hitler counted for less than the fact that as a result of the pact, the Communist party had been discredited, divided, and outlawed. The final loss of a potential ally made the Federation more, and not less, willing to resist Hitler. The signing of the German-Soviet nonaggression pact divested France of an awkward and dangerous ally. Moreover, the subsequent outlawing of the French Communists meant that wartime France would once again be able to restore social order and discipline. War was no longer a vehicle for revolution but a potential means for securing the badly shaken fabric of French society.[60]

As war began to appear inevitable, even some who had stubbornly opposed war over Czechoslovakia stood firm over Poland. On the eve of the war Philippe Henriot wrote an article for *Gringoire* entitled "Paix oui, guerre à terme non." He argued that if Hitler were determined to go to war with the west, there was little point in stalling for time by making further concessions. He listed all the reasons why France now had the stronger hand. Italy would only support Hitler, if at all, "with a sense of despair." The Soviets, no longer allies, would stay prudently out of the conflict and remain neutral vis-à-vis Poland. Hitler's troops were spread across a broad front, many were still raw recruits, and the officer corps was of low caliber. In addition, many of his troops were conscripts from Austria and Bohemia, German morale was bad, and food stocks were low.

By contrast, the morale of France and England has never been and perhaps never will be as high, as calm and as determined. Neither bluster nor puerile illusions. Because the question has never been

60. *Journal Officiel*, January 26, 1939, p. 219; *La Nation*, August 9, September 2, 1939.

and perhaps never will be more clearly put. It is no longer the case, as it was two years ago, of a people that was divided, disoriented, unarmed, isolated and ruined by two years of the Popular Front which wanted to lead them to the slaughterhouse for a cause which seemed obscure. Today the nation is aware, renewed, recovered, re-armed, sure of its allies and this is reflected in the formula that one hears everywhere and which is the essential truth of the hour: since we cannot deal with that faithless man of prey, who is simultaneously as ruthless as a plague and as tortuous as a pettifogger, what is the point of delaying the inevitable. Therefore, if he wishes, by capitulation, to save the peace, we are agreed. But, if, having discovered that the game is going badly for him, he only wants to postpone the war, the answer is no.

Henriot's record under the Vichy regime has obscured the fact that on the eve of the Second World War he was quite willing to die for Danzig.[61]

The revival of the traditional nationalistic bellicosity of the Federation was due in some measure to external developments. Since March the aggressiveness of Hitler had become more marked, and it was difficult to deceive oneself about the threat that he represented. Many in the party had reconciled themselves to the Munich settlement by insisting that it would mark the last concession; Hitler's demands on Danzig seemed like the last straw. But internal developments played the major role in the party's change of attitude. The great fear of revolution, so prevalent in September, 1938, had disappeared with the end of the Popular Front and the collapse of the working-class movements. The critical precondition for resistance to Hitler had at last been attained.

The shift in the party's position on foreign affairs closely followed the changing fortunes of the domestic Left. The party began to abandon its traditional stance in 1935, at the same time as

61. *Gringoire*, August 31, 1939. Henriot later helped obscure this fact about himself in Philippe Henriot, *Comment mourut la paix* (Paris, 1941). He denounced the "*bellicistes,*" who refused to negotiate with Hitler and who insisted on such unreasonable conditions as the evacuation of Poland.

the formation of the Popular Front. It did not begin to regain its former posture until the Popular Front definitively collapsed at the end of 1938. The connection between the two phenomena is undeniable. The Republican Federation abandoned its unbending nationalism from fear of the social and political consequences of the Popular Front. Although fear of war or fear of losing played a part in the determination of the party's attitude during those critical three years, the major determinant was fear of revolution.

VII. *Vichy*

The Vichy regime temporarily ended the political chaos and social insecurity of the 1930s and restored an order that was far closer to the ideal of French conservatives than the later Third Republic had been. Old values appeared to be restored, and the enemies of the conservatives were destroyed or driven underground. The new order of Vichy seemed to pave the way for a revival of a France that had degenerated in the twentieth century. But the return to social stability came at a price—a crushing French defeat and diplomatic and military domination by France's traditional enemy. At best the new regime shared power with the occupier, and in order to retain what authority had been left to it, it was drawn into a policy of increased collaboration with Germany. Torn between patriotic sentiment and a desire to recapture the secure and stable France they had once known, most French conservatives opted to support the Vichy regime and accepted collaboration as unpleasant but unavoidable. A few went beyond this *"collaboration d'état"* [1] and actively supported the nation that they assumed would be dominant in postwar Europe. Only a tiny minority among French conservatives were moved by hostility to the Germans and fidelity to the republican tradition to oppose the Vichy regime from the outset.

There was much in the Vichy regime that appealed to the Republican Federation. The new government promised a return to the traditional values that had been lost in the latter days of the Republic, restored to conservatives, if rarely their political

1. The expression is from Stanley Hoffman, "Collaboration in France during World War II," *Journal of Modern History*, XL (1968), 375–95.

power, at the least their social and moral authority, and initiated many of the reforms the Federation had clamored for in the 1930s. For many in the party, the Vichy interlude came as a relief from the frighteningly unstable days of the late 1930s. But the party's adhesion to Vichy was not quite unanimous and not without some afterthoughts. A few of the party's leaders opposed the regime from very nearly the beginning, and the Federation retained some of its traditional nationalism as well as some measure of its liberalism. Even while praising the positive accomplishments of Vichy, members of the party often regarded certain features of the regime with distaste, notably its collaboration with Germany and certain of its totalitarian innovations. Although the Federation ceased all political activity during the Vichy regime, enough of the party apparatus remained intact and enough of its directing personnel remained in public life to permit an examination of the response of these conservatives to the *ordre nouveau* of 1940–1944.

Although the Federation substantially regained its nationalistic instinct during the months before the outbreak of war, its preoccupation with the domestic Left remained intense. During the "phony war" the Federation supported the Daladier government, but it grew increasingly impatient at its lethargic prosecution of the war against France's enemies, both within and without. After the signing of the German-Soviet pact in August, 1939, and especially after the Soviet invasion of Finland, the Federation treated the Germans and the Communists, French and foreign, as equally dangerous enemies. Louis Marin argued that the invasion of Finland proved once and for all that in spite of apparent differences, Nazis and Communists were united by identical methods. Philippe Henriot told the Chamber that it was no longer possible to draw a distinction between Stalin and Hitler. "There is," he affirmed, "no enemy number one and enemy number two, there are two enemy number one's." René Dommange, an affiliated deputy, went further and suggested that Germany was only the enemy of France, whereas Communism was the enemy both of France and of civilization. In fact, many deputies of the Federation showed far more enthusiasm for a war with the Soviet Union than one against Hitler. In March, 1940, Jean Fernand-Laurent complained of France's ambiguous relationship with the Soviet Union. Surely, he suggested, the ally of Germany and the assassin of Poland and Finland might legitimately be considered an enemy of France. Later noting that the war against Germany had reached a stalemate, he argued that the only way to regain the initiative was to attack Germany's ally, the Soviet Union. Had France intervened more energetically in support of the Finns, she could have attacked Germany through its Russian flank.[2] Wartime censorship and political discretion prevented members of the Federation from making this kind of proposal very often. Nonetheless, Fernand-Laurent clearly betrayed a widespread feeling that war with Germany was not complete without one against the Soviet Union. This sanguine attitude toward the stalemate on the German front and the desire for adventurous campaigns against Russia helped prepare the country for the Vichy regime.

The Federation demanded the vigilant repression of domestic traitors but restricted its attention almost exclusively to the Communists. The party refused to admit the existence of pro-German elements on the Right and treated those who warned of a Nazi fifth column as paranoid scaremongers. When Henri de Kerillis attempted to warn of the dangers of the pro-German elements within France, Xavier Vallat, Georges Cousin, André Parmentier, and Philippe Henriot savagely attacked him. Three of these four would soon show how correct Kerillis had been.[3]

The Republican Federation, like most French political parties, did not play a very distinguished role in the last days of the Third Republic. Louis Marin, since May 10 a minister of state in Paul Reynaud's government, was one of those who most firmly opposed the armistice and who counseled continuing the strug-

2. *La Nation*, November 25, December 23, 1939; *Journal Officiel*, January 16, 1940, p. 48, March 22, 1940, p. 400; *Chambre des Députés, Comités secrets*, March 19, 1940 (Paris, 1948).

3. *Journal Officiel*, January 16, 1940, pp. 29–34.

gle in North Africa.[4] Once the armistice had been signed, however, neither Louis Marin nor any other member of the party seriously resisted the schemes of Pierre Laval and Marshal Pétain. Forty-three of the party's deputies voted full powers to the Marshal on July 10, 1940, and the rest either abstained or did not take part in the vote.[5]

The sudden collapse of France, the demoralizing retreat of parliament to Bordeaux and then to Vichy, and the chaotic and confused state of the nation left the deputies of the Federation ill prepared to resist the clever maneuvering of Laval. Jean Crouan, for example, had escaped from a prisoner-of-war camp and had walked 450 kilometers in the previous two weeks to arrive in Vichy early in the morning of July 9. The deputy from the Finistère did not grasp the significance of the issues being voted upon and "followed blindly" the advice of his colleagues on July 10. No one in the Federation, including Louis Marin, provided any leadership for the frightened and confused deputies. Marin distrusted Pétain, but he had been badly shaken by the defeat and by the defeatist sentiments of his associates. Consequently, he limited himself to preaching resistance in the corridors. Even in this capacity, he hardly constituted a pole of resistance to the Marshal. When Georges Roulleaux-Dugage, deputy from the Orne, confronted the president of the Republican Federation on the eve of the July 10 vote, asking him anx-

4. After the war, Louis Marin maintained that the partisans of continued resistance were in the majority in Reynaud's cabinet and that Reynaud should not have surrendered the government to those, led by Pétain, who wanted an armistice. Louis Marin, "Contributions à l'étude des prodromes de l'armistice," Revue d'histoire de la deuxième guerre mondiale, I (1951), 1–26. See also his testimony before the high court of justice at Pétain's trial. Le Procès du Maréchal Pétain (Paris, 1945), 63–72. On Marin's role in the government, see particularly Jean-Noël Jeanneney (ed.), Jules Jeanneney: Journal Politique (Paris, 1972), 61, 68, 70, 73–74; Paul Baudouin, Neuf mois au gouvernement (Paris, 1948), 150, 161, 163, 169.

5. Joseph Bastide and André Baud declared their abstentions; Joseph Denais and Bernard de la Groudière were in Algeria, having departed from Bordeaux on the Massila; Marin, Camille Blaisot, André Daher, Vincent Inizan, Emile Lardier, Jacques du Luart, Bernard de Coral, Fernand Wiedemann-Goiran, and Ernest Sourioux did not take part in the vote. Alexandre Duval was absent from the session, and André Parmentier was a prisoner of war. All the rest voted for Vichy.

iously what the party should do the next day, Marin's only reply to his repeated inquiries was a resigned and bitter "Pff." Although Marin never hid his distrust for Pétain, he did not vote against giving him full powers but simply refused to take part in the vote.[6]

Perhaps in more normal circumstances some members of the Federation might have had reservations about granting full power to Pétain. But many obviously welcomed the vote of July 10 as a long-awaited opportunity to modify the political structure of France. Indeed, some were clearly in an indecent hurry to bury the Republic and replace it with an authoritarian alternative. Seven deputies of the Federation—Vallat, Vallette-Viallard, Cousin, Poitou-Duplessy, Temple, Boucher, and d'Aramon—were among the sixty-nine parliamentarians who signed the Bergery Declaration. The declaration, drafted by the Radical Gaston Bergery and presented before the National Assembly on July 10, condemned the war as having been unnecessary, unwise, and unconstitutional and demanded that the Republic be replaced by a new and radically different government. The new regime was to undertake a policy of "collaboration" with Germany and was to institute an authoritarian national and social "new order" at home. The declaration recognized the universal drift toward "a national form of socialism" and urged that the new France have "a regime which accords with those of continental Europe."[7] Besides revealing instinctive authoritarian tendencies, the deputies who signed the Bergery Declaration betrayed an early eagerness to abandon all resistance to the Germans.

These seven deputies were, of course, a small minority of the Federation's representatives as well as a minority of the sixty-nine signatories, eight of whom were Socialists. But even among

6. Crouan's resistance dossier, in Marin Papers, carton 75; Henri Becquart, *Au temps du silence* (Paris, 1945), 159; Xavier Vallat, *Le Nez de Cléopâtre* (Paris, 1957), 182, 185; François de Saint-Just, *Une Bataille perdue* (Paris, 1964), 116.

7. The text of the Bergery Declaration is taken from Jacques de Launay (ed.), *Le Dossier de Vichy* (Paris, 1967), 291–99.

those deputies who retained their unconditional hostility to Germany there was a general feeling that France needed a fundamental change of regime. Henri Becquart, although outraged by the terms of the armistice, voted full powers to Pétain and afterward admitted: "I definitely wanted the constitution changed and I agreed that the chance to do so without too much difficulty might not come again and hence we should seize the opportunity." To Becquart, voting against granting the Marshal full powers meant losing "the opportunity to get rid of institutions whose exhaustion and growing harmfulness were clear." He insisted that modifying the constitution in a more authoritarian and disciplined direction did not imply collaboration with Germany. On the contrary, only a new constitution could provide France with the basis for a future *relèvement*. "We should," he wrote, "have made the national revolution by calling on the country for heroic resistance and not by preaching cowardly resignation." Since Becquart admittedly considered Pétain's foreign policy prior to July 10 to have been "disastrous," it was at best exceedingly naïve to have expected the Marshal to mount a "heroic resistance." Moreover, it cannot have escaped him that the constitution could have been modified without granting such sweeping powers to Pétain. But Becquart, like most of the deputies of the party, submitted to a willing suspension of disbelief and closed his eyes to the possible consequences of his act. Under the circumstances that prevailed at Vichy, the bulk of the deputies of the Federation, like their fellow parliamentarians, willingly abdicated their responsibilities and abandoned a Republic that few of them still cherished.[8]

With the fall of the Republic, the Republican Federation ceased all political activity, and *La Nation* abruptly ceased publication after May, 1940. The party's headquarters were dispersed, and most former leaders of the Federation went their own way. The Federation's reaction to the new regime can to some degree be traced through its branch in the Rhône. Under

8. Becquart, *Au temps du silence*, 176, 183.

Vichy, Victor Perret decreed that all political struggles must immediately cease so that all political energies could be channeled into the Légion Française des Combattants. Nonetheless, the Federation of the Rhône retained its esprit de corps for several years. Former leaders of the Federation continued to meet under the auspices of the Foyers sociaux du Rhône, and it continued to refer to *militants* by the office they had held in the Federation. Well into 1941 the local branch of the Federation still held reunions on social occasions. Perret and his associates continued to publish a weekly newspaper, although the name changed from *L'Union Républicaine* to *La Renaissance Nationale*.

L'Union Républicaine had published no defeatist sentiments; all its contributors had been partisans of a *guerre à l'outrance*.[9] Once Pétain had been granted full powers, however, the newspaper expressed the warmest approval of the Marshal and hailed him as the only man capable of saving France. Octave Lavalette declared that it was impossible "not to be, with all one's heart and all one's mind, behind Marshal Pétain and the courageous men who surrounded him and support him." Victor Perret announced that the initial measures taken by the Vichy government corresponded to the deeply felt wishes of the Federation. He wrote: "It is with a profound satisfaction and an immense moral joy that we see the establishment of a new order from which will be excluded the abuses, the various forms of favoritism, the demagogy so destructive to human effort, the intrigues, the financial disorders, the shameful plurality of offices and finally, *la république des camarades* which prepared our ruin and our defeat." Perret and Lavalette admitted that the new regime would be more authoritarian than its predecessor and that henceforth Frenchmen would be less free. However, both

9. Although men like Octave Lavalette had been lukewarm in their opposition to Germany prior to 1939, during the war the Union Républicaine showed no signs of defeatism. On the eve of the French collapse, Perret, Denais, Lavalette, and even Henriot were calling for continued resistance. See *L'Union Républicaine du Rhône*, June 8, 1940.

agreed that such sacrifices were inevitable if France were to restore her greatness. Lavalette did not think that it mattered that "certain liberties, more nominal than real" should be lost if this "momentary sacrifice is necessary to assure the recovery of France, after which . . . all legitimate liberties will regain their proper place." The time had come, Perret informed his readers, for Frenchmen once again to discipline themselves and to "abandon certain liberties and submit to certain demands and privations."[10]

No one regretted the passing of the Republic. In November, 1940, the *Union Républicaine* changed its name to *La Renaissance Nationale* because the word *republican* in the title was "equivocal." Perret explained that he did not want his readers to conclude that the old title "implied a regret for institutions that have been abolished or a fidelity to a form of government which has been definitively eliminated by the very debacle which it prepared." Alexandre Bosse-Platière affirmed that "the elective regime lowered and perverted the moral sense of the people." Jean Fernand-Laurent defended the Vichy regime against the charge of having been imposed from above. He granted that the National Revolution was primarily the work of the Marshal, but he insisted that it had been accepted with "an undeniable and quasi-unanimous popular élan." As far as he was concerned, "the masses" were only "an instrument, aware or unaware, good or bad, depending on who is leading them." He also asserted: "We have always maintained that the masses . . . in no way aspire to control but, on the contrary, wish to be led."[11] The deputy for the sixteenth arrondissement of Paris had not, in fact, openly expressed such sentiments prior to the coming of the Vichy regime. The new order left members of the Federation free to air views about the democratic republic that they had heretofore preferred to leave unsaid.

10. *L'Union Républicaine du Rhône*, July 14, 29, 1940.
11. *La Renaissance Nationale*, November 15, 21, 1941. The *Annuaire de la Presse* for 1944 indicates that at least two dailies in Lyon managed to retain the word *republican* in their titles.

The early domestic legislation of the Vichy government clearly pleased the former members of the Federation of the Rhône. The new regime attempted to remodel French society along lines that the Republican Federation had always approved. It restored religion to its proper place, the family once again became the focus of social life, authority took precedence over anarchy, and social harmony replaced the idea of class struggle. Social legislation no longer reflected the irresponsible dictates of foreign-controlled labor unions, but it reflected instead a sensible concern for the spiritual as well as the social well-being of Frenchmen of all classes. The peasantry and the artisans, who represented the real strength of the nation, now received priority over the once-favored urban proletariat, who had been led astray and had helped betray its motherland. The Freemasons, the bête noire of all patriotic and Christian Frenchmen, had at last been dissolved and their occult dictatorship destroyed. The false liberty and the demagogy of the old regime had been replaced by the spiritual values and social duty of the new order. In short, the new national trinity—*Travail, Famille, Patrie*—suited the Federation very well.

Spokesmen for the Federation thought they saw in the new order the promise of a return to an earlier and more stable preindustrial society and economy. Shortly after the defeat Jean Duquaire, a former executive member of the Federation of the Rhône, wrote: "In the middle of the debris of the industrial order we perceive that if the earth is at times a harsh friend, it is at least a sure friend." Victor Perret expressed the hope that under the new regime France was "witnessing the blossoming of professional and artisanal organizations . . . which assure dignity, and the possibility of a relative degree of independence to the man possessed of the *joie de vivre* and the love of his trade." He hoped to see "a social transformation favorable to the union between all classes," "the collaboration between capital and labor" and "economic recovery by means of quality production."[12]

Marshal Pétain struck a responsive chord in the Federation

12. *L'Union Républicaine du Rhône*, July 29, 1940.

when he denounced the moral and cultural decadence of the old regime. The new government, it was hoped, would restore the vigor and purity of Frenchmen in general and its youth in particular. Victor Perret welcomed the Chantiers de Jeunesse, which would produce "virile men, upstanding, courageous, clever, and adroit while at the same time possessing healthy minds, pure hearts and simple souls, prepared for the real life of family, of work, of society and the motherland." The passing of the Republic stimulated hopes for a cleansing of public morals. Guy St. Laumer, an executive member of the Federation, promised that henceforth French radio and cinema would feature fewer "stories of sordid love affairs and adulteries, licentious songs, and all the other 'scandalous depravities'" that had tempted prewar youth.[13]

In general, the former members of the Republican Federation found themselves very much at home in the France of Marshal Pétain, and their attachment to the new order represented more than a reluctant resignation to the French defeat. Yet despite its general approbation of the new regime, there were aspects of Vichy that the Federation did not endorse. Although *La Renaissance Nationale* energetically attacked Freemasons, virtually the only reference to Jews in the newspaper was one brief reminder that Jews had often associated closely with Freemasons under the Third Republic. Although Xavier Vallat had formerly been closely associated with the Federation of the Rhône, his name was never mentioned after he became head of the Commissariat général aux questions juives. Similarly, the speeches of such pro-Nazi converts as Philippe Henriot ceased to appear in the pages of *La Renaissance Nationale*. The themes of fascists like Jacques Doriot and Marcel Déat found no echo among the members of the Federation of the Rhône, and their newspaper reproached (albeit obliquely) Déat for his criticisms of traditional conservatives.[14] The men of the Rhône stood solidly behind Pé-

13. *Ibid.*, September 8, 1940; *La Renaissance Nationale*, December 15, 1941.
14. *L'Union Républicaine du Rhône*, October 18, 1940. *La Renaissance Nationale*, December 15, 1941, ridiculed (but on the last page) both Déat and "the remarkable *bobards* that he peddles."

tain, but they distrusted the more dynamic and racist figures in Paris. Long before the prospect of an allied victory made discretion advisable, these former party members drew a distinct line between the Marshal, whom they fully trusted, and the fascist element, whom they did not. For them the Vichy regime was to be a conservative restoration and not a fascist adventure.

Furthermore, the sweeping attacks on the old regime and the parliamentary system then in vogue made some members of the Federation uneasy. Despite their newly articulated contempt for past institutions, they had been active politicians in the Third Republic and had taken electoral politics seriously. Without wishing to question the present regime or to deny the obvious flaws in the old system, representatives of the Federation insisted that the detractors of the Third Republic should distinguish between those who had corrupted the parliamentary republic and those who had served it honorably and tried to reform it. It was irritating to discover that some of the most vocal critics of the parliamentary republic had been apolitical in the previous decade and had done nothing to prevent the disaster of 1940. Victor Perret admitted that the Republic had been "rotten" and that universal suffrage had been "stupid"; he did not dispute that a change of regime had been "indispensable." But, "to harp forever on the same string," as did some of the critics of the Republic, served only to blur the distinction between those who had served France under the previous regime and those who had merely used France. Alexandre Bosse-Platière protested against the tendency to damn all political parties as "the cause of our misfortunes." He noted that at the first congress of the Légion Française des Combattants speaker after speaker had lumped together all of the prewar politicians, Radicals and Socialists, with the conservatives of the Republican Federation. It struck him as fundamentally unjust that the hardworking and dedicated members of the Federation should be castigated as "politicians"—particularly when such injurious remarks issued from those who had often shirked from their duty during the 1930s. A former *militant* Joseph Pouzen, commenting on the career of Victor Perret after his death in August, 1941, noted that it was now fashionable to malign former political leaders. Such scorn, he objected, was unfair because under the Third Republic "to be a *militant* in one of those great nationalistic parties whose name has not yet been forgotten, was the equivalent of being a militant legionnaire in today's National Revolution."[15]

To demonstrate that having been an active member of the Republican Federation and being a loyal supporter of the Marshal were not incompatible, many members of the Federation insisted that the Vichy government had merely implemented the program of the Federation. In November, 1940, Perret announced that the Vichy government had "realized, one after another, all the articles of the program which we unsuccessfully advocated for thirty years." Former *militants* frequently argued that if the Federation had been heeded during the Third Republic, the disaster of 1940 could have been avoided and the Marshal would not now have to attempt to rebuild France under such difficult circumstances. Joseph Denais, initially warmly pro-Vichy, even felt that the Republican Federation still had a role to play in the new France. The Federation's "deputies and *militants*" had "rendered the resurrection of our country possible," and to continue to contribute to the effort of national regeneration they need only "persevere in the paths that they have always followed." He also recommended that each member of the party "keep as closely in touch as possible with his departmental union and with the Republican Federation at large."[16]

For several years under titles like "The Marshal has fulfilled the wishes of the FR," the former members of the Federation claimed the parentage of the new order. Victor Perret pronounced such reforms as Vichy's old age and family legislation to be "precisely as conceived by the Republican Federation" and claimed that the Federation had been "the advanced champions

15. *La Renaissance Nationale*, June 29, July 31, November 30, 1941.
16. *L'Union Républicaine du Rhône*, July 29, September 28, 1940, November 8, 1941.

of the new order." Bosse-Platière, in a revealing statement, declared: "Thanks to us, Marshal Pétain found a state of mind which permitted him to implement his reforms."[17] Statements like these would one day seem like damning evidence against the Republican Federation. At the time they were made, however, these affirmations were part of an attempt to legitimize the prewar record of the party for the benefit of those who might have found the old *modérés* insufficiently imbued with the spirit of the new order. They also suggest that although the Federation welcomed the comparative domestic stability of Vichy, it retained a nostalgia for *la république conservatrice*, which had regrettably disappeared in the chaos of the 1930s.

During the first two years of the Vichy regime, members of the Republican Federation of the Rhône enthusiastically approved most of the domestic legislation of the new government. On questions of foreign policy they were far more circumspect. Most did not want to speculate on the outcome of the war, and they rarely went beyond vague references to possible future European cooperation. In 1941 Perret admitted that some *modérés* objected to the current discussions between the government and the Reich for "an honorable and independent collaboration." Without directly addressing the issues of Franco-German collaboration, he reminded his readers: "We have committed grave errors so let us accept our misfortunes and go back to work."[18] Since foreign policy was no longer the affair of the common man, he proposed that former members of the Federation leave such complex problems in the capable hands of the Marshal. His attitude reflected his faith in Pétain but also his unwillingness to face the disquieting issues raised by the fact of collaboration with Germany.

For the most part, members of the party confined their observations on foreign policy to expressing a certain Anglophobia. It was England that had coddled Germany after the First World War, it was England that had failed to support France in 1940,

17. *La Renaissance Nationale*, April 27, June 29, 1941.
18. *Ibid.*, June 29, 1941.

and it was England that had killed French sailors at Mers-el-kebir and now appeared to have designs on the French Empire. Bosse-Platière remembered the English persecution of Joan of Arc and concluded that history taught that France had "only one secular and hereditary enemy: England."[19] For most members of the Federation, a distrust for perfidious Albion did not imply a corresponding enthusiasm for Nazi Germany, and most commentators remained discreetly silent about the possibility of a German victory.

Nonetheless, a few former members of the Federation diverged from their colleagues on the question of foreign policy and pronounced in favor of active collaboration with Nazi Germany. France, they asserted, had been vanquished, and her only chance for recovery lay in cooperation with Germany. Bosse-Platière argued: "It was we who committed the folly of attacking them and they beat us"; consequently, "if they offer us the opportunity of constructing the new order, why should we refuse?" Siding with the Allies and the Gaullists would only lead France back into a war from which she had so mercifully escaped. It would mean sacrificing France to the imperialist ambitions of the Anglo-Saxons and to the revolutionary designs of their Bolshevik ally. In response to those who accused him of betraying France, Bosse-Platière replied that, although France had been soundly crushed by Germany and could reasonably expect very little from her, she had been offered a chance to rebuild Europe. "Had we been in their position, would we have had their generosity? One might well doubt it. We are privileged people, those who suffer least from the war. Look around you and compare."[20] For Bosse-Platière collaboration with Germany had real advantages for France. It was not merely a question of assisting the war machine of France's former enemy but one of voluntarily contributing to the new European order that would arise after the war.

19. *Le Réveil du Beaujolais*, June 4, 1941. Bosse-Platière ceased active collaboration with *La Renaissance Nationale* at the end of 1941, but he continued to write editorials in the local *Réveil* until the middle of 1943.
20. *Ibid.*, June 4, September 2, 1941.

Octave Lavalette, who became editor of *La Renaissance Nationale* after Perret's death, also stressed the importance of "European collaboration," insisting that on this question "sentiment must cede to reason." He revealed his absolute sincerity about the value of collaboration by his defense of the Service de Travail Obligatoire. Imposed on Vichy by the Germans in February, 1943, the terms of the Service de Travail Obligatoire obliged France to provide Germany with a quarter of a million young men to work in the factories of the Reich in return for several minor administrative advantages and a modification of the status of French prisoners of war. This measure, by which France made heavy sacrifices in return for token concessions, demonstrated clearly what collaboration with the Germans really meant. No measure was more unpopular, and none did more to stimulate the growth of resistance to the regime and the occupying forces. Lavalette, however, defended the Service de Travail Obligatoire on the grounds that the limited advantages that France gained were all that she had a right to expect under the present circumstances. France had to learn that she could not be an idle spectator in the momentous struggle against Bolshevism. "One fact that the country is beginning to perceive is that France, like all European nations, must play its role in the defense of the continent against the Bolshevik tide." He saw the crusade against Bolshevism as one "in which France participates by her work and which others carry out in deadly and bitter combat." In the all-important struggle against Communism, France had the easier task. While Germans were dying on the eastern front, French youth had only to spend two years of forced labor in Germany. For Lavalette it was well worth the price. The Service de Travail Obligatoire might be "deeply painful," but it presented "advantages for the moment and above all for the future" because "by these sacrifices, France buys the right to take part in the reconstruction of our continent and to take part, not as a defeated nation obliged to accept the conditions of the victor, but as an associate, who is entitled by the services she has rendered, to work for the organization of

Europe and to take her place in it instead of having to accept a Europe made by others."[21]

The Service de Travail Obligatoire was the type of measure that caused many early converts to Pétainism to pause and reconsider. For Lavalette it involved "tasks consented to freely and loyally fulfilled." The former propaganda delegate of the Republican Federation of the Rhône believed that the need to construct a new, antirevolutionary Europe outweighed the traditional fear and distrust of Germany.

When they defended the policy of Franco-German collaboration, Lavalette and Bosse-Platière assumed that the new order would be a German one, and the prospect did not disturb them. Bosse-Platière pointedly observed that a German military defeat would "bring with it the immediate Bolshevization of the country." Without a "stable" Germany the forces of order in France would not be able to contain the domestic revolutionary elements. The Allies could not be trusted to preserve the social order, for had they not joined with the Soviet Union? Should the Allies win, Bosse-Platière wondered, "Who would stop the irresistible wave of Asiatics?"[22] Given the ubiquitous threat of Communism, Germany was not only the probable but also the preferable victor.

No other contributors to *La Renaissance Nationale* expressed enthusiasm for collaboration. After the Allied landing on North Africa and the German occupation of the south of France, much of the earlier admiration for the Vichy regime evaporated. Previous contributors either ceased to write or submitted increasingly innocuous articles. Joseph Denais, whose reservations about the Marshal's foreign policy had already earned him a period of detention, now limited his articles to technical discussions of finance or historical examinations of the failures of Joseph Caillaux or Ledru-Rollin. The National Revolution and the new order ceased to generate much excitement, and the French Empire and its potential greatness absorbed most of the attention. *La*

21. *La Renaissance Nationale*, December 15, 1941, February 28, June 15, 1943.
22. *Le Réveil du Beaujolais*, April 27, 1943.

Renaissance Nationale did denounce the "Communist-inspired terror" and the threat of civil war. Increasingly, it challenged the pretensions of Gaullist "émigrés," who had deserted France in her darkest hour. But most writers were deliberately vague, and their analyses of events usually degenerated into reiterations of the spiritual values of Catholicism. The change of tone from the earlier, more exuberant days of the Vichy regime reflected the growing disillusionment with the policy of the government and the general loss of faith in the "double game" of the Marshal. In some cases a desire to avoid becoming a target of the ever more active resistance prompted a gradual withdrawal from the political scene. Bosse-Platière admitted in August, 1943, that he had been threatened for his collaborationist articles. Although he insisted that he would not be deterred by the empty threats of Gaullist traitors, he soon ceased to write editorials in his newspaper. Only Octave Lavalette continued to defend both the Vichy regime and collaboration until the end, insisting that an Allied victory would mean at best "economic and political serfdom" and at worst "total bondage under the iron yoke" of Russian Communism.[23]

The former members of the Federation who contributed to *La Renaissance Nationale* welcomed the Vichy regime. Not only did it seem to be the only possible alternative under the circumstances, but the basic premises on which the Pétain government was founded were precisely those ideals with which the Federation had been most sympathetic. Far from regretting the changes made by Pétain, many in the Federation felt that he had created a healthier and saner society. He had been faithful to the true France, the *pays réel*, which had suffered under the later Republic. In short, they rallied with few reservations to the National Revolution. The less appealing aspects of the Vichy regime—the terror, the tortures, the deportations—they chose to ignore.

23. *Ibid.*, August 18, 1943; *La Renaissance Nationale*, January, 1944.

The foreign policy of the Vichy government was another question. The majority in the Federation supported the Marshal because he seemed to represent a buckler against Germany while simultaneously restoring the spiritual and social health of a defeated France. Collaborating as junior partner with Germany appealed to far fewer in the party. When it became clear that Pétain was an ineffective shield against the Germans and their French agents, they ceased to give the regime their active support. Only a handful, like Bosse-Platière and Lavalette, approved of collaboration with Nazi Germany. For them, it was not enough to purge France of her foreign elements, her Freemasons, and Communists. One had to make the world safe for a stable, ordered society, and this necessitated the final eradication of the Bolshevik menace. The image of Germany as a bulwark against Communism loomed larger than that of Germany as an occupying and exploiting power. Whereas most of the former members of the Federation converted their earlier support for Vichy into a cautious *attentisme* by 1943, a few were willing to support the regime and all that it had come to stand for until the end.

It is, of course, unlikely that *La Renaissance Nationale* spoke for all members of the Federation of the Rhône. Those who strongly disagreed with the journal's policies could not dissent publicly and may have severed relations with their former colleagues. Pierre Burgeot, former deputy from the sixth arrondissement of Lyon, refused a post from the Vichy government and associated with a number of resistance groups after 1941. Near the end of the occupation, his open antagonism to the regime earned him threats from the Milice and obliged him to go into hiding. Claude Chaland, a former president of the youth section of the Federation of the Rhône, and Edouard Roure-Robur and Paul Montrochet, both executive members of the party, were all active in the resistance around Lyon. On the other hand, when the Vichy government appointed mayors to communes with populations between 2,000 and 10,000, at least twelve in the Rhône were former members of the Republican Federation, half of whom had belonged to the party's executive.[24] The fact that for the first year of the new regime the Federation continued to meet socially suggests that initially most members of the party shared the views of Perret. In the final analysis, it seems unlikely that the sentiments of the bulk of the Republican Federation of the Rhône differed substantially from those expressed in *La Renaissance Nationale*.

What can be said of the directing personnel of the national Republican Federation during the Vichy period? The most striking aspect of their role is that, by and large, they were not prominent either in the resistance or in the government of Vichy. Vichy might have restored a France that conservatives found more appealing, but it did not in any sense give them political power. Former Socialists, Radicals, and members of the Alliance Démocratique, as well as apolitical technocrats, were at least as well represented in the directing circles of Vichy as were former members of the Republican Federation. None of the major personalities in the government belonged to the Federation, and of the 192 members of the Vichyite Conseil National only 6 had been members of the Federation in 1939. Although several members of the Federation earned notoriety under the Vichy regime, none held any real political power.[25]

The most notorious former member of the Federation was Philippe Henriot. In spite of his prewar patriotism, Henriot became a devoted collaborator and an outspoken proponent of French Nazism. He was a leading member of the Milice and even enrolled his son in the SS. His dedication to the new regime was total: Maurice Martin du Gard described him, not without irony, as having "the courage of ignorance, the simple

24. *L'Union Démocratique du Rhône* (a newspaper established by former members of the Federation in 1944) listed the resistance activities of its members on May 20, 1945. *La Renaissance Nationale*, April 27, 1941.

25. Robert O. Paxton, *Vichy France* (Princeton, 1972), 258–59. The six members of the Conseil National included François Martin, Emmanuel Temple, Augustin Michel, Pierre de Monicault, Emile Taudière, and Jean Crouan. Former members—including Georges Pernot, François Peissel, Manuel Fourcade—also sat on the Council.

heart of a soldier of God." What Henriot brought to Vichy was neither ideological originality nor political ability but the gift of his remarkable oratory. He gave weekly and, upon becoming minister of propaganda in 1944, twice daily propaganda broadcasts. His performance was so impressive that some people allegedly altered their meal hours in order not to miss it. Henriot's total conversion to Nazism resulted less from any prewar predilection for fascism than from a desire to compensate for his intellectual mediocrity by selling his one gift to whoever would buy. Although little more than a hired orator, Henriot stuck doggedly by his task until the resistance executed him on June 28, 1944.[26]

If Henriot was an intellectual cipher, Xavier Vallat was not; and his contribution to Vichy was a direct continuation of one of his prewar preoccupations. After a brief period as director of the Légion Française des Combattants, Vallat became director of the Commissariat général aux questions juives. As such he had the responsibility for implementing measures designed to deprive French Jews of their civil rights, their property, and their position in society. Vallat had always been deeply concerned about the "excessive influence" of the Jews, and the early measures of the Vichy regime were intended to restrict dramatically this influence. But Vallat did not seek the physical extermination of French Jewry. When the German authorities began to press the Vichy government to coordinate its Jewish policy with that of the Reich, Vallat began to resist. Although reluctantly permitting the deportation of foreign Jews, he refused to cooperate with the deportation of French Jews and reportedly warned some Parisian Jews of their impending arrests. By early 1942 the occupation forces ordered Vallat to resign in favor of a far purer anti-Semite, Darquier de Pellepoix. Vallat

26. Maurice Martin du Gard, *La Chronique de Vichy, 1940–1944* (Paris, 1948), 432–33. See the assessment of Jacques Debû-Bridel, *L'Agonie de la Troisième République* (Paris, 1948), 185. As Jean Galtier-Boissière later noted, Henriot could as easily have followed the path of Maurice Schumann and donated his voice to the BBC, "Histoire de la Guerre, 1939–1945," *Crapouillot*, n.s., V (1946?), 355–57.

afterward claimed that in his official capacity he did more good than harm, but he nonetheless profited from the defeat of France to settle an old score with French Jews and was willing, to a degree, to cooperate with the Germans to do so.[27]

Several deputies of the Federation held prominent posts in the administration of the Vichy regime. The most notorious was André Parmentier, former deputy from the Nord. A prisoner of war in 1940, Parmentier had been repatriated in August, 1941, and shortly afterward accepted a post as prefect of the Vosges. He later became regional prefect at Rouen and finally head of Darnand's Sûreté Générale. His eagerness to round up Frenchmen for deportation to Germany caused the resistance to publicly condemn him to death in August of 1943.[28] François Martin, the deputy from the Aveyron, accepted the post of prefect of the Tarn-et-Garonne in December, 1941. Although he later claimed to have been among the ranks of the anticollaborators and although he was overtly hostile to the Milice, he was not forced to resign his post until February, 1944. Martin's fellow deputy from the Aveyron, Emmanuel Temple, also accepted the post of prefect of Algers shortly before the Allied landing in 1942. He later fought with the free French in Tunisia and Italy.[29]

While a handful of former members of the Federation accepted more or less important posts in the Vichy government, a few members of the Federation were not seduced by the Vichy

27. See Robert Aron, *Histoire de Vichy* (Paris, 1946), 420; Xavier Vallat, *Le Procès de Xavier Vallat (présenté par ses amis)* (Paris, 1948), esp. 242–51; Yves-Frédéric Jaffré, *Les Tribunaux d'exception, 1940–1962* (Paris, 1962), 162–65; Vallat's deposition in Hoover Institution, *France During the German Occupation, 1940–1944* (3 vols.; Stanford, 1957), II, 534–37.

28. The text of his condemnation is given in Aron, *Histoire de Vichy*, 595–96. It was never carried out, and in 1949 Parmentier's case was dismissed. See Peter Novick, *The Resistance Versus Vichy* (New York, 1968), 32n. See also Parmentier's deposition in Hoover Institution, *France During the German Occupation*, I, 334–37. This three-volume work consists largely of self-justificatory statements by former collaborators. Its bias and distortion were amply demonstrated by Pierre Arnould *et al.*, *La France sous l'occupation* (Paris, 1959).

29. Martin's deposition in Hoover Institution, *France During the German Occupation*, I, 414–31; see also the report of the postwar parliamentary *jury d'honneur*, *Journal Officiel*, December 28, 1945, p. 8634. Temple's deposition in Hoover Institution, *France During the German Occupation*, II, 711–12.

experience and entered into active resistance. The most notable was Louis Marin. Marin remained in Vichy after the armistice, apparently unable to obtain permission to return to his native Nancy. At Vichy he gave the appearance of a bewildered and confused figure, unable to grasp the reality of the defeat. Maurice Martin du Gard described him as "looking a bit lost, the phantom of parliamentarianism, his bow tie soiled." But Marin made no effort to hide his distrust of the Marshal and his opposition to the entire Vichy government. During the early stages of the Vichy experience, Marin's undisguised hostility did not disturb Pétain, who regarded him as a harmless relic of the Third Republic. But his uncompromising attitude in respect to the Vichy government impressed Pertinax in New York. André Weil-Curiel remembered hearing Marin "thundering" against the capitulation during his daily walk in the Parc Thermal at Vichy and noted that in late 1940 Marin was one of the very few *modérés* who had not completely endorsed Pétain![30]

Neither Pétain nor Laval was prepared to arrest Marin for fear of the diplomatic ramifications of such an act. After November, 1942, and the total German occupation of France, however, both the Germans and the Milice placed Marin under constant surveillance. Marin, nonetheless, worked actively in the resistance, maintaining personal representatives on the Conseil National de la Résistance and the Front National. Although occupying the same building as the police, he managed to join the Hihi information network and regularly forwarded to London information on the state of the German armed forces in France and other information drawn from his daily contact with diplomatic circles. As an agent in the Direction général des études et recherches, he held the rank of captain in the Forces Françaises Libres. By 1944 his activities had aroused the suspicion of the

30. André François-Poncet, "Notice sur la vie et les travaux de Louis Marin," *Institut de France, Académie des Sciences Morales et Politiques*, 1964, no. 3, p. 32; Mme. Louis Marin, *Louis Marin, 1871–1960* (Paris, 1973), 191–205; Martin du Gard, *La Chronique de Vichy*, 152–53; Jeanneney, *Jules Jeanneney*; Pertinax, *Les Fossoyeurs* (2 vols.; New York, 1943), I, 304n.; André Weil-Curiel, *Le Temps de la honte: éclipse en France* (Paris, 1946), 96.

Gestapo and the Milice. Joseph Darnand included Louis Marin among the former leading figures of the Third Republic whom he intended to eliminate. Marin initially ignored warnings that his life was threatened, but after the assassination of Maurice Sarraut, elements of the resistance in Lyon insisted that Marin leave Vichy immediately. On March 18, 1944, he escaped from Vichy to Lyon, shaved off his famous moustache, dyed his hair, and went into hiding. Three weeks later he was flown to London, where over the BBC he violently denounced Marshal Pétain.[31]

Other individual members of the Republican Federation, including Joseph Denais, Camille Blaisot, Jean Crouan, Henri Becquart, Pierre Burgeot, Jean Guiter, and Pierre Vallette-Viallard possessed legitimate and respectable resistance records. In 1940 Blaisot refused the post of departmental councilor and worked for the resistance in Normandy. He was arrested in March, 1944, and deported to Dachau, where he died shortly before the liberation of the camps. Becquart and Vallette-Viallard established contact with resistance organizations in their departments after 1942 and participated actively in the struggle against the Germans. Particularly in the eastern departments, leaders of the Republican Federation participated in anti-German activities. Louis Biétrix, deputy from the Doubs, was imprisoned for seven months because of his anti-German attitudes. André Baud, deputy from the Jura, was arrested several times for helping residents of Alsace-Lorraine escape to the nonoccupied zone. He later became president of the departmental committee of liberation. Jean Bernex, deputy from the Haute-Savoie, was ultimately deported to Buchenwald and released by the Allies. Alfred Oberkirch from the Bas-Rhin, known for his anti-German sentiments even before 1919, was hunted by the Gestapo and forced to take refuge in Switzerland.

31. Mme. Marin, *Louis Marin*, 198–99; *Chambre des Députés, Rapport fait au nom de la commission chargée d'enquête sur les événements survenus en France de 1933 à 1944* (deposition of Louis Marin), III, 657.

Geoffroy de Montalembert, deputy from the Seine-Inférieure, was arrested and deported by the Germans.[32]

Some members of the Federation who initially played an active role in the Vichy government later rallied to the resistance. In 1940 François Valentin, Louis Marin's protégé, broke with his patron and accepted a post of director general of the Légion Française des Combattants. Early in 1942 when the government decided to use the Légion as a recruiting grounds for the Service d'Ordre Légionnaire, an elite body led by Joseph Darnand and inspired by the SS, Valentin quit. His disillusionment with the Vichy regime grew, and he soon went into hiding. In August, 1943, on the third anniversary of the founding of the Légion, he published a manifesto in which he admitted his past mistakes and expressed the desire to unburden his conscience at last. The Vichy government, he declared, had betrayed France and was no longer worthy of support; patriotic Frenchmen had no choice but to oppose the regime and enter into the resistance. Valentin commanded a battalion of the French Forces of the Interior in the Tarn, and after August, 1944, he fought as a captain in the regular French army.[33]

As late as November, 1941, Jean Crouan, deputy from the Finistère, accepted a post on the Vichy National Council. He did so reluctantly and, as he later claimed, because he still thought that Pétain "was playing a clever game intended to *rouler les Boches.*" At the same time he reported having persistently hampered German activities within his commune. As mayor he drafted false lists of individuals eligible for deportation to German labor camps—eliminating all those who were actually in a position to be deported. In 1943 he provided shelter

32. The most detailed description of the resistance activities of members of the Federation is in *L'Union Démocratique du Rhône*, May 20, 1945; see also Henri Noguères, *Histoire de la résistance en France* (3 vols.; Paris, 1967–71), II, 229; *La Nation*, April 24, 1945; *La Liberté de Normandie*, May 8, 1945; *Journal Officiel*, May 4, 1945, p. 2524, June, 30, 1945, p. 3970, August 24, 1945, p. 5285.

33. François Vallentin to Xavier Vallat, in Olivier d'Ormesson, *François Valentin, 1909–1961* (Paris, 1964), 85–88, 96–97, 607; Aron, *Histoire de Vichy*, 607; *Journal Officiel*, December 28, 1945, pp. 112–13.

for five downed American airmen and subsequently helped them escape. The Germans discovered Crouan's activities, arrested him in June, 1943, sentenced him to death, and deported him to Dachau where he was liberated in May, 1945.[34] Both Crouan and Valentin were early partisans of the Vichy regime whose change of heart came late but was obviously genuine and clearly demanded courage.

Nonetheless, the resistance record of the Republican Federation included only a few individual members. Although the Federation formally adhered to the Conseil National de la Résistance with Jacques Debû-Bridel as Louis Marin's delegate, the two men represented little more than themselves. The Federation had been invited to join the CNR in 1943 in order to give that body a more balanced political coloration. As its historian notes, the affiliation of the Federation involved a certain "arbitrariness" since the party was not officially engaged in any clandestine activity and the majority of its members were known to sympathize with Pétain.[35] In fact, in spite of the undeniable courage of a few men in the party, the resistance record of the Federation as a whole was meager. If outright collaborators like Henriot, Vallat, and Parmentier were exceptional, so were resisters of the first hour. After the liberation, the party had difficulty in finding genuine *résistants*. The problem of nominating members to the Consultative Assembly provided an example.

When in November, 1944, the Assembly was expanded to include representatives from all points on the political spectrum, the Republican Federation was allowed to nominate three additional representatives. The Assembly specified that all those who had voted full powers to Pétain or who had held office under Vichy would be automatically excluded, but it was prepared to make exceptions for those who could demonstrate that, in spite of earlier errors, they had made a valuable contribution to the resistance. Jacques Poitou-Duplessy was one of the Federation's nominees who had voted Pétain full powers and who was

34. Crouan's resistance dossier, in Marin Papers, carton 75.
35. René Hostache, *Le Conseil National de la Résistance* (Paris, 1958), 121.

rejected by the Assembly's credentials committee because his resistance activity was insufficient. He chose to challenge this decision; and to the evident embarrassment of Louis Marin, the issue was debated before the Assembly, and the resistance dossier of Poitou-Duplessy was made public.

The credentials committee noted that in addition to having voted full powers to Pétain, Poitou-Duplessy had been a member of the Vichyite Conseil Départemental until May 30, 1944. It also read a telegram from the departmental Comité de la Liberation in the Charente, which protested the seating of Poitou-Duplessy, denounced him as a "notorious collaborator," and cited his pro-Vichy articles in Le Réveil Charentais.[36] In his defense Poitou-Duplessy claimed that when he voted for Pétain he had been unaware of the Marshal's intentions.[37] He had remained a departmental councilor because he felt that under the German occupation "men of character" should remain at their posts in order "to maintain the public spirit, restrain the demands of the enemy and even to denounce his exactions."[38] At the session of the departmental council on May 31, 1944, he had denounced the policy of the Marshal and expressed a hope for an Allied victory. He was consequently removed from his post and threatened by the local Milice. Poitou-Duplessy read letters from genuine resisters, who testified that during the occupation he had opposed Laval and aided refugees from the Gestapo. The liberation committee in the Charente, he argued, was simply trying to settle old political scores. The Assembly was unimpressed and, with the exception of six former members of the Republican Federation, voted his exclusion.

The case of Jacques Poitou-Duplessy was not exceptional. François Halna du Fretay, one of the Federation's senators from the Finistère, and Ernest de Framond, deputy from the Lozère,

36. The state of the Bibliothèque Nationale's collection of the Réveil Charentais for the war years makes it impossible to verify this charge.
37. Since Poitou-Duplessy was one of the signers of the Bergery Declaration, this defense has a hollow ring.
38. Journal Officiel: Assemblée Consultative Provisoire, November 17, 1944, pp. 296–303.

had records that were very similar.[39] Like many French conservatives, they had at first welcomed the Vichy regime and had later—often very much later—become disillusioned with Pétain and had engaged in acts of resistance. Denouncing Pétain a week before the Normandy landing was perhaps not a very significant act of resistance, but Poitou-Duplessy did expose himself to some personal risk by his defiance of the regime. But even taken at its face value, the record of Poitou-Duplessy was that of a typical Vichyite rather than that of a typical *résistant*. Political memories were short in 1944, and even a relatively undistinguished resistance record could get a man a seat on the Consultative Assembly. It was a telling comment on the history of the Republican Federation that it was reduced to nominating Jacques Poitou-Duplessy.

39. See the reports of the *jury d'honneur* for Frammond, *Journal Officiel*, December 15, 1945, p. 8298; for Halna du Fretay, *Journal Officiel*, October 21, 1945, p. 6764.

Epilogue

There was no place in the Fourth Republic for the Republican Federation. Insofar as the party was identified with anything, it was associated with the more sclerotic features of the Third Republic and the more sordid aspects of Vichy. Fresher and more credible parties competed for the allegiance of the *modérés*. Louis Marin and Jacques Debû-Bridel, nonetheless, again began to publish *La Nation* (this time as a one-page daily), and a number of former leaders reformed the party executive. The party created a commission to wrestle with the problem of altering its image to attract new generations of voters. The commission toyed with the idea of adopting the name Parti Républicain Libéral and announced that the party now belonged to the Center. The party excluded members who had been compromised during the occupation and refused to intervene on behalf of the imprisoned Xavier Vallat or the former Vichyite prefect, François Martin. At the same time it held out the possibility of collaboration or even fusion with the Alliance Démocratique, moderate Radicals, and the Parti Démocrate Populaire.[1]

Although the Federation reestablished its prewar organizations in Paris and the Rhône, in most departments its cadres had been seriously compromised under the Vichy regime. Moreover, many former *Pétainistes* in the party deeply resented

1. The *Carnet de Bureau de la Fédération Républicaine*, a record of executive meetings in 1945 and 1946, in Marin Papers, carton 70 (hereafter cited as *Carnet*), June 8, 29, July 5, 1945; report of the Commission de Réorganization, in Marin Papers, carton 73; *L'Union Démocratique du Rhône*, July 29, 1945. Marin vetoed the proposed change of name. Xavier Vallat, *Feuilles de Fresnes* (Annonay, 1971), 50. In these prison notebooks Vallat acidly observed that Guiter had forgotten that during the occupation he had sought similar interventions from Vallat on behalf of Parisian Jews.

Marin's anti-Vichy posture and refused to cooperate with the Federation. Throughout 1945 local organizers complained about the difficulty of attracting either new members or significant financial aid.[2]

In the cantonal elections of October, 1945, the Republican Federation won only 269 seats compared with the 519 seats that it had held between 1934 and 1937. In the legislative elections of the same year the Federation presented only twelve former deputies of the party, none of whom ran as official candidates of the Republican Federation. Nine were elected and, over Marin's opposition, opted to join thirty other conservatives in a group called the Unité Républicaine. Although Marin initially agreed to join the group, he refused to accept its discipline and within a month was expelled.[3]

The relative feebleness and inactivity of the postwar Republican Federation contrasted markedly with the energetic style of the two major newcomers to conservative politics, the Mouvement Républicain Populaire and the Parti Républicain de la Liberté. The Mouvement Républicain Populaire (MRP), born in Lyon in 1944, was a Christian Democratic party in the tradition of the Parti Démocrate Populaire but with far more members and a broader geographical base. A young party, untainted either by the chaos of the Third Republic or by Vichy, it enjoyed instant success during the immediate postwar period, attracting five million votes in October, 1945, and becoming one of the three major parties in France. Despite its liberal and progressive leaning, the MRP was a political haven for conservatives in the early postwar years. Far less of a political liability than a party like the Federation, the MRP took over many Catholic strongholds and attracted some of the former leaders of the Federation. Alfred Oberkirch, former deputy from the Haut-Rhin, joined the new party as did the longtime president of the

2. Joseph Denais to Marin, March 8, 1945, in Marin Papers, carton 73; report from the Loire to the Commission de Réorganization, n.d., in Marin Papers, carton 73; letters to Marin from the Rhône, December 12, 1945, in Marin Papers, carton 70; from the Eure-et-Loire, February 16, 1946, from the Bouches-du-Rhône, January 28, 1946, all in Marin Papers, carton 73.

3. Le Monde, November 30, December 1, 1945.

Republican Federation of the Bouches-du-Rhône, Dr. Jules Monge.[4]

Ideologically closer to the Republican Federation and a greater immediate threat was the Parti Républicain de la Liberté (PRL). Founded in December, 1945, by Joseph Laniel and André Mutter,[5] the PRL planned to unite "the scattered forces of the old nationalist parties that were dismantled by the war and the occupation." Predictably, the new party promised to be highly organized and disciplined. The PRL immediately attracted many former members of the Federation. Despite pleas from some party loyalists, the federations of the Seine and the Rhône voted to join the PRL; and François de Wendel offered the new party his financial support. By January, 1946, the executive of the Republican Federation formally considered fusion with the new party. Louis Marin strenuously resisted fusion, unwilling to relinquish control over a party he had led for twenty years and convinced that the new party would be a political flash in the pan. After a heated debate the executive refused to join the PRL, but most of the *militants* and all of the deputies except Louis Marin adhered to the new party. The rump of the Federation continued to meet into the middle of 1946, examining as Jean Guiter once plaintively put it, *"ou va la Fédération?"* At the end of the year isolated branches of the Federation were still asking about the party's future. The Federation never revived, although as late as 1948 the executive of the party continued to meet to handle legal formalities. A Republican Federation of France, presided over by old party hands, existed as late as 1953, apparently as a nonparliamentary ally of the Indépendants.[6]

4. Report to the Commission de Réorganization in Marin Papers, carton 73.

5. Mutter had belonged to the Republican Federation, then to the Parti Social Français in the 1930s; Laniel had been affiliated with the Alliance Démocratique.

6. Joseph Laniel, "Le Parti Républicain de la Liberté," *Revue de Paris*, May, 1946, p. 59; *Le Monde*, April 1, 1946; minutes of the executive of the Republican Federation of the Seine, January 12, 1946, in Marin Papers, carton 73; *Carnet*, January 25, June 13, 1946, February 4, 1948; letter to the Federation from its branch in the Gironde, 1946?, in Marin Papers, carton 82; flyer, 1953, in Marin Papers, carton 70. Robert Pimienta, a longtime *militant* from the Oise, served as principal link between the Federation and the Indépendants.

Even without the rivalry of the Parti Républicain de la Liberté, the postwar disappearance of the Federation was inevitable. The Federation had possessed little enough dynamism before the war and far too little to carry it across the giant gap of defeat and the Vichy experience. By 1945 the Federation was clearly a relic of the past and seen as such by contemporaries. A postwar article on "Les Chevaliers de la Triste Figure" accurately captured the dilemma of the "poor but honest Federation." Don-Quixote-like, the Federation continued to tilt at prewar windmills, unaware (or pretending to be so) of changes in France brought by the previous six years. Wearily trotting out the slogans of the 1930s, clearly unattuned to the world of postwar France, striving hopelessly to portray itself as a leading force in the resistance—this decaying group of conservatives continued to act as if it were the pivot of French politics.[7] The Republican Federation of France was a spent force in politics, soon quietly abandoned by even its most dedicated former *militants*.

7. Maurice Clavel, *L'Epoque*, September 22, 1945.

Bibliography

ARCHIVAL SOURCES

Archives de la Préfecture de Police, Paris. Cartons 326 (Croix de Feu), 327 (Parti Social Français), 328 (Jeunesses Patriotes), 329 (Parti Républicain National et Social), 336, 337, 341 (Parti Populaire Français).

Archives Nationales, Paris. Louis Marin Papers, preserved in the *Archives Privées*, no. 317 (cartons 70, 73, 74, 75, 79, 82, 85, 88).

OFFICIAL DOCUMENTS

Chambre des Députés, 14ᵉ législature: Notices et Portraits, 1928. Paris: Imprimérie de la Chambre des Députés, 1929.

Chambre des Députés, 15ᵉ législature: Notices et Portraits, 1932. Paris: Imprimérie de la Chambre des Députés, 1933.

Chambre des Députés, Comités secretes, 1939–1940. Paris: Annales de l'Assemblée Nationale, 1948.

Chambre des Députés, Rapport fait au nom de la commission chargée d'enquête sur les événements survenus en France de 1933 à 1944. 9 volumes.

Chambre des Députés, Rapport fait au nom de la commission chargée de réunir et de publier les programmes électoraux des candidats aux élections législatives des 1ᵉʳ et 8 mai 1932. (Barodet)

Chambre des Députés, Rapport fait au nom de la commission chargée de réunir et de publier les programmes électoraux des candidats aux élections législatives des 26 avril et 3 mai 1936. (Barodet)

Chambre des Députés, Rapport fait au nom de la commission d'enquête chargée de rechercher les causes et les origines des événements du 6 février 1934. 4 volumes.

Journal Officiel de la République francaise: Débats parlementaires, Assemblée Consultative, 1944–45.

Journal Officiel de la République française: Débats parlementaires, Chambre des Députés, 1929–40.
Journal Officiel de la République francaise: Débats parlementaires, Sénat, 1929–40.
Journal Officiel de la République française: Documents parlementaires, 1945.
Le Procès du Maréchal Pétain. Paris: Imprimérie des Journaux Officiels, 1945.

NEWSPAPERS AND PERIODICALS

Paris Party Press
Les Devoirs des Femmes, 1935–39
Jeunesse, 1934–38
Les Libertés Communales, 1926–37
La Nation, 1925–40, 1945–46

Other Paris Newspapers
L'Action Française, 1929–32; 1936–38
L'Alliance Démocratique, 1933–39
L'Aube, 1932–36
Aux Ecoutes, 1929–38
Brumaire, 1932–37
Bulletin-Correspondance de l'Association Nationale Républicaine, 1903–1908
Candide, 1935–39
Le Charivari, 1929–37
Choc, 1935–38
Correspondance politique et agricole, 1908–20
Crapouillot, 1929–39
La Croix, 1907–12
L'Echo de Paris, 1929–37
L'Epoque, 1937–38, 1945
L'Ere Nouvelle, 1929–32
Le Figaro, 1903–14
Le Flambeau, 1934–37
Gringoire, 1935–39
L'Humanité, 1929–30
Je Suis Partout, 1931–39
Le Jour, 1936–38

Le Journal des Débats, 1929–32
La Lanterne, 1903–12
La Liberté, 1936–38
Les Libertés Républicaines du XIXe, 1937
La Libre Parole, 1905–14
Marianne, 1934–36
Le Matin, 1929–32
Le Monde, 1945–46
Le National, 1929–38
L'Ordre, 1929–39
L'Ouvrier Libre, 1938
La Patrie, 1932
Le Petit Bleu, 1929–32, 1936–38
Le Petit Démocrate, 1928–39
Le Petit Journal, 1937–38
Le Petit Parisien, 1936–38
Politique, 1929–36
Le Populaire, 1929–30, 1936–38
La République Française, 1903–12
La Revue de Paris, 1929–38
La Revue Hebdomadaire, 1929–38
Le Temps, 1929–39
Vendémiaire, 1935–38

Party Press of the Departments

L'Action Sociale et Nationale (Seine), 1930–35
Bulletin Mensuel de la Fédération Républicaine de Rambouillet (Seine-et-Oise), 1932
Bulletin Mensuel de la Fédération Républicaine du Calaisis (Pas de Calais), 1928–34
L'Entente Républicaine Démocratique de Hazebrouck (Nord), 1932–39
La Liberté de l'Aude, 1926–27
La Liberté du Morbihan, 1921–24
L'Oise Nationale, 1936
La Renaissance Nationale (Rhône), 1940–44
Le Réveil du Calaisis (Pas de Calais), 1934–36
Le Sud-Est Républicain de Toulouse (Haute-Garonne), 1933–36
L'Union Démocratique du Rhône, 1944–45

L'Union Républicaine de l'Aube, 1930–34
L'Union Républicaine du Rhône, 1931–40
Voir Clair en Politique (Seine-Inférieure), 1931–39

Sympathetic Local Newspapers

L'Abeille Jurassienne, 1932
Le Courrier de la Montagne (Doubs), 1932
La Dépêche Vendéenne, 1936–38
L'Eclair de l'Est (Meurthe-et-Moselle), 1932, 1936
La Gazette d'Annonay (Ardèche), 1929–40
Le Glaneur de la Manche, 1936–37
L'Indépendant de l'Arrondissement de Rambouillet (Seine-et-Oise), 1932
Le Journal de Rouen (Seine-Inférieure), 1922–27, 1929–39
La Liberté de l'Ain, 1932
La Liberté du Sud-Ouest (Gironde), 1936–38
Le Mortainais (La Manche), 1937
Le Nouvelliste (Rhône), 1936
Le Petit Courrier (Maine-et-Loire), 1932
Le Petit Loir-et-Cher, 1929–39
La Province, 1931–38
Le Réveil Charentais, 1929–40
Le Réveil du Beaujolais (Rhône), 1932–44

The Press of Neighboring Conservatives

L'Alerte (Jeunesses Patriotes, Rhône), 1929–38
L'Attaque (Parti Populaire Français, Rhône), 1936–38
Le Chardon (Jeunesses Patriotes, Meurthe-et-Moselle), 1932–34
Le Flambeau de Flandre, Artois et Picardie (Parti Social Français), 1937–38
L'Heure Française (Parti Social Français, Bouches-du-Rhône), 1936–38
Le P.S.F. Autunois (Saône-et-Loire), 1938–39
Le Petit Breton (Parti Démocrate Populaire, Finistère), 1936
Le Ralliement du Nord (Parti Social Français), 1937–38
Réalité (Parti Social Français, Aisne), 1937–38
La République Lyonnaise (Action Française, Rhône), 1929–36
Samedi (Parti Social Français, Loire-Inférieure), 1937–38
Volontaire 36 (Parti Social Français, Rhône), 1936–38

BOOKS

Anderson, Malcolm. *Conservative Politics in France.* London: Allen & Unwin, 1975.

Arnould, Pierre, *et al. La France sous l'occupation.* Paris: Presses Universitaires de France, 1959.

Aron, Robert. *Histoire de Vichy.* Paris: Fayard, 1946.

Barral, Pierre. *Le Département de l'Isère sous la IIIe République, 1870–1940.* Paris: Armand Colin, 1962.

Baudouin, Paul. *Neuf mois au gouvernement.* Paris: La Table Ronde, 1948.

Beau de Loménie, Emmanuel. *Le Débat de ratification du traité de Versailles.* Paris: Denoel, 1945.

————. *La Mort de la Troisième République.* Paris: Denoel, 1951.

————. *Les Responsabilités des dynasties bourgeoises.* Vols. III, IV, V. Paris: Denoel, 1954–73.

Becquart, Henri. *Au temps du silence.* Paris: Editions Iris, 1945.

Benoist, Charles. *Souvenirs.* Vol. II. Paris: Plon, 1934.

Berl, Emmanuel. *La Politique et les partis.* Paris: Editions Rieder, 1932.

Bonnard, Abel. *Les Modérés.* Paris: Grasset, 1936.

Bonnefous, Edouard, and Georges Bonnefous. *Histoire politique de la Troisième République.* Vols. II–VII. Paris: Presses Universitaires de France, 1959–67.

Bonnet, Serge. *Sociologie politique et religieuse de la Lorraine.* Cahiers de la fondation nationale des sciences politiques, no. 181. Paris: Armand Colin, 1972.

Bonnevay, Laurent. *L'Histoire politique et administrative du conseil generale du Rhône.* Lyon: Editions Joannes Desvigne, 1946.

————. *Les Journées sanglantes de février 1934.* Paris: Flammarion, 1935.

Boulard, F. *Essor du déclin du clergé français.* Paris: Editions du Cerf, 1950.

Bourgin, Georges. *Manuel des partis politiques en France.* Paris: Editions Rieder, 1928.

Buché, Josephe. *Essai sur la vie et l'oeuvre d'Edouard Aynard.* Lyon: A. Rey, 1921.

Cameron, Elizabeth R. *Prologue to Appeasement: A Study in French Foreign Policy.* Washington: American Council on Public Affairs, 1942.

Cathala, Pierre. *Eloge de Henri Barboux*. Mesnil sur l'Estrée: Firmin-Didot, 1921.

Charlot, Jean. *L'U.N.R.: Etude du pouvoir au sein d'un parti politique*. Cahiers de la fondation nationale des sciences politiques, no. 153. Paris: Armand Colin, 1967.

Chastenet, Jacques. *Histoire de la Troisième République*. Vols. III–VII. Paris: Hachette, 1952–63.

Chavardès, Maurice. *Une Campagne de presse: la droite française et le 6 février 1934*. Paris: Flammarion, 1970.

———. *Le Six février 1934*. Paris: Calmann-Levy, 1966.

Chopine, Paul. *Six ans chez les Croix de Feu*. Paris: Gallimard, 1935.

Corcos, Fernand. *Catechisme des partis politiques*. Paris: Editions Montaignes, 1928, 1932.

Coston, Henry, ed. *Dictionnaire de la politique française*. Paris: Publications Henry Coston, 1967.

———. *Partis: Journaux et hommes politiques d'hier et d'aujourd'hui*. Paris: Lectures françaises: 1960.

Creyssel, Paul. *La Rocque contre Tardieu*. Paris: Sorlot, 1938.

Debû-Bridel, Jacques. *L'Agonie de la Troisième République*. Paris: Le Bateau Ivre, 1948.

De la Rocque, Edith, and Gilles de la Rocque. *La Rocque tel qu'il était*. Paris: Fayard, 1962.

De la Rocque, François. *Autour des élections: Principes d'arbitrage du mouvement Croix de Feu*. Paris: Le Flambeau, 1936.

Delperrie De Bayac, J. *Histoire de la Milice, 1918–1945*. Paris: Fayard, 1969.

Denais, Joseph. *Un Apôtre de la liberté: Jacques Piou*. Paris: La Palatine, 1960.

Dominique, Pierre. *Vente et achat*. Paris: Denoel, 1937.

Doty, C. Stewart. *From Cultural Rebellion to Counterrevolution: The Politics of Maurice Barrès*. Athens: Ohio University Press, 1976.

Dumont-Wildon, Louis. *Louis Marin*. Paris: Denoel, 1937.

Dupeux, Georges. *Le Front populaire et les élections de 1936*. Cahiers de la fondation nationale des sciences politiques, no. 99. Paris: Armand Colin, 1959.

Duverger, Maurice. *L'Influence des systèmes électoraux sur la vie politique*. Cahiers de la fondation nationale des sciences politiques, no. 16. Paris: Armand Colin, 1950.

———. *Political Parties*. New York: Science Editions, 1963.

Einaudi, Mario, and François Goguel. *Christian Democracy in Italy and France.* Notre Dame: University of Indiana Press, 1952.

Faber, Paul. *Discours, Paris, Conseil Municipal, Inauguration officielle, de la Place Louis Marin.* Paris: n.p., 1967.

Fernand-Laurent, Camille (Jean). *Un Peuple ressuscite.* New York: Brentano, 1943.

Flandin, Pierre-Etienne. *Politique française, 1919–1940.* Paris: Editions nouvelles, 1947.

Folliet, Joseph. *Pacifisme de droite, bellicisme de gauche.* Paris: Editions du cerf, 1938.

Fourcade, Jacques. *La République de la province.* Paris: Grasset, 1936.

Fournel, E. *Manuel de politique française.* Paris: Editions des portiques, 1933.

Frédérix, Pierre. *Etat des forces en France.* Paris: Gallimard, 1935.

George, Margaret. *The Warped Vision: British Foreign Policy, 1933–1939.* Pittsburgh: University of Pittsburgh Press, 1965.

Goguel, François. *Géographie des élections françaises de 1870 à 1951.* Cahiers de la fondation nationale des sciences politiques, no. 27. Paris: Armand Colin, 1951.

―――. *La Politique des partis sous la IIIe République.* Paris: Seuil, 1946.

Guerin, Jean, and Bernard Guerin. *Des hommes et des activités autour d'un demi-siècle.* Bordeaux: Editions B.E.B., 1957.

Halévy, Daniel. *La République des comités.* Paris: Grasset, 1934.

―――. *La République des Ducs.* Paris: Grasset, 1937.

Hamon, Augustin. *Les Maîtres de la France.* 3 vols. Paris: Editions sociales internationales, 1937.

―――. *Voici Les Deux Cents Familles.* Hanoi: n.p., [1936].

Harvard de la Montagne, Robert. *Histoire de l'Action Française.* Paris: Amiot-Dumont, 1950.

Henriot, Philippe. *Comment mourut la paix.* Paris: Editions de la France, 1941.

―――. *Le 6 février.* Paris: Flammarion, 1934.

Hoover Institution. *France During the German Occupation.* 3 vols. Stanford: Stanford University Press, 1957.

Hostache, René. *Le Conseil National de la Résistance.* Paris: Presses Universitaires de France, 1958.

Irving, R. E. M. *Christian Democracy in France.* London: Allen and Unwin, 1973.

Jacques, Léon. *Les Partis politiques sous la IIIe République*. Paris: Receuil Sirey, 1913.

Jaffré, Yves-Frédéric. *Les Tribunaux d'exception, 1940–1962*. Paris: Nouvelles Editions Latines, 1962.

Jeanneney, Jean-Noël. *François de Wendel en République: L'Argent et le pouvoir, 1914–1940*. Paris: Editions du Seuil, 1976.

———, ed. *Jules Jeanneney: Journal Politique*. Paris: Armand Colin, 1972.

Joll, James, ed. *The Decline of the Third Republic*. St. Anthony's Papers, no. 5. London: Chatto and Windus, 1959.

Jolly, Jean, ed. *Dictionnaire des parlementaires françaises*. 7 vols. Paris: Presses Universitaires de France, 1960–72.

Jonas, Erasmus. *Die Volkskonservativen, 1928–1933*. Dusseldorf: Droste, 1965.

Jouvenel, Robert de. *La République des camarades*. Paris: Grasset, 1914.

Kerillis, Henri de, and Raymond Cartier. *Faisons le point*. Paris: Grasset, 1931.

Kleinclausz, André. *Histoire de Lyon*. Vol. III. Lyon: Pierre Maison, 1952.

Lachapelle, Georges. *L'Alliance Démocratique*. Paris: Grasset, 1935.

———. *Elections législatives des 22–29 avril 1928, Resultats Officiels*. Paris: Roustan, 1928.

———. *Elections législatives des 1er et 8 mai 1932, Resultats Officiels*. Paris: Le Temps, 1932.

———. *Elections législatives des 26 avril, 3 mai 1936, Resultats Officiels*. Paris: Le Temps, 1936.

Larmour, Peter J. *The French Radical Party in the 1930's*. Stanford: Stanford University Press, 1964.

Launay, Jacques de, ed. *Le Dossier de Vichy*. Paris: Julliard, 1967.

Laurens, Franklin D. *France and the Italo-Ethiopian Crisis, 1935–1936*. The Hague: Mouton, 1967.

Lavau, Georges E. *Partis politiques et réalités sociales*. Cahiers de la fondation nationale des sciences politiques, no. 38. Paris: Armand Colin, 1953.

Le Clère. Marcel. *Le 6 février*. Paris: Hachette, 1967.

Léger, B. *Les Opinions politiques des provinces françaises*. Paris: Recueil Sirey, 1936.

Leiserson, Avery. *Parties and Politics*. New York: Alfred A. Knopf, 1958.

Lewinsohn, Richard. *L'Argent dans la politique.* Paris: Gallimard, 1931.

Marabuto, Paul. *Les Partis politiques et mouvements sociaux sous la IVᵉ République.* Paris: Receuil Sirey, 1948.

Marin, Louis. *Le Traité de paix.* Paris: H. Floury, 1920.

Marin, Mme. Louis. *Louis Marin, 1871–1960: Homme d'Etat, Philosophe et Savant.* Paris: the author, 1973.

Martin du Gard, Maurice. *La Chronique de Vichy, 1940–1944.* Paris: Flammarion, 1948.

Maxence, Jean-Pierre. *Histoire de dix ans.* Paris: Gallimard, 1939.

Meynaud, Jean. *Les Groupes de pression en France.* Cahiers de la fondation national des sciences politiques, no. 95. Paris: Armand Colin, 1958.

————. *Nouvelles études sur les groupes de pression en France.* Cahiers de la fondation nationale des sciences politiques, no. 118. Paris: Armand Colin, 1961.

Micaud, Charles A. *The French Right and Nazi Germany, 1933–1939.* Durham, N.C.: Duke University Press, 1943.

Nipperdey, Thomas. *Die Organization der deutschen Parteien vor 1918.* Dusseldorf: Droste, 1961.

Noguères, Henri. *Histoire de la résistance en France.* Vols. I–III. Paris: Laffont, 1967–71.

Norman, Gilles. *Politiques et hommes politiques.* Vol. II. Paris: Perrin, 1925.

Novick, Peter. *The Resistance Versus Vichy.* New York: Columbia University Press, 1968.

Ormesson, Olivier d'. *François Valentin, 1909–1961.* Paris: Berger-Levrault, 1964.

Ostrogorski, Moshe Y. *Democracy and the Organization of Political Parties.* New York: Macmillan, 1902.

Paxton, Robert O. *Vichy France: Old Guard and New Order.* Princeton: Princeton University Press, 1972.

Pertinax (André Giraud). *Les Fossoyeurs.* 2 vols. New York: Editions de la Maison Française, 1943.

Plumyene, Jean, and Raymond Lasierra. *Les Fascismes françaises, 1923–1963.* Paris: Seuil, 1963.

Ponthière, Maurice. *Les Partis de droite.* Paris: Librairie de documentation politique, 1914.

Pozzo di Borgo, Duc. *La Rocque: fantôme à vendre.* Paris: Sorlot, 1938.

Pressac, Pierre de. *Les Forces historiques de la France*. Paris: Hachette, 1928.

Pujo, Maurice. *Comment la Rocque a trahi*. Paris: Sorlot, 1938.

Raymond-Laurent, Jean. *Le Parti Démocrate Populaire*. Le Mans: Imprimérie Commerciale, 1965.

Rebatet, Lucien. *Les Décombres*. Paris: Denoel, 1942.

Rémond, René. *Les Catholiques, le communisme et les crises, 1929–1939*. Paris: Armand Colin, 1960.

———. *Là Droite en France de 1815 à nos jours*. 2 vols. Paris: Aubier, 1968.

Rémond, René, et al., eds. *Léon Blum, Chef du gouvernement, 1936–1937, Actes du colloque*. Paris: Armand Colin, 1967.

Robbe, Fernand. *Le Parti Social Française et le Front de la Liberté*. Paris: Société d'Editions et d'Abonnements, 1937.

Robert, Adolphe, and Gaston Cougny, eds. *Dictionnaire des parlementaires françaises*. 5 vols. Paris: Bourloton, 1889–91.

Rossi-Landau, Guy. *La Drôle de guerre*. Paris: Armand Colin. 1972.

Rowse, A. L. *All Souls and Appeasement*. London: Macmillan, 1961.

Rudaux, Philippe. *Les Croix de Feu et le PSF*. Paris: Editions France-Empire, 1967.

Saint-Just, François de. *Une Bataille perdue*. Paris: Editions du Scorpion, 1964.

Schmidt, Martin E. *Alexandre Ribot: Odyssey of a Liberal in the Third Republic*. The Hague: Martinus Nijhoff, 1974.

Scott, William Evans. *Alliance Against Hitler*. Durham: Duke University Press, 1965.

Shapiro, David, ed. *The Right in France, 1889–1919*. St. Anthony's Papers, no. 13. London: Chatto and Windus, 1962.

Sherwood, John M. *Georges Mandel and the Third Republic*. Stanford: Stanford University Press, 1970.

Siegfried, André. *Tableau des partis en France*. Paris: Grasset, 1930.

———. *Tableau politique de la France de l'ouest sous la troisième République*. 2nd ed. Paris: Armand Colin, 1963.

Soucy, Robert. *Fascism in France: The Case of Maurice Barrès*. Berkeley: University of California Press, 1972.

Soulier, A. *L'Instabilité ministerielle sous la troisième république*. Paris: Recueil Sirey, 1939.

Sternhell, Zeev. *Maurice Barrès et le nationalisme français*. Cahiers de la fondation nationale des sciences politiques, no. 182. Paris: Armand Colin, 1972.

Suarez, Georges. *Pour un parti central*. Paris, Denoel et Steele, 1936.

Tannenbaum, Edward R. *The Action Française*. New York: Wiley, 1962.

Thibaudet, Albert. *Les Idées politiques de la France*. Paris: Stock, 1932.

————. *La République des professeurs*. Paris: Grasset, 1927.

Thompson, Neville. *The Anti-Appeasers*. London: Oxford University Press, 1971.

Tucker, William R. *The Fascist Ego: A Political Biography of Robert Brasillach*. Berkeley: University of California Press, 1976.

Vallat, Xavier. *Feuilles de Fresnes*. Annonay: the author, 1971.

————. *Le Nez de Cléopâtre*. Paris: Les Quatre Fils d'Aymon, 1957.

————. *Le Procès de Xavier Vallat (presenté par ses amis)*. Paris: Editions du Conquistador, 1948.

Veuillot, François. *La Rocque et son parti*. Paris: Plon, 1938.

Weber, Eugen. *Action Française: Royalism and Reaction in Twentieth Century France*. Stanford: Stanford University Press, 1962.

Weil-Curiel, André. *Le Temps de la honte: éclipse en France*. Paris: Editions du Myrtle, 1946.

Werth, Alexander. *France and Munich*. New York: Harper, 1939.

————. *France in Ferment*. New York: Harper, 1935.

————. *Which Way France*. New York: Harper, 1937.

Weygand, Jacques. *Weygand mon père*. Paris: Flammarion, 1970.

Willard, Claude. *Quelques aspects du fascisme en France avant le 6 février 1934*. Paris: Editions Sociales, 1961.

Williams, Philip M. *Crisis and Compromise: Politics of the Fourth Republic*. London: Archon Books, 1964.

Wolf, Dieter. *Doriot, du communisme à la collaboration*. Paris: Fayard, 1969.

Wolfers, Arnold. *Britain and France Between Two Wars*. New York: Harcourt and Brace, 1940.

ARTICLES

Albertini, R. von. "Partei-organization und Parteibegriff in Frankreich, 1789–1940." *Historische Zeitschrift*, CXCIII (1961), 529–600.

Beau de Loménie, Emmanuel. "Verrons nous se faire un regroupement national." *La Revue Hebdomadaire*, September 28, 1935, pp. 400–412, October 5, 1935, pp. 62–75, October 19, 1935, pp. 321–30, October 26, 1935, pp. 472–85, November 9, 1935, pp. 222–33, November 16, 1935, pp. 357–66, November 30, 1935, pp. 598–616, December 14, 1935, pp. 201–27.

Borne, E. "Du côté de la droite classique." *La Vie Intellectuelle*, January, 1955, pp. 66–73.

Debû-Bridel, Jacques. "La crise des partis." *La Revue Hebdomadaire*, January 21, 1933, pp. 326–48.

Dovine, Georges. "Philosophie d'un scrutin: le suicide des partis nationaux." *La Revue Hebdomadaire*, June 4, 1932, pp. 84–104.

Fohlen, Claude. "Les partis politiques en France de 1919 à 1933." *Historiens et Géographes*, no. 215 (January, 1969), 304–14.

François-Poncet, André. "Notice sur la vie et les travaux de Louis Marin." *Institut de France, Académie des Sciences Morales et Politiques*, 1964, no. 3, pp. 1–32.

Fusilier, Raymond. "Les Finances des partis politiques." *Revue politique et parlementaire*, CCXI (1953), 258–76.

Hoffman, Stanley. "Collaboration in France during World War II." *Journal of Modern History*, XL (1968), 375–95.

———. "Quelques aspects du regime de Vichy." *Revue française de science politique*, VI (1956), 46–59.

Lalevée, Henri. "Un grand Français d'origine vosgienne: Louis Marin, 1871–1960." *Bulletin de la Société Philomathique Vosgienne*, LXIX (1966), 97–106.

Laniel, Jospeh. "Le Parti Républicain de la Liberté." *Revue de Paris*, May, 1946, pp. 58–62.

Leduc, Jean. "Les Rois de la République: La Famille de Wendel." *Documents politiques, diplomatiques et financiers*, January, 1930, pp. 47–48.

Machefer, Philippe. "Les Croix de Feu, 1927–1936." *L'Information Historique*, January–February, 1972, pp. 28–34.

———. "Le Parti Social Français en 1936–37." *L'Information Historique*, March–April, 1972, pp. 74–80.

———. "L'Union des droites: Le PSF et le Front de la Liberté, 1936–1937." *Revue d'histoire moderne et contemporaine*, XVII (1970), 112–26.

Marin, Louis. "Contributions à l'étude des prodromes de l'armistice." *Revue d'histoire de la deuxième guerre mondiale*, I (1951), 1–26.

Martin, Benjamin F., Jr. "The Creation of the Action Libérale Populaire: An Example of Party Formation in Third Republic France." *French Historical Studies*, IX (1976), 660–89.

Mennevée, R. "Parlementaires et Financiers." *Les Documents politiques diplomatiques et financiers*, April, 1928; April, 1930; March, 1932; August, 1933; February, 1936.

Millet, Raymond. "Notes sur les partis modérés." *L'Esprit*, June, 1939, pp. 205–12.

Nipperdey, Thomas. "Die Organization der bürgerlichen Parteien in Deutschland vor 1918." *Historische Zeitschrift*, CLXXXV (1958), 550–602.

Olivesi, Antoine. "La droite à Marseille en 1914: Aspects de la géographie électorale, de la structure sociale et de l'opinion politique des milieux modérés marseillais." *Provence Historique*, VIII (1957), 175–99.

Osgood, Samuel M. "The Front Populaire: Views from the Right." *International Review of Social History*, IX (1964), 189–201.

Rémond, René. "Les anciens combattants et la politique." *Revue française de science politique*, V (1955), 267–90.

————. "Explications du six février." *Politique*, n.s., I (1959), 218–30.

Renouvin, Pierre. "Discours prononcé le 25 avril 1967 à l'occasion de l'inauguration de la Place Louis Marin." *Institut de France, Académie des Sciences Morales et Politiques*, 1967, no. 6, pp. 1–12.

Ribot, Alexandre. "Georges Picot." *La Revue Hebdomadaire*, February 11, 1911, pp. 141–70.

Sanvoisin, Gaetan. "L'Oeuvre de M. Louis Marin." *La Revue Hebdomadaire*, February 27, 1932, pp. 474–93.

————. "La responsabilité présente des modérés: histoire des deux mois." *La Revue Hebdomadaire*, August 17, 1929, pp. 351–60.

Soucy, Robert. "French Fascism as Class Conciliation and Moral Regeneration." *Societas*, I (1971), 287–97.

————. "French Fascist Intellectuals in the 1930s: An Old New Left?" *French Historical Studies*, VIII (1974), 445–58.

Suarez, George. "Les Croix de Feu." *Le Document*, June, 1935, .pp. 6–21.

Thierry, Joseph. "Le Parti républicain modéré." *La Revue Hebdomadaire*, March 26, 1910, pp. 478–87.

Vivenot, Monique. "Un homme politique lorrain: Louis Marin et L'Allemagne, 1905–1933." *Bulletin de l'Association Inter-universitaire de l'Est*, VIII (1966), 295–303.

Warren, Edouard de. "La République des Modérés." *La Revue de Paris*, February 15, 1929, pp. 233–49.

Weber, Eugen. "New Wine in Old Bottles, Les Familles Spirituelles de la France." *French Historical Studies*, I (1959), 200–224.

THESES AND DISSERTATIONS

Anderson, Malcolm. "The Parliamentary Right in France, 1905–1919." D. Phil. dissertation, Oxford, 1961.

Maizy, H. "Les groupes anti-parlementaires républicaines de droite de 1933 à 1939." Thèse d'institut politique, Paris, 1951.

Phillipet, Jean. "Les Jeunesses Patriotes et Pierre Taittinger, 1924–1940." Memoire de l'institut des études politiques, Paris, 1967.

Siemiatycki, Myer. "Geusdism and Anti-Collectivism in Roubaix-Wattrelos: A Study of the Legislative Elections between 1893–1906." M.A. thesis, University of Sussex, 1971.

Index